lonely planet

POCKET
PARIS

Mary Winston Nicklin, Alexis Averbuck,
Jean-Bernard Carillet, Fabienne Fong Yan,
Rooksana Hossenally, Nicola Leigh Stewart,
Rowan Twine, Peter Yeung

Contents

Top: Paris Plages (p33)
Bottom: Jardin du Luxembourg (p182)

Plan Your Trip 4

The Journey Begins Here ... 4
Our Picks ... 6
Perfect Days ... 20
Get Prepared ... 24
When To Go ... 26
Getting There ... 28
Getting Around ... 29
A Few Surprises ... 32

POCKET **PARIS**

Explore Paris — 37

Eiffel Tower & Western Paris — 39
Champs-Élysées & Grands Boulevards — 55
Louvre & Les Halles — 69
Montmartre & Northern Paris — 89
Le Marais — 107
Bastille & Eastern Paris — 123
The Islands — 141
Latin Quarter — 157
St-Germain & Les Invalides — 177

Paris Toolkit — 209

Family Travel — 210
Accommodation — 211
Food, Drink & Nightlife — 212
LGBTIQ+ Travellers — 214
Health & Safe Travel — 215
Responsible Travel — 216
Accessible Travel — 218
Nuts & Bolts — 219
Language — 220
Index — 222

★ Top Experiences

Eiffel Tower — 42
Arc de Triomphe — 58
Palais Garnier — 59
Musée du Louvre — 72
Basilique du Sacré-Cœur — 93
Les Puces de St-Ouen — 94
Cimetière du Père Lachaise — 126
Notre Dame — 144
Sainte-Chapelle — 150
Conciergerie — 151
Panthéon — 160
Jardin des Plantes — 161
Jardin du Luxembourg — 182
Musée d'Orsay — 183
Église St-Sulpice — 186
Musée Rodin — 187
Hôtel des Invalides — 188

Worth a Trip

Bois de Boulogne — 66
Bois de Vincennes — 138
Les Catacombes — 202
Château de Versailles — 206

The Journey Begins Here

Where else can you play pétanque in a Roman amphitheatre, gawk at impressionist masterpieces and drink a cocktail with Hemingway's ghost? Such an embarrassment of riches could only be Paris. The city is a multi-layered *millefeuille* of culture just waiting for you to sink your teeth into. As a long-time Paris resident, I'm often struck by its magic. I'll be at an exhibit opening, or digging into a divinely delicious bistro meal or listening to a band during the Fête de la Musique, and suddenly be bowled over by the beauty of Paris, smitten by its irrepressible joie de vivre.

Mary Winston Nicklin
marywinstonnicklin.com
Mary Winston Nicklin is a Franco-American writer and editor based on the Left Bank of Paris.

St-Germain des Prés (p177)
POSITIVETRAVELART/SHUTTERSTOCK

THE BEST
Architectural Experiences

Packed with architectural stunners that are instantly recognisable, Paris has a timeless familiarity for visitors. Famous monuments have become synonymous with the city itself – some even spawning international copycats.

Ascend the **Eiffel Tower**, its wrought-iron spire soaring over the skyline. No one could imagine Paris without it. (pictured above; p42)

Stand in awe of **Notre Dame**, the city's geographic and spiritual heart, meticulously restored by 2000 artisans after the devastating 2019 fire. (p144)

Visit the **Louvre** at night for the marvellous ambience of this immense palace-turned museum. (p72)

Climb to the top of the 130m-high Butte de Montmartre to admire the white-domed **Basilique du Sacré-Cœur**. (pictured above; p93)

Go ghost hunting for the Phantom of the Opera at the opulent 19th-century **Palais Garnier** that inspired the hit book and musical. (p59)

Gape at Napoléon's tomb beneath the gold dome in the 17th-century **Hôtel des Invalides** built as a residence for disabled war veterans. (p188)

Right: Hôtel des Invalides (p188)

PLAN YOUR TRIP

THE BEST
Culinary Experiences

As a world food capital, Paris is a bastion of French culinary tradition, drawing international chefs to sharpen their knives in Michelin-starred kitchens. It's also a multicultural hub boasting global flavours. Believe the hype – Paris is a fabulous feast.

Get your picnic from your market of the day *(paris.fr)*, like **Le Marché des Enfants Rouges** with fresh produce stalls and counter-service eateries. (p117)

Splurge on a Michelin-starred lunch at legendary **La Tour d'Argent** (pictured above) or try Substance, Le George or Pavyllon. (p172)

Experience **Le Procope**, one of the oldest cafes in Paris, with a spectacular dining room in which traditional French fare is elegantly served. (p191)

Indulge in **pastry paradise** – there's never been a better time to find pastry nirvana in Paris with master *pâtissiers* like Claire Damon drawing lines to their jewellery-box shops. (p198)

Shop for foodie delights on **rue Montorgueil**, a bustling market street that's a vestige of the historic Les Halles marketplace. (pictured above; p82)

Right: Le Marché des Enfants Rouges (p117)

FROM LEFT: KIEV.VICTOR/SHUTTERSTOCK, HJBC/SHUTTERSTOCK, MO WU/SHUTTERSTOCK

THE BEST
Green Experiences

While Paris is Europe's most densely populated capital, it's easy to find outdoor havens. Parks serve as communal backyards for apartment-dwelling residents, and sprawling lawns like the Champ de Mars beckon for picnics.

Wander the **Jardin du Luxembourg**, an urban oasis with a special place in Parisians' hearts – a playground for young and old. (p182)

Search for famous tombs amidst the greenery in the city's biggest cemetery, **Cimetière du Père Lachaise**, a bastion of biodiversity. (p126)

Soak up the symmetry and grandeur of the **Jardin des Tuileries**, designed by André Le Nôtre in the 17th century. (p80)

Discover the natural treasures of **Jardin des Plantes**, the historic botanical garden. (p161)

Explore **Bois de Boulogne**, the former royal hunting ground brimming with rose gardens, tropical greenhouses and more. (p66)

Embrace summer in Paris, paddling lazily around the central isles of Lac Daumesnil in the **Bois de Vincennes**. (p138)

Jardin du Luxembourg (p182)

FOKKE BAARSSEN/SHUTTERSTOCK

THE BEST

Art Experiences

With an illustrious artistic pedigree – Renoir, Picasso and Van Gogh worked here – Paris is one of the world's great art repositories. In addition to famous museums, smaller establishments feature every imaginable genre.

Make the trip to the Frank Gehry–designed contemporary art centre, **Fondation Louis Vuitton**, resembling a glass-panelled ship sailing over the Bois de Boulogne. (pictured above; p66)

Soak up the medieval magic at **Musée de Cluny**, housed in a 15th-century mansion built on Roman thermal baths. (p166)

Admire the world's largest collection of Claude Monet works in **Musée Marmottan Monet**, a sumptuously decorated former hunting lodge. (p50)

Marvel at Auguste Rodin's former workshop, showroom and garden at **Musée Rodin**, filled with sculptural masterpieces such as *The Kiss*. (pictured above; p187)

Get lost in the **Louvre**, once a fortress and now the world's most visited museum – it's embarking on a restoration project to better welcome its nearly nine million annual visitors. (p72)

FROM LEFT: KIEV.VICTOR/SHUTTERSTOCK, GILMANSHIN/SHUTTERSTOCK

THE BEST

Panoramic Experiences

The cityscape of Paris is best admired from above. As the capital's tallest building, the Eiffel Tower offers sublime panoramas, but other vantage points abound.

Drink in the views along with a killer cocktail at one of the city's rooftop hotspots such as **Maggie** at the Hôtel Rochechouart. (p104)

Take in some of Paris' best vistas atop the magnificent **Arc de Triomphe** on the Champs-Élysées. (pictured above; p58)

Get dizzying, bird's-eye views of Paris from the top of the **Eiffel Tower**, with a flute of Champagne in hand. (p42)

Ascend to the 56th floor of the **Tour Montparnasse**, considered an eyesore when it opened in 1973, for Eiffel Tower views from the observation deck. (p205)

Gaze out at central Paris from the panoramic terrace of the **Galeries Lafayette** department store – for free. (pictured above; p64)

Right: Eiffel Tower, seen from the Tour Montparnasse (p205)

FROM LEFT: RADOSLAW MACIEJEWSKI/SHUTTERSTOCK, PAULOALBERTO82/SHUTTERSTOCK, VERMILION2006/SHUTTERSTOCK

THE BEST
New Experiences

Paris may seem timeless, but it isn't static. Constant renovations add to its sparkle, while revolutions in urban planning have added green pedestrian spaces and new transportation links. However often you visit, there are always new thrills to discover.

Gape at the results of the restoration of **Grand Palais**, the glass-capped monument built for the 1900 Exposition Universelle (World's Fair). (pictured above; p63)

Watch the magical summertime spectacle as the hot-air-balloon-inspired **Paris 2024 Cauldron** rises over the Tuileries (until the 2028 Games in Los Angeles). (p80)

Check out the 'urban forest' around the **Hôtel de Ville** – Paris is planting greenery galore as part of its environmental initiatives. (pictured above right; p114)

Admire contemporary art at **Fondation Cartier's** dazzling new home designed by Jean Nouvel. (p83)

Dance the night away at **Mia Mao** in a former industrial hall of La Villette – an electro scene giving Berlin a run for its money. (p100)

Right: Paris 2024 Cauldron by Mathieu Lehanneur, Jardin des Tuileries (p80)

THE BEST

Nightlife Experiences

The reputation of the demure Parisian goes out the window when you click into nightlife mode. Cafes morph into bars and edgy alt-scene venues fill for live music. Dive in.

Take part in the **vinyl revival** – listening bars are having a moment in Paris as records come back in style. (p101)

Enjoy the cocktail renaissance at glitzy hotel bars like the **Hôtel de Crillon**, backstreet speakeasies and former hostess bars in hip SoPi ('south Pigalle'). (p65)

Catch a jazz concert at a storied club like **Caveau de la Huchette** (p169) or the **Duc des Lombards** (p83).

Dance the night away at **Café de la Danse** located at the beating heart of Bastille nightlife. (p132)

Join moviegoers at an iconic arthouse cinema such as **Le Champo** near Odéon. (p170)

Explore the northern Paris music scene – venues include Cigale, Elysée-Montmartre and **Le Zénith**. (p103)

Caveau de la Huchette (p169)

THE BEST

Riverine Experiences

Flanked by famous monuments, the Seine River is Paris' lifeblood. The Left and Right Banks are connected by 37 bridges, and the quays are a UNESCO World Heritage Site. It's central to Parisian life.

Go sightseeing on the Batobus, indulge in a gourmet meal or hire your own captained boat on a **Seine cruise**. (p46)

Drink an *apéro* (apéritif) or catch a concert on one of the **converted houseboats** moored on the Seine. (pictured above; p196)

Fall under the spell of island life on **Île St-Louis**, settling in at a cafe or listening to buskers on the **Pont St-Louis** (p153).

Hire a boat from **Akwa Experience** to explore the Bassin de la Villette and the Canal de l'Ourcq, a Seine tributary. (p102)

Dive into the Seine at one of the designated **summer swimming spots** after a colossal clean-up made the river swimmable again in time for the 2024 Olympics. (pictured above; p134)

Browse the *bouquinistes*' **green stalls** on the riverbanks, likened to an open-air bookshop. (p168)

FROM LEFT: JEANLUCICHARD/SHUTTERSTOCK, FRANCK LEGROS/SHUTTERSTOCK

Marché aux Puces de St-Ouen (p94)

THE BEST

Market Experiences

Street markets are social gatherings for the entire neighbourhood. Nearly every quarter has its own market at least once a week, where tarpaulin-topped trestle tables bow beneath fresh, cooked and preserved delicacies.

Explore the maze of markets at the **Marché aux Puces de St-Ouen**, the world's largest antiques market, brimming with treasures. (p94)

Pick up a bouquet at the **Marché aux Fleurs Reine Elizabeth II**, the charming flower market renamed in 2014 in honour of the UK's Queen Elizabeth II. (p154)

Stroll **rue Mouffetard**, the cobbled market street dating from the Middle Ages that's packed with gourmet boutiques and market stalls. (p167)

Shop at **Marché d'Aligre**, a street favourite with chefs and locals, its stalls fronting specialist shops stocking cheeses, coffee, chocolates, meat, seafood and wine. (p132)

Admire the glorious bounty at **Marché Biologique Raspail**, Paris' top organic food market. (p192)

Best for Kids

Go on a treasure hunt looking for the **pixelated mosaics** created by French street artist Invader, racking up points on the app. (p116)

Gape at vintage merry-go-rounds at the whimsical **Musée des Arts Forains** inside the old Bercy wine warehouses. (p133)

Delve into science at the huge industrial-style children's exploratorium, **Cité des Sciences et de l'Industrie**, complete with La Géode immersive cinema. (p103)

Craft outdoor adventures in the **Jardin du Luxembourg** (p182) with its merry-go-round and toy sailboats, the giant **Bois de Boulogne** (p66) or **Tuileries** (p80) and Seine river parks.

Sign up for an entertaining children's workshop at one of Paris' multitude of museums, such as the **Musée des Arts et Métiers**, dedicated to the history of scientific invention and human ingenuity. (p116)

Best for Free

Admire Delacroix murals inside the **Église St-Sulpice** – some of Paris' most magnificent buildings are free-to-enter places of worship, filled with exquisite art and treasures. (p186)

Amble the world's first elevated park, the **Coulée Verte**, atop a 19th-century railway viaduct. (p130)

Wander through the astounding permanent collections at the **Musée d'Art Moderne de Paris** – municipal museums *(parismusees.paris.fr)* are free! (p52)

Enjoy many free hours of entertainment at the *brocantes* and **flea markets** that pop up all over the city. (p116)

Catch a concert on the street, bridges or in a garden pavilion anytime of year, especially during the annual **Fête de la Musique**. (p132)

Seek out an art show at the **Collège des Bernardins**, a former Cistercian college dating from the 13th century that's now a Latin Quarter cultural centre. (p167)

Perfect Days

Paris is compact, making it easy to travel between neighbourhoods. These itineraries cover key sights and offbeat wonders, but leave time for wandering – this is a city for flâneurs.

DAY ONE

Only Have One Day?

MORNING
Start your day at newly restored **Notre Dame** (pictured above; p144). Cross the **Pont St-Louis** (p153) to explore Île St-Louis then continue into the Latin Quarter to see the **Arènes de Lutèce** (p165) and the market delights of **rue Mouffetard** (p165).

AFTERNOON
Laze in the lovely **Jardin du Luxembourg** (p182), or pop by a storied cafe like **La Palette** (p194) for coffee and people-watching. Swoon over impressionist masterpieces in the **Musée d'Orsay** (p183).

EVENING
Catch a concert at one of the jazz clubs along the **rue des Lombards** (p83) such as Sunset/Sunside, Duc des Lombards or Le Baiser Salé.

Canal St-Martin (p102)

DAY TWO
A Weekend Trip

MORNING

IM Pei's glass pyramid is your compass point to enter the labyrinthine **Louvre** (p72). Once you've had your fill, stroll through the elegant **Jardin des Tuileries** (pictured above; p80) or the **Jardin du Palais Royal** (p80). Tap into the soul of the former Les Halles wholesale markets along **rue Montorgueil** (p82).

AFTERNOON

Scope out Victor Hugo's house in **Place des Vosges** (p114), then wander through the Marais' narrow streets to uncover hidden gardens, treasure-filled museums and trendy boutiques.

EVENING

The lively Bastille neighbourhood calls for a cafe crawl. Catch live music at **Les Disquaires** (p131), **Supersonic** or **Café de la Danse** (p132).

DAY THREE
A Short Break

MORNING

Montmartre's slinking streets lined with ivy-clad buildings are enchanting places to meander, especially in the early morning. Visit **Sacré-Cœur** (p93), then head to the **Canal St-Martin** (p102), spanned by wrought-iron bridges, to stroll the shaded towpaths.

AFTERNOON

Western Paris, a culture-packed district, is home to the world's largest Monet collection at the **Musée Marmottan Monet** (p50), contemporary art at the **Palais de Tokyo** (p52) and Asian masterpieces at the **Musée Guimet** (p52). Sunset is the best time to ascend the **Eiffel Tower** (pictured above; p42) for dizzying views.

EVENING

Nothing beats a sultry, Seine-side party at night. Check out the **floating bars and nightclubs** (p196) moored near Invalides.

If You Have More Time

Paris is made for walking and off-the-radar promenades provide a different perspective of the city: the **Coulée Verte** (p130) is a greenway on a former elevated railway that inspired New York's High Line, and the Petite Ceinture, 'the Little Belt', offers an immersion in nature on an old train track. Further afield, outdoor enthusiasts appreciate the city's two 'green lungs': the **Bois de Vincennes** (p138) and **Bois de Boulogne** (p66).

A Seine **river cruise** (p46) gives you a front-row seat to the scenery as it glides by the city's famous monuments.

A more offbeat aquatic adventure is a cruise through the locks of the **Canal St-Martin** (p102).

For pinch-me panoramas, climb the mighty **Arc de Triomphe** (p58), the monstrous **Tour Montparnasse** (p205) or the **Galeries Lafayette** (p64) terrace overlooking the back of the **Palais Garnier** (p59), Paris' opulent opera house, where you can go behind the scenes on a guided tour.

Seine river cruise (p46)

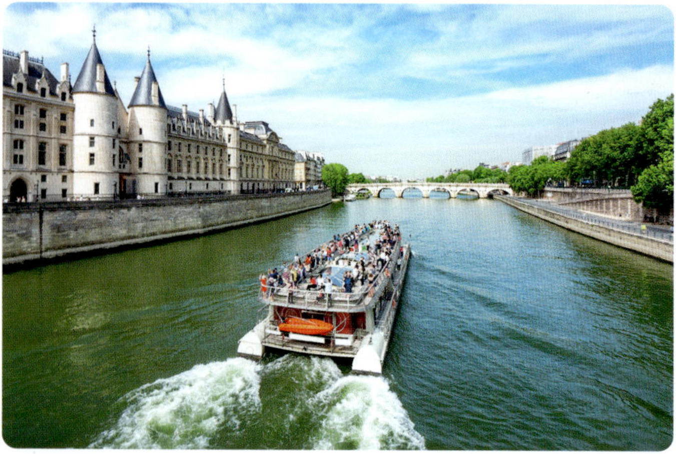

MISTERVLAD/SHUTTERSTOCK

A City Day Trip

Nothing prepares you for your first glimpse of the **Château de Versailles** (pictured above; p206). France's most opulent palace sprawls across 2300 rooms, which once housed the entire royal court. It's an easy day trip on the RER C from central Paris (30 minutes from the Champ de Mars station).

Book your ticket online in advance for a guaranteed time slot. To access areas that are otherwise off-limits, take a 90-minute guided tour of the King's Private Apartments, enlarged by Louis XV so he could escape the nosy court.

For lunch, reserve Alain Ducasse's **Ore** (p207) within the château, or book the acclaimed **Bistrot du 11**, outside the palace on rue de Satory.

On a Rainy Day

Shelter in a cinema such as the **Odéon** (p170) arthouse favourites, marvel at myriad museums in the **Le Marais** (p115), watch an opera at the **Palais Garnier** (pictured above; p59) or catch a cabaret in **Pigalle** (p98). What's more, the city's churches – free to access – are resplendent repositories of fine art, also sometimes setting the stage for concerts.

Exploring the **passages couverts** (p78), the glass-roofed covered galleries pioneered in the 19th century, offers an elegant shopping experience protected from inclement weather. Many of these atmospheric passageways connect (for example, passage des Panoramas, passage Jouffroy and passage Verdeau); you can cover ground while sheltered from the rain.

Get Prepared

BOOK AHEAD

Three months before
Book opera, ballet or cabaret tickets; check events calendars for festivals; and make reservations for high-end/popular restaurants.

One month before
Sign up for a local-led tour and start narrowing down your choices of museums, pre-purchasing tickets online where possible to minimise ticket queues.

One week before
Check the weather forecast and pack your comfiest shoes to walk Paris' streets.

Manners Matter

Always greet and say goodbye to anyone you interact with, such as shopkeepers, using *bonjour* (*bonsoir* at night) and *au revoir*. It's not viewed as a formality but as basic respect.
Take your time at meals or in cafes – eating is relaxation in Paris.
Talking about money (salaries or spending outlays) in public is taboo. Food and drink aside, conversations often revolve around philosophy, art and sports.

Clothes

As the cradle of *haute couture,* Paris is chic: don your smarter threads. Parisians have a finely tuned sense of aesthetics. They favour style and simplicity – classic items – over bling, mixing basics from chain stores with designer pieces and vintage finds. You'll also stand out less as a tourist and therefore be less of a target for pickpockets.

Bring sturdy shoes whatever the season, whether trainers, which are ubiquitous, or walking shoes.

Things to Know

Shops Particularly in smaller upmarket boutiques and at market stalls, staff may not appreciate you touching the merchandise until you have been invited to do so, nor taking photographs.

Speech Overall, communication tends to be formal and reserved, but this shouldn't be mistaken for unfriendliness. Parisians don't speak loudly – modulate your voice to a similarly low pitch.

Terms of address *Tu* and *vous* both mean 'you', but *tu* is only used with people you know very well, children or animals. Use *vous* until you're invited to use *tu*.

Waitstaff Attract attention with a subtle gesture or glance. Never use *'garçon'* (literally 'boy') to summon a waiter, rather 'Monsieur' or 'Madame'.

TIPPING

Tipping isn't expected in France – service is included in the restaurant bill. Reserved for good service.

5–10%
Restaurants
For excellent service

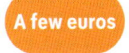
A few euros
Bars and cafes
Left on the table

Round up
Taxi
To the nearest euro

€1–2
Hotel porters
Per bag

DAILY BUDGET

Budget: Less than €100

- Dorm bed: **from €32**
- Espresso/glass of wine/*demi* (half-pint of beer)/cocktail: **from €2/4/4/10**
- Metro ticket: **€2.50**
- Filled baguette: **€4.50–6.50**
- Frequent concerts and events: **free**

Midrange: €200–300

- Double room: **from €160**
- Two-course meal: **€24–50**
- Admission to museums: **free to around €22**
- Admission to clubs: **free to around €30**

Top End: More than €300

- Double room at historic luxury hotel: **from €250**
- Gastronomic restaurant *menu:* **from €60/100**
- Private two-hour city tour: **from €200**
- Premium ticket to opera/ballet performance: **from €160**

Currency
Euro (€)

Language
French

Time
Central European Time (GMT/UTC plus one hour)

MICHAEL BARAJAS/SHUTTERSTOCK

PICKPOCKET WARNING

Beware of pickpockets who occasionally target busy tourist areas, such as metro line 1 and beneath the Arc de Triomphe and Eiffel Tower. Keep bags zipped. Do not leave phones in your back pocket or out on a restaurant terrace table.

When To Go

Paris is a feast of culture and entertainment in every season, from the glittering lights of December to summer's many festivals.

A highlight of virtually all travellers' lifetime itineraries, Paris is a magnet for all. Spring (especially April and May) and autumn (particularly September and October) are ideal with gentle weather and fewer crowds. Summer (June to August) is the main tourist season. Daylight can last around 16 hours, 'beaches' – complete with sunbeds, lounge chairs and palm trees – line the banks of the Seine, Paris Pride rocks the June streets and shoppers hit the summer *soldes* (sales). But many establishments close during August when Parisians generally leave on holiday. Sights are quieter and prices are lower during winter (November to February).

The Big Events

December/January: The **New Year's Eve** fireworks show over the Arc de Triomphe (p58) and the Champs-Élysées is sensational.

June: The **Fête de la Musique** (p132) welcomes in summer on the solstice with fabulous staged and impromptu live performances of all genres on footpaths, squares and in venues all over the city.

July: The last of 21 stages of the **Tour de France**, the prestigious, 3500km-long cycling event, finishes with a race up the av des Champs-Élysées on the third or fourth Sunday of July.

14 July: The capital celebrates **France's national day** with a morning military parade along av des Champs-Élysées, accompanied by a fly-past of fighter aircraft and helicopters. Fireworks light up the sky above the Champ de Mars (p46) by night.

Paris Weather

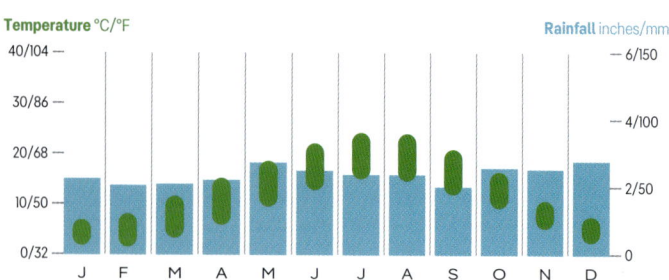

Fête des Vendanges (p97), Montmartre

Artsy & Cultural

February: During **Chinese New Year**, parades throng the **13e arrondissement** and firecrackers light up the night.

April & May: For four weeks each spring, the **Banlieues Bleues**, a jazz, blues and R&B festival, is held at venues in Paris' outer suburbs.

June: The Latin Quarter (p157) comes alive with the bookish **Quartier du Livre** festival, and **Nuit Blanche** brings contemporary art installations to the city streets for one 'White Night' ('All Nighter').

September–December: During **Journées Européennes du Patrimoine** (European Heritage Days) on the third weekend in September, you can get exclusive access to off-limits buildings. Montmartre's grape harvest is celebrated over five days during October's **Fête des Vendanges** (p97) and the months-long **Festival d'Automne** showcases the arts in venues throughout the city.

ACCOMMODATION LOWDOWN

Paris' plentiful accommodation spans all budgets, but it is often fully booked well in advance, particularly during peak times (April to October, as well as public and school holidays). Reservations are essential at these times, but are also recommended year-round. Prices are generally lowest in winter, outside of Fashion Week.

✈ Getting There

Paris is the main point of entry for visitors to France. Most international airlines fly to Aéroport Charles de Gaulle (CDG) or Orly. Five major train stations offer international services.

From the Airport to the City Centre

By RER Train or Metro

Trains are the best way to get to and from Paris' airports. The RER B line from Charles de Gaulle crosses under the middle of Paris, with stops including Gare du Nord, Châtelet–Les Halles, St-Michel–Notre Dame and Luxembourg. Some trains run express through the suburbs, saving about 10 minutes. An even faster express route is slated for 2027.

From Orly, you can connect to the city via the driverless line 14 of the metro, or on the RER B after taking the Orlyval shuttle.

By Taxi

Allow 40–80 minutes to central Paris. Take an official taxi from the clearly marked ranks at each terminal's Arrivals level. The government mandates fixed prices for taxis to the Right and Left Banks. Note that rideshare services do not have access to Paris' fast taxi lanes, so they're more susceptible to traffic jams.

By Bus

The Roissybus connects CDG airport with the Opéra district in about an hour. Buses run every 15 minutes during the day (20 minutes at night). The Orlybus was discontinued in March 2025.

Other Points of Entry

Eurostar

The high-speed London–Paris line (2¼ hours) runs from St Pancras International to Gare du Nord. Fees start from €44. 'Snap' tickets *(snap .eurostar.com/rw-en)* offer reduced last-minute fares. Eurostar also operates routes to Brussels, Antwerp and Amsterdam.

Coach

Companies like FlixBus and BlaBlaCar operate long-distance routes. Book far ahead to bag cheap tickets.

TGV

The SNCF operates high-speed TGV trains to international destinations. Partnerships with Renfe, Lyria and Trenitalia reach Spain, Switzerland and Italy, respectively.

Getting Around

The Paris metro is fast and convenient, while the comprehensive bus system allows you to sightsee while travelling. A surge in new bike lanes and infrastructure has prompted a cycling revolution. For many, however, walking the beautiful streets is the way to go.

Metro & RER
The fastest way to get around, the metro runs from about 5.30am to around 1.15am (about 2.15am on Friday and Saturday evenings). Serving the suburbs, RER trains save time crossing the city because they have fewer stops in the centre.

Bus
With no stairs, buses are widely accessible and are good for parents with prams/strollers and people with limited mobility. Bus lines complement the metro: for some journeys a bus is the more direct – and scenic – way to go. Stops show schedules, routes and often the waiting time until the next bus.

Walking
Easily navigable, Paris is a walker's paradise. The city is so compact you can actually traverse it in about two hours. Serious urban hikers can explore several Grandes Randonnées (long-distance trails) in Paris, including the GR75, a 50km loop around the city that was launched in 2017 in support of Paris' bid for the 2024 Olympic and Paralympic Games.

FROM LEFT: IVAN MARC/SHUTTERSTOCK, GENOVA/SHUTTERSTOCK

--- **ESSENTIAL APP** ---
Download **Bonjour RATP**, the app from the Paris metro authority, to get real-time traffic updates, itinerary options and tickets.

Boat

Combining scenery and convenience, the **Batobus** *(batobus.com)* is a handy hop-on, hop-off service stopping at nine key destinations along the Seine. In warmer months the service runs regularly through the day and offers the chance for a river cruise at a fraction of the price of a tour boat.

Cycling

The Vélib' bike-share scheme has over 20,000 bikes, both classic (green) and electric (blue), at nearly 1480 docking stations in the city and surrounding region. In Paris proper, stations are found every 300m. Buy a subscription online *(velib-metropole.fr/en)* or at docking stations. There are single-trip, day and multi-way options. Other bike-sharing service operators include Lime and Dott. Before choosing your bike, be sure to check the tyres, brakes and gears. Be aware of the rules of the road, and note that some cycling lanes share traffic with buses.

Taxi & Rideshare

Find taxis at official stands or via companies such as **Taxis G7** *(g7.fr)*. There are queues of cabs at major train stations. Flag one on the street if the roof sign is green. Taxis must accept payment by credit card. The *prise en charge* (flag fall) is €3 (if using the app, it's €4 to order immediately, €7 in advance). The minimum journey cost is €8. Aside from airport trips, which are a fixed flat-rate fare, the cost of the taxi journey is determined by the taximeter located inside the vehicle – strictly regulated by law.

Public Transport Essentials

Navigo Easy Card

The cheapest, easiest way to use Paris' public transport is via the Navigo Easy card. Sold for €2 at metro and RER ticket windows and RATP-affiliated outlets (eg tobacconists and markets), this credit-card-sized fare card is used for all your ticketing needs; or charge up a virtual one on the RATP app. Navigo, like London's Oyster card or Hong Kong's Octopus card, is a system that provides a full range of fare options. As Paris phases out paper tickets, Navigo Easy cards are the future. You can load the reusable, contactless card with tickets, which are then deducted for each ride.

Understanding the Fares

As of January 2025, a new fare system was put into place which eliminates the confusing zone system. Previously ticket prices were higher for trips to the suburbs, including Versailles. Now you can travel all over the Île-de-France region by train for the price of a single, one-way fare of €2.50. The ticket is valid for a duration of two hours. Note that buses and trams have a different price, which is set at €2. You can load a variety of ticket types onto a Navigo Easy card: metro-train-RER, bus-tram, RoissyBus, Paris airports, Navigo Day Pass. Use one of the multilingual machines found at metro and train stations, get assistance from an RATP agent at the service window or load tickets via the RATP app on your phone.

Navigo Day Pass

If you anticipate using public transport a lot on a single day, the Navigo Day Pass is better value at €12 for unlimited rides on all transportation modes in the Île-de-France (excluding airport access).

TRAVEL COSTS

Metro ticket
€2.50

Vélib' bike single ride
€3

Bus fare
€2

— **DON'T FORGET TO VALIDATE** —

Validate your Navigo pass or ticket for each journey, and have it handy to show to ticket inspectors.

RUSH HOUR

The Paris region public transport system is the busiest in the world after Tokyo with 9.4 million trips every day. If your plans are flexible, consider travelling outside the peak hours of 8am to 10am and 5pm to 7pm. Commuting Parisians pack the trains and they can become uncomfortably crowded. Always allow passengers to get off the trains before you hop on, and don't sit in a *strapontin* (folding seat) during rush hour.

PIERRE LABORDE/SHUTTERSTOCK

🎁 A Few Surprises

Paris isn't just the headline sights. The city is also full of unexpected treasures, if you keep an eye out.

See the Signs

The city's 700 **historic markers** were created by renowned designer Philippe Starck in the shape of an oar – a reference to the ship in the Paris coat of arms. If you read French, you can glean insights about fascinating historic events, people and lost monuments. Look up to find plaques on buildings and walls, which detail the famous residents who lived there, such as the author Colette at the **Palais Royal** (p80) garden and James Joyce on the **rue du Cardinal Lemoine** (p169) in the Latin Quarter.

Philippe Auguste Wall

Over the centuries, Paris has been encircled by defensive walls. The oldest that you can still see today is the **Enceinte de Philippe Auguste** (p111), named for the king who constructed it in the 12th century. Remnants include mysterious towers and crumbling ramparts on both sides of the Seine. The longest stretch abuts the sports court of the Collège Charlemagne in the 4e. There's also a tower hidden in the Jardin des Rosiers–Joseph Migneret in the Marais district.

Urban Street Furniture

Street benches, lamps, newspaper kiosks, fountains and even trash cans/rubbish bins are part of the urban fabric, designed with aesthetics in mind. Named for the architect who designed it in the 1860s, the **Davioud double-seated public bench** is a much-loved urban emblem. The reclining green lawn chairs in the **Jardin du Luxembourg** (p182) are as famous as the cast-iron, ornamental **Wallace Fountains** that were donated in the 19th century by Sir Richard Wallace, the affluent British art collector, to bring clean drinking water to the city. Still in use today, these fountains are usually painted green, though you'll find a red one in Chinatown in the 13e. Free public toilets called **sanisettes** were designed by famous designer Patrick Jouin and come complete with water drinking fountains installed on the outside. Numbering 400, these toilets can be found on a Paris Je T'aime map: parisjetaime.com/eng/article/public-toilets-a696.

Paris Piscines

In the summer months, **Paris Plages** ushers in a season of open-air swimming. The Seine opens three lifeguard-patrolled swimming spots (p134), and the **Bassin de la Villette** offers three clean-water-zoned swimming pools. Year-round, the swimming options are enticing. You can watch the Seine boats sail by from the floating swimming pool, **Piscine Joséphine Baker**, near Bercy. Others are historic landmarks that add a dash of style to your paddle. The art deco **Piscine Pontoise** in the Latin Quarter dates from the 1930s and has night openings – particularly moody – or try the minimalist, white **Piscine de la Butte aux Cailles** or the maximalist **Piscine Molitor**. **Piscine Georges Vallerey**, which was built for the 1924 Olympic Games, got a make-over for the 2024 Games.

Street Art

Paris is a hotbed for street art. Look for the stencilled heroines of **Miss. Tic**, graffiti by Jef Aérosol and pixelated video game–inspired mosaics by **Invader** (p116), among other popular artists. Spot massive murals by the likes of international greats Shepard Fairey, D*Face and Inti in an open-air museum along bd Vincent Auriol in the 13e *arrondissement*. The **Boulevard Paris 13** is a joint initiative launched by

Piscine Joséphine Baker

Tour St-Jacques

the Galerie Itinerrance and the 13e *arrondissement* mayor's office, and maps are available *(itinerrance.fr)*.

Look Down

Once an ancient Roman road, the rue St-Jacques is the oldest street in Paris. It's part of the pilgrimage route to Santiago de Compostela in northwestern Spain – the starting point in Paris is the **Tour St-Jacques**, a marvellously sculpted Gothic tower that's the only vestige of the 16th-century church St-Jacques-de-la-Boucherie, destroyed during the Revolution. Pilgrims often wear scallop shells around their necks, or dangling from their backpacks, and this symbol can be found in **bronze medallions** embedded in the footpath on the street all the way through the 14e *arrondissement*.

Another treasure hunt is to look for the medallions marking the 'lost river' of Paris. A tributary to the Seine, the **Bièvre** once ran through the 13e and 5e *arrondissements* before it became so polluted that it was covered over and incorporated into the sewage system by the early 20th century.

You'll also notice **Arago medallions** marking the Paris meridian, the line of longitude that was used before the Greenwich meridian became the global standard. Dutch artist Jan Dibbets created them as a homage to the French physicist who developed the Paris meridian. You can even see the Arago markers inside the Louvre.

Go Underground

Beneath the cobblestone streets and elegant boulevards of Paris, there's a sprawling underground realm. The buildings admired on the surface were constructed from limestone excavated from a maze of subterranean quarries, some of which today house **Les Catacombes** (p202), one of the world's largest ossuaries. Layers of metro tunnels, sewers and hidden hideouts punctuate this alluring underground domain.

Visitors can glimpse the archaeological layers, including Gallo-Roman ruins, at the **Crypte Archéologique** (p147) hidden under the Notre Dame forecourt. See vaulted 15th-century cellars inside the **M Musée du Vin**, where monks once stored their barrels in former quarries beneath Passy (p50). Tour the air raid shelter converted into a command post by the Resistance during WWII at the **Musée de la Libération de Paris**. On a **Canauxrama** cruise of the **Canal St-Martin** (p102), sail through tunnels beneath the 11e *arrondissement*, looking up to see the crypts buried beneath the **Bastille** (p130). And you can get a glimpse of so-called metro ghost stations while riding lines 8 and 9 – the abandoned St-Martin station is now sometimes used for illuminated advertising campaigns.

Reinvented Spaces

Abandoned industrial buildings have been reborn as vibrant cultural playgrounds and hybrid venues, revitalising entire neighbourhoods. Near Gare de Lyon train station in eastern Paris, **Ground Control** (p135) occupies a former SNCF warehouse – browse the shops, take part in a yoga class, listen to live music or grab a beer from the food court. In northern Paris, **Le 104** (p103) is a contemporary art gallery and community centre housed in a former municipal funeral home. What's more, it morphs into a dance floor for the city's youth to practise routines. Other happening hybrid venues include **La REcyclerie** (p99), **La Gare – Le Gore** and **Césure** (p171).

OFFBEAT PARIS

Walk in the footsteps of Honoré de Balzac in the **charming house** (p50) where the author escaped his creditors in Passy.

Party in a former train station at **Le Hasard Ludique** (p99), along the former railway known as the Petite Ceinture (Little Belt).

Hide in St-Germain's secret gardens such as **Jardin Catherine-Labouré** (p193), on the grounds of a former 17th-century convent.

Meet artists and browse studios and exhibits at the massive art incubator **POUSH** (p100) in Aubervilliers.

Wander the leafy lanes of **Cimetière du Montparnasse** (p205), final resting place of icons like Man Ray, Simone de Beauvoir and Serge Gainsbourg.

Explore Paris

Eiffel Tower & Western Paris	39
Champs-Élysées & Grands Boulevards	55
Louvre & Les Halles	69
Montmartre & Northern Paris	89
Le Marais	107
Bastille & Eastern Paris	123
The Islands	141
Latin Quarter	157
St-Germain & Les Invalides	177

Worth a Trip

Bois de Boulogne	66
Bois de Vincennes	138
Les Catacombes	202
Château de Versailles	206

Paris' Walking Tours

Walk the 16e's Awesome Architecture	48
Champs-Élysées to Palais Garnier	60
Walk the Covered Passages	78
Walk Mythic Montmartre	96
Walk Through Time in Le Marais	110
Explore Jewish Traditions	112
Walk the Artisans' Courts	128
Walk the Islands	152
Walk the Latin Quarter's Essentials	164
Walk Quintessential St-Germain	190
Walk the Villagey 14e	204

People enjoying the Seine's quays (p154)
JEANLUCICHARD/SHUTTERSTOCK

Researched by
Mary Winston Nicklin

Explore
Eiffel Tower & Western Paris

Ascend the Eiffel Tower and all of Paris is at your *pieds*. To your west, the panoramas unfurl past the Trocadéro to the elegant 16e *arrondissement,* flanked by the Seine and the glorious green Bois de Boulogne (p66). In centuries past, Passy village was home to luminaries such as Balzac, before it was annexed to the city in 1860. Nowadays, must-try restaurants vie for your attention alongside standout museums – the most of any Paris district. The architecture is another draw, with art nouveau residences, art deco buildings and modernist villas commissioned by well-heeled residents. Above it all, the scene-stealing tower sets even the most hardened hearts aflutter.

Getting Around

 Metro & RER
To reach the Eiffel Tower, take the metro line 6 to Bir-Hakeim, or RER C to Champ de Mars–Tour Eiffel. Traverse the 16e from north to south on line 9 (Trocadéro to Exelmans).

 Walking
This is the easiest way to appreciate the 16e's village ambience. Plus, you can admire the architecture as you stroll.

 **Bicycle**
Numerous bike lanes, plus the Vélib' bike-share scheme, make cycling easy and convenient in the 16e. Travel from Trocadéro to Auteuil in just 10 minutes.

THE BEST

CITY ICON Eiffel Tower (p42)

ART INSPIRATION Musée Marmottan Monet (p50)

OPEN-AIR MARKET Marché Président Wilson (p50)

AQUATIC ADVENTURE Seine River cruise (p46)

HIDDEN DELIGHT Maison de Balzac (p50)

Eiffel Tower (p42)
STEPHEN RICHARD MCADAM/SHUTTERSTOCK

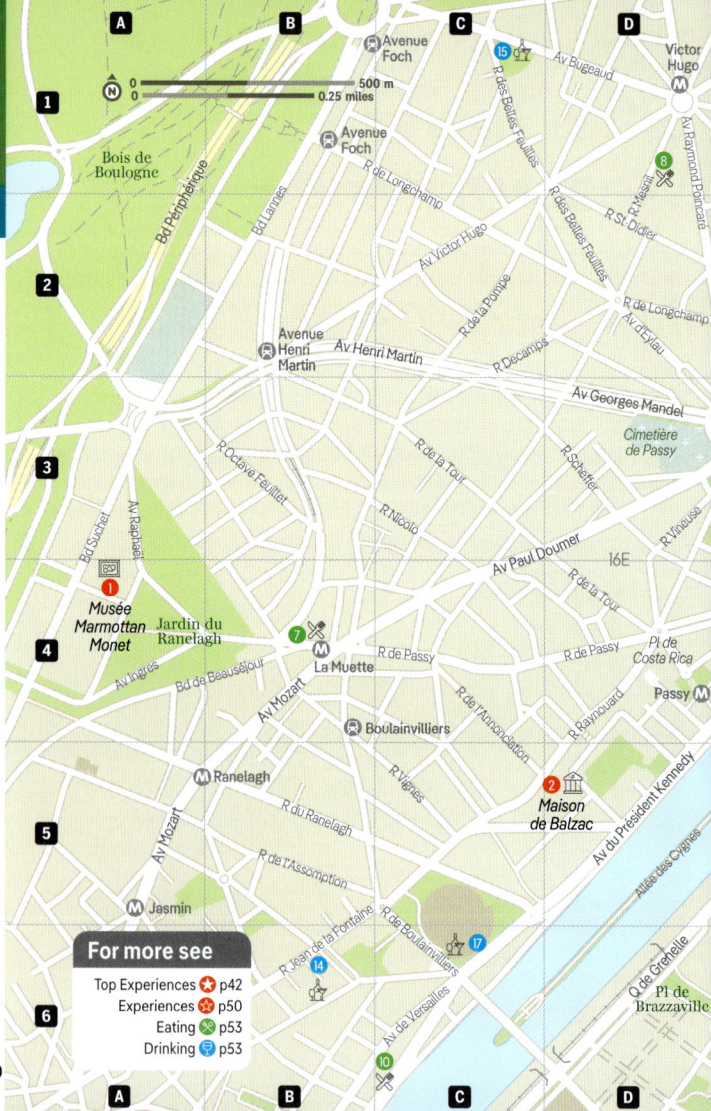

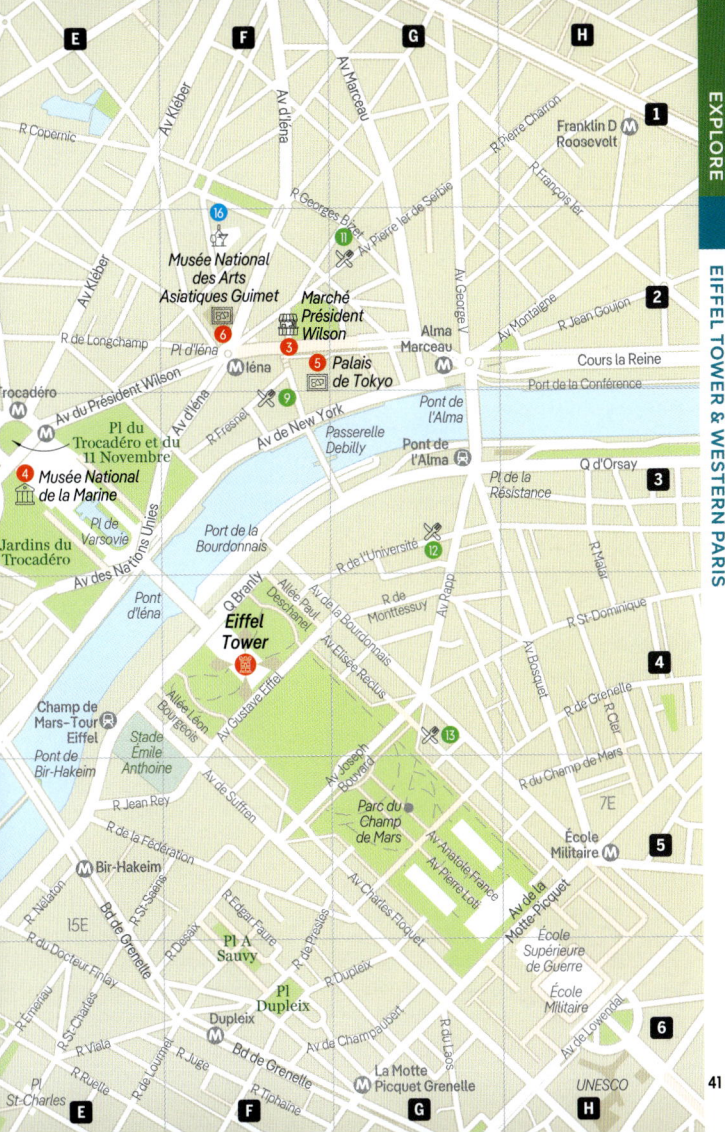

★ **TOP EXPERIENCE**

Eiffel Tower

Piercing the city skyline, Paris' icon beckons. Experience the Eiffel Tower in myriad ways, from a daytime trip to a glittering evening ascent. Even though nearly seven million people visit annually, few would dispute that each time is unique – it's something that simply has to be done once.

MAP P40 **F4**

PLANNING TIP
Book tickets well in advance and bring a jacket – it can be breezy at the top. Note that the top floor may close during heavy winds.

Scan this QR code for full opening hours and to book ahead.

Exploring an Icon
Named after its designer, Gustave Eiffel, the Tour Eiffel was built for the 1889 Exposition Universelle (World's Fair). It took 300 workers, 2.5 million rivets and two years of nonstop labour to assemble. Upon completion, the tower became the tallest human-made structure in the world (324m) – a record held until the 1930 completion of New York's Chrysler Building. A symbol of the modern age, it faced opposition from Paris' artistic and literary elite, and the 'metal asparagus', as some snidely called it, was originally slated to be torn down in 1909. It was spared only because it proved an ideal platform for the transmitting antennas needed for the newfangled science of radiotelegraphy. Now a local nickname for the tower is La Dame de Fer (Iron Lady).

1st Floor
Of the tower's three floors, the 1st (57m) has the most space, with a broad wooden deck for lounging, but the least impressive views. The glass-enclosed **Pavillon Ferrié** houses an immersion film along with a small cafe, pizza bar and souvenir shop. On the outer walkway follow a

JEANLUCICHARD/SHUTTERSTOCK

discovery circuit to learn more about the tower's ingenious design and history. Check out the sections of glass flooring that offer a dizzying view of the ant-like people walking on the ground far below. This level also hosts the restaurant **Madame Brasserie**. The 1st floor's commercial areas are powered by two sleek wind turbines within the tower.

2nd Floor

Views from the 2nd floor (115m; pictured above) are grand – impressively high but still close enough to see the details of the city below. Pinpoint locations in Paris and beyond using telescopes and panoramic maps placed around this level. Story windows give an overview of the lifts' mechanics, and from this vantage point, you can gaze through glass panels to the

QUICK BREAK
The tower's eateries range from snack bars to sit-down 1st-floor Madame Brasserie or 2nd-floor Le Jules Verne. Nearby, don't get tourist-trapped: rue de l'Exposition has a good range, from Le P'tit Troquet to Ryukishin Eiffel.

PAINT JOB

Every seven years, a 50-person night crew repaints the tower. It's sported six different colours throughout its lifetime, most recently the original golden shade conceived by Gustave Eiffel.

JEANLUCICHARD/SHUTTERSTOCK

ground. Also up here are toilets, souvenir shops, a macaron bar and Michelin-starred restaurant **Le Jules Verne** (accessible by a dedicated lift in the south pillar).

Top Floor (Summit!)

Views from the wind-buffeted top floor (276m) stretch up to 60km on a clear day. At this height the sweeping panoramas are more thrilling than detailed. You'll exit the lift onto a glass-enclosed level with directional panels orienting many of the world's cities. Then take one of the two small sets of metal stairs to the highest tier, which is open-air. Celebrate your ascent with a glass of bubbly from the **Champagne bar** at this topmost level – or opt for mineral water, lemonade and macarons. Afterwards, peep into Gustave Eiffel's restored top-level **office** where wax models of Eiffel and his daughter Claire greet Thomas Edison. Somewhat unbelievably, there are also toilets up here.

Ticket Purchases & Queues

Even on a good day the base of the Eiffel Tower can be a chaotic scrum of confused travellers. A bit of preparation can cut down on joining that fray, and save time waiting in often atrocious queues, especially in high season (June to September) and during holidays like Easter. Generally attendance is lowest on Tuesdays, Wednesdays and Thursdays.

External Security

Nowadays, bullet-proof glass barriers surround the tower's base. Visitors must pass through external security at one of the two entrances to the glass enclosure on av Gustave Eiffel. The two exits are on quai Branly. The security lines are divided between walk-in visitors, people with pre-booked tickets, and people with reservations at the restaurants. You are allowed through this point without a ticket if you just want to stroll the gardens directly under the tower itself.

Tickets

Once inside, there are ticket booths (with long queues) at the south pillar. It is well worth pre-booking online to reduce waiting. And, at certain times, only people with pre-booked lift tickets to the top will be allowed up there (ie sometimes there are no tickets available on the day). But most days you can buy a stairs ticket or a stairs-plus-ticket-to-the-top. If you can't reserve your tickets ahead of time, expect lengthy waits both for tickets and for lifts. Pre-purchasing tickets online gives you an allocated time slot and means

NIGHTLY SPARKLES
Every hour on the hour, the entire tower sparkles for five minutes with 20,000 6-watt lights. They were first installed for Paris' millennium celebration in 2000 – it took 25 mountain climbers five months to install the current bulbs and 40km of electrical cords. For the best view of the light show, head across the Seine to the Jardins du Trocadéro.

CHAMP DE MARS
Running southeast from the Eiffel Tower, the grassy green jewel of the Parc du Champ de Mars – an ideal summer picnic spot – was originally used as a parade ground for the cadets of the 18th-century École Militaire (Military Academy). This school in the vast French-classical building commissioned by Louis XV at the southeastern end of the park counts Napoléon Bonaparte among its illustrious graduates.

you enter straight away to go through a second security check just before the lift or stairs. Print your ticket or show it on your phone.

Taking the Stairs

The climb consists of 327 steps to the 1st floor and another 347 steps to the 2nd floor. The stairs to the top are not open to the public for safety reasons. You must buy a lift ticket at the base or online (there are no ticket sales for the top on the 2nd floor). Plan for 10 to 20 minutes between floors, depending on your fitness level.

Top-Floor Lift

Ascend as far as the 2nd floor (either on foot or by lift), and from there a separate lift goes up to the top floor (closed during heavy winds). This lift to the top is only accessible by walking up a small flight of stairs to the 2nd-floor mezzanine where the lift is located. Note that the top floor and stairs aren't accessible to people with limited mobility. Pushchairs must be folded in lifts, and bags or backpacks larger than aeroplane-cabin size aren't allowed. You will need your ticket to access the lift, after, once again, waiting in a queue.

Seine River Cruises

Taking to the Seine on a river cruise (pictured right) is an idyllic way to view the Eiffel Tower. **Bateaux Parisiens** runs hour-long circuits with audioguides in 14 languages and themed lunch and dinner cruises. **Vedettes de Paris** offers one-hour cruises from its base at the foot of the Eiffel Tower.

ADISA/SHUTTERSTOCK

The hop-on, hop-off **Batobus** stops at the Eiffel Tower. **Green River Cruises** has pontoon boats you can privatise. Chef Alain Ducasse oversees the floating restaurant **Ducasse sur Seine** on a luxurious electric boat, where both lunch and dinner are served. The only Michelin-starred cruise is aboard the **Don Juan II**, an art deco–style yacht kitted out with a fireplace, wooden panelling and brass fixtures. The multicourse dinner *menu* is by chef Frédéric Anton of Le Jules Verne fame.

ONLINE VISITOR'S GUIDE

The info-packed website *(guide. toureiffel.paris)* can be accessed via the tower's wi-fi. Near the west pillar, the information booth has brochures and information on guided tours and activities for kids.

WALKING TOUR

Walk the 16e's Awesome Architecture

The Passy and Auteuil areas of the 16e are a festival of art nouveau, art deco and modernist masterpieces. A stroll through this district is a chance to admire architecture that was innovative and avant-garde in its time, and still turns heads today.

START	END	LENGTH
Cité de l'Architecture et du Patrimoine	Le Corbusier studio-apartment	5km; 3 hours

1. Stunning Museum

Start at the **Cité de l'Architecture et du Patrimoine**, a standout museum with Eiffel Tower views framed through enormous windows. You'd be hard-pressed to find a grander setting to show off France's architectural achievements.

2. Lessons in Luxury

Exit the Palais de Chaillot and skirt the square de Yorktown, named for the famous battle of the American Revolutionary War. The **Jean Fidler building**, at 1 av Paul Doumer, is considered an iconic luxury edifice from the inter-war period. Resembling an ocean liner, it was inaugurated at the 1937 World's Fair.

3. Concrete Pioneer

Continue on rue Benjamin Franklin (named for the fellow who lived at 66 rue Raynouard) until you reach 25bis with an elaborate inlaid floral facade (1904). Designed in reinforced concrete by the Perret Brothers, this **apartment building** had revolutionary features, including the 'free plan' that later inspired Le Corbusier. Along rue Raynouard, peek at Balzac's house with the Eiffel Tower in the backdrop.

4. Art Nouveau Marvel

Rue Jean de la Fontaine is flanked with architectural stunners by Hector Guimard (1867–1942). The art nouveau pioneer was behind the gorgeous, nature-inspired entrances for the Paris metro. Guimard's glory is **Castel Béranger**, at 16 rue Jean de la Fontaine. It won the award for Paris' best façade in 1898 – spot wild seahorses climbing the stone.

5. Hector Guimard's Home

Across the street, take a look at the **Cravan bar** (p53), a destination for cocktail enthusiasts inside a Guimard-designed building with art nouveau tiles and mirrors. Continue down rue Jean de la Fontaine to **122 av Mozart**. This is where Guimard built his home and studio, an asymmetrical celebration, in 1909.

6. Modernist Villa

Walk through the village of Auteuil to reach **Maison La Roche**, a groundbreaking modernist villa constructed by Le Corbusier and Pierre Jeanneret between 1923 and 1925. Now home to the Fondation Le Corbusier, this UNESCO-listed site is open to visitors (online booking required). The carefully curated furniture is as eye-catching as the experimental interiors.

7. UNESCO Sites

To continue your immersion in Le Corbusier's architecture, explore another UNESCO-listed property near Boulogne-Billancourt. Le Corbu's **studio-apartment** occupied two floors of the world's first glass-fronted apartment building, which he designed between 1931 and 1934. On your way there, take a gander at the Hotel Molitor pool complex, an art deco icon built in 1929.

EXPERIENCES

Immerse Yourself in Art at Musée Marmottan Monet
ART MUSEUM

MAP: ❶ P40 **A4**

Housed in the Duc de Valmy's former hunting lodge (well, let's call it a mansion), the **Musée Marmottan Monet** *(marmottan.fr/en; adult/child €14/free)* is home to the world's largest Claude Monet collection. Take this unique chance to immerse in a real cross-section of the artist's work, beginning with paintings such as the seminal *Impression, soleil levant* (1872), passing through numerous water-lily studies, before moving on to abstract pieces. Masterpieces to look out for include *La barque* (1887), *Cathédrale de Rouen* (1892), *Londres, le Parlement* (1901) and the various *Nymphéas* (water lilies).

With acres of gilt and plush Empire-style furnishings, the mansion almost eclipses the art collection. Head-turning decor includes a bed that once belonged to Napoléon, an enormous wood desk sculpted with winged lions and a splendid geographic clock by porcelain powerhouse the Manufacture de Sèvres. Upstairs, don't miss the ensemble of paintings by Berthe Morisot, the famed female impressionist. Temporary exhibitions, included in the admission price, are usually superb.

Follow in Balzac's Footsteps
WRITER'S HOME

MAP: ❷ P40 **D5**

Transport yourself back in time at the pretty, three-storey house where realist novelist Honoré de Balzac (1799–1850) hid from his creditors to live and work from 1840 to 1847. (He used a pseudonym, and visitors had to pronounce a special password.) This is a small pocket of old-school Passy, and you can look over the wall at the rue Berton, a cobbled lane that served as Balzac's secret exit. The **Maison de Balzac** *(maisondebalzac.paris.fr/en; adult/child €9/free)* is perfect for fans of literature and letters – you'll even spy the porcelain coffee pot that famously fuelled his all-nighters. The app (there's wi-fi on-site for downloading) is crammed with audio commentary, including fascinating details about how Balzac maintained his manically intense work habits. Settle in at the on-site **Rose Bakery** cafe for fresh-baked treats, soups and quiche – garden tables with the Eiffel Tower high in the distance make the perfect setting to contemplate your next great work.

Pick Up Picnic Supplies at Marché Président Wilson
STREET MARKET

MAP: ❸ P40 **F2**

Stroll the open-air **Marché Président Wilson** across from Palais de Tokyo, where fresh-cut flowers crowd vendors of heirloom vegetables, fish and artisanal charcuterie. Adored by the city's top chefs, this lively market brims with the highest-quality products: poultry from Maison Priolet, Normandy-grown fruit from Moulin de l'Abbaye and cheese from Les Fromages de Sophie. Looking for lunch? You'll also find food stands with readymade meals you can pack up for a picnic, including Japanese street food, spice-topped Lebanese flatbread and crêpes. The many temptations are available Wednesday and Saturday mornings, and it's one of the most convenient options to reach in the 16e.

Ride the Waves at the Musée de la Marine   MUSEUM

MAP: ④ P40 E3

Located in the western wing of Palais de Chaillot, the **Musée National de la Marine** *(musee-marine.fr/en.html; adult/child €11/free)* doesn't just celebrate France's grand naval adventures from the 17th century until the present day (with model ships galore). This maritime museum is a sensory immersion in all things related to the sea, from cargo routes to open-ocean sailing races, from pollution to the mysterious shipwrecks that have fuelled the human imagination. It all comes to life thanks to interactive touchscreens, movies and more. A massive six-year makeover unveiled in 2023 completely transformed a fusty old museum into a must-visit cultural attraction that keeps Parisians coming back for more. Kids can't get enough. In a first for a Paris museum, there's even a special 'zen' room for children with autism.

Discover Modern Art at Palais de Tokyo   MUSEUM

MAP: ⑤ P40 F2

Soaring columns, art deco friezes...what exactly is that palace

WORLD'S FAIR LEGACY
Starting in the 19th century, World's Fairs drew massive crowds to gape at exhibitions designed to showcase the latest in technology, culture and industry. Paris played host to seven such events, for which staggering architectural monuments were constructed. The Palais de Chaillot, dating to 1937, is perched above fountain-bedecked gardens facing the Eiffel Tower. Today the eastern wing houses the Cité de l'Architecture et du Patrimoine, devoted to French architecture, as well as the Théâtre National de Chaillot, staging dance and theatre. The Musée National de la Marine and the Musée de l'Homme (tracing human evolution) are housed in the western wing.

on the Seine? **Palais de Tokyo** *(palaisdetokyo.com; adult/child €13/free)* was created for the 1937 Exposition Internationale. Nowadays the western wing is Europe's largest contemporary arts centre. The concrete-and-steel interior is a slick host for interactive exhibitions and installations. Eating, drinking and entertainment options are fun: Bambini and Forest, with tables in the central courtyard over a reflecting pool with the Eiffel Tower in the distance, and basement nightclub Yoyo.

In the east wing, **Musée d'Art Moderne de Paris** *(mam.paris.fr/en)* displays a vast permanent collection that's free to access. Monumental installations include an entire room of Matisse murals, and Raoul Dufy's *La Fée électricité,* a fresco depicting the history of electricity. The room is so dazzling that visitors sit on stools, transfixed, losing themselves in the effervescent colours. Look out for excellent temporary exhibitions (not free).

Transport Yourself to Asia at the Musée Guimet   MUSEUM

MAP: 6 P40 F2

Musée National des Arts Asiatiques Guimet *(guimet.fr/en; adult/child €13/free)* is France's foremost Asian arts museum, housing a superb collection from all corners of the continent. In fact, it's possible to observe the gradual transmission of both Buddhism and artistic styles along the Silk Road in some of the museum's pieces, from the 1st-century Gandhara Buddhas from Afghanistan and Pakistan to the later Central Asian, Chinese and Japanese sculptures. Above all, it's a place where you'll want to get lost in beauty – from the neoclassical rotunda in the historic library to the Khmer courtyard. In this elegant space there are delights at every turn. Keep an eye out for Tibetan mandalas, centuries-old terracotta horses from China and the world's largest collection of Khmer artefacts outside Cambodia. For a quick bite, try family-style Korean dishes at Hannok restaurant. In the summer months, the panoramic rooftop is a hip spot for lunch, snacks and evening cocktails with a DJ-spun soundtrack on the weekends.

LISTINGS

Best Places for...

€ Budget €€ Midrange €€€ Top End

See p40 for map of locations

Eating

Classic French

La Rotonde de la Muette €€
7 B4

This celebrated brasserie is a local institution, with velvet banquettes, wood panelling and brass light fixtures. Don't miss the Grand Marnier soufflé. *7am-midnight*

Le Petit Rétro €€
8 D1

An art nouveau time capsule from 1904, classified a historic monument, serving traditional treats like *steak-frites*. *noon-2.30pm & 7.30-10.30pm*

Les Marches €€
9 F3

Red-chequered tablecloths on bistro tables set the scene at this classic joint. *noon-2.30pm & 7.30-10.30pm*

Worth the Splurge

Comice €€€
10 C6

A friendly husband-and-wife team run this Michelin-starred favourite. *7-9pm Mon-Fri, sometimes Sat*

Substance €€€
11 G2

Let yourself be wowed by Chef Matthias Marc's multicourse tasting menu. *noon-1.30pm & 7.30-9pm Mon-Fri*

Near the Eiffel Tower

Les Deux Abeilles €€
12 G3

Homemade delights await at this old-fashioned tearoom that's adored by regulars. *9am-7pm Tue-Sat*

Arnaud Nicolas €€
13 G4

The charcuterie maestro artfully stocks a boutique and runs this restaurant. *noon-2.30pm & 7-10pm Tue-Sat*

Drinking

Cocktails in the 16e

Cravan
14 B6

Sip some of the city's best drinks inside an art nouveau building by Hector Guimard. *6-11pm Wed-Sat*

St James Paris
15 C1

In a wood-panelled library, or on the dreamy terrace, try creative drinks highlighting ingredients from the hotel's garden. *7pm-midnight*

Midi-Minuit
16 F2

The bar at Ducasse Baccarat, inside a stunning mansion, is run by mixologist Margot Lecarpentier of Combat fame. *noon-midnight*

Le Belair
17 C6

Retro glamour at this hip spot at the Maison de la Radio, with a dance floor and DJ sets. *6.30pm-2am Thu-Sat*

Explore
Champs-Élysées & Grands Boulevards

Researched by Nicola Leigh Stewart

The Champs-Élysées and Grands Boulevards area is grandiose in layout – it's possible to play an epically proportioned game of connect the dots here. The main landmarks – the Arc de Triomphe, place de la Concorde, place de la Madeleine and the Opéra – are joined by majestic boulevards, each lined with harmonious rows of Haussmann-era buildings. Monumental vistas will easily keep your eyes occupied but high-end shops and elegant department stores are this district's raison d'être. Beyond the fashion overload, there's a bevy of impressive historic monuments and art museums to keep you entertained.

Getting Around

 **Walking**
Paris is an easy city to walk around, and strolling up the famed Champs-Élysées is the best way to see it.

 Metro
There are a few key metro stations along the Champs-Élysées, including Charles de Gaulle–Étoile, Champs-Élysées–Clemenceau and Concorde.

 Taxi
If you're visiting some of the fancier addresses around the Champs-Élysées you might want to arrive by taxi. Your ride might even include a drive around the manic place de l'Étoile, anchored by the Arc de Triomphe.

THE BEST

PHANTOM'S LAIR Palais Garnier (p59)

ART MUSEUM Petit Palais (p62)

MONUMENT MUST Hôtel de la Marine (p63)

FASHION FUN La Galerie Dior (p63)

PARIS VIEWS Arc de Triomphe (p58)

Arc de Triomphe (p58)
ERIC ISSELEE/SHUTTERSTOCK

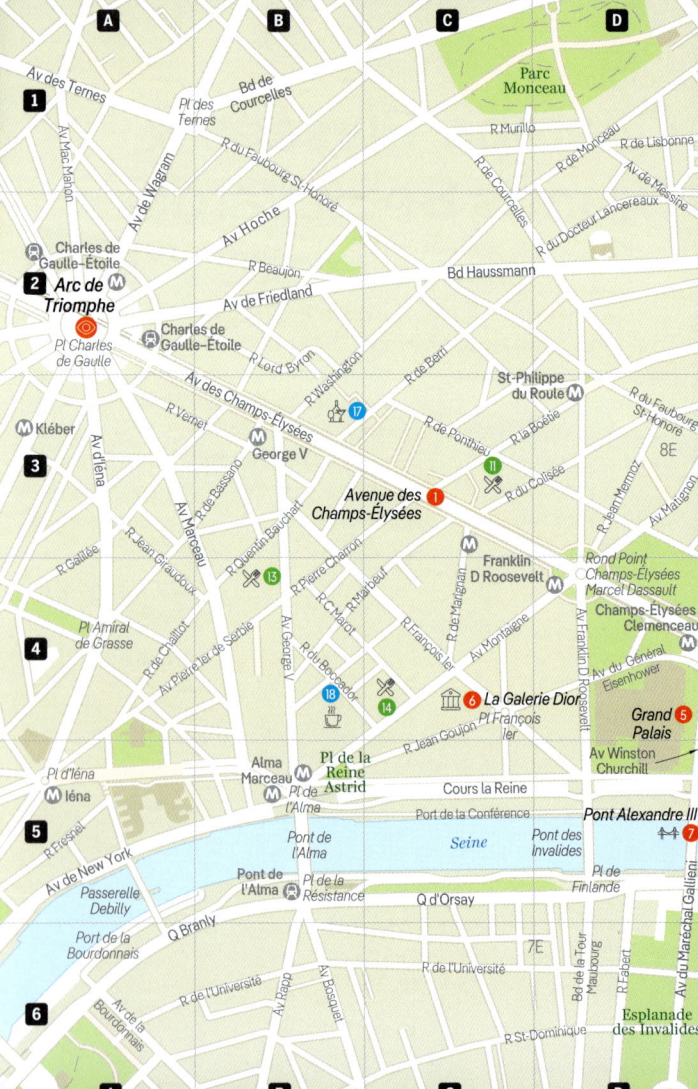

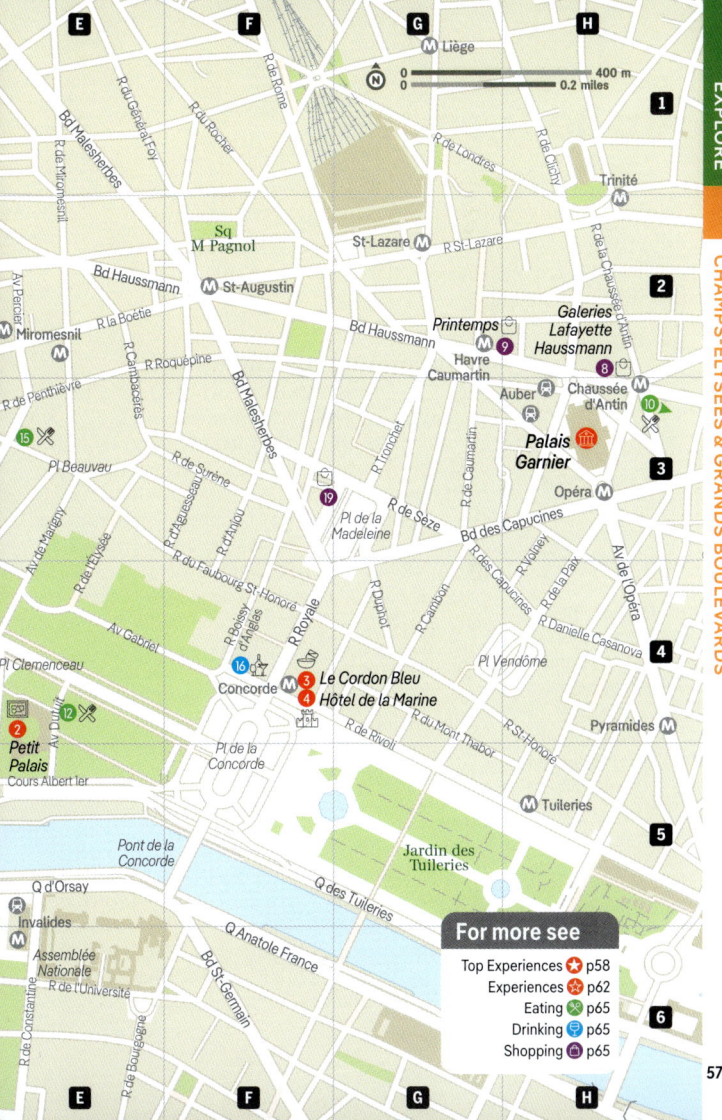

⭐ **TOP EXPERIENCE**

Arc de Triomphe

Napoléon's armies never did march through the Arc de Triomphe showered in honour, but the monument has nonetheless come to stand as the very symbol of French patriotism. For visitors, it's the sublime panoramas from the top that are the draw.

MAP P56 **A2**

PLANNING TIP
First thing in the morning is usually your best chance to find a quiet moment at this busy attraction, though sunset is the most beautiful. Book tickets online for a time slot.

A Symbol of Peace & Remembrance

Napoléon commissioned the Arc de Triomphe after his victory at the Battle of Austerlitz in 1805, but by the time it was finished in 1836, the emperor had abdicated, died, and the monarchy had made its brief return. Beneath the arch at ground level lies the Tomb of the Unknown Solider. Honouring the 1.3 million French soldiers who lost their lives during WWI, the Unknown Solider was laid to rest in 1921, beneath an eternal flame, which is rekindled daily at 6.30pm. Visitors can watch the event or catch it on the live video inside the museum.

The 200 original steps will take you up to the museum and a further 40 lead up to the terrace – easily one of the best views in Paris. Note it's closed during adverse weather conditions and during official ceremonies.

Sunset Splendour

Two days a year, you can see the sun fall right through the arch's centre, usually on or around 10 May and 1 August (the exact date isn't posted on the website but you can find it through a Google search). To get the ultimate shot, don't stand at the arch itself but further back on the Champs-Élysées.

Scan this QR code for full opening hours and to book ahead.

⭐ **TOP EXPERIENCE**

Palais Garnier

Few other Paris monuments have provided artistic inspiration in the way that the Palais Garnier has. From Degas' ballerinas to Gaston Leroux' Phantom and Chagall's ceiling, the layers of myth painted on gradually over the decades have bestowed an air of mystery and drama to its ornate interior.

Design Dream

MAP P56 **H3**

In an emperor power move, Napoléon III commissioned a new Paris opera house to his liking after an assassination attempt at the former opera house on nearby rue Le Peletier. Charles Garnier was just 35 years old, and as yet unknown, when he won the commission to build it. He surprised everyone including Empress Eugénie, who was less than impressed when Garnier presented his designs.

Once inside, the 'show' starts not in the auditorium but on another stage: the grand staircase. Garnier purposefully designed the staircase with sweeping steps and balconies to observe who was sashaying up it. In the auditorium, he flattered high society by choosing red velvet seating to complement the gold, saying that the pink tinge reflected on women's faces helped them look 'more youthful and radiant'.

Tour Highlights

Crowning the space is a fresco ceiling by Marc Chagall, a recent design addition, and the opera house's impressive chandelier, which inspired an event in Gaston Leroux' *The Phantom of the Opera* when it fell from the ceiling in 1896.

Aside from the auditorium, one of the Palais Garnier's most prestigious rooms is the Grand Foyer, inspired by the Hall of Mirrors at Versailles and recently restored to its full splendour.

PLANNING TIP
Book online in advance – it's not guaranteed you'll get a same-day ticket at the box office. A private group tour takes you behind the scenes. Otherwise the audio tour is excellent.

Scan this QR code for full opening hours and to book ahead.

WALKING TOUR
Champs-Élysées to Palais Garnier

Strolling down the Champs-Élysées is a chance to take in landmark monuments and architectural beauties from fin-de-siècle Paris. This museum-rich neighbourhood is rich with history, and the vistas from both the Arc de Triomphe and the place de la Concorde are unparalleled. Take the time to soak it all in – this walk has plenty of breaks along the way.

START	END	LENGTH
Arc de Triomphe	Palais Garnier	4km; 3 hours

1 'Most Beautiful Avenue'
Starting from the **Arc de Triomphe** (p58), stroll down the 2km of the tree-lined Champs-Élysées with its many designer and luxury stores. The avenue might be the most famous in the world, but not for its food. If you need a pit stop, try Ladurée and L'Occitane x Pierre Hermé (for macarons) and Flora Danica (for coffee and a cinnamon roll).

2 Magnificent Monuments
Turn right down av Winston Churchill to visit the art nouveau **Petit Palais** (p62), built as a fine-art museum for the 1900 Paris Exposition. Look out for the Statue of General Charles de Gaulle on your way, and the Winston Churchill statue on the corner of the museum towards the Pont Alexandre III. Opposite the museum, you'll find the grand glass-roofed **Grand Palais** (p63).

3 Historic Square
Once you've got your art fix, cross over the Champs-Élysées and through the gardens on the allée Marcel-Proust. Continue to **place de la Concorde**. Sculptures on the edge of the city's biggest square represent major French cities. Near the gold-tipped Egyptian obelisk in the middle, look for the plaque that marks the execution site of King Louis XVI and Marie Antoinette.

4 Grandiose Church
Cross the street and take rue Royale towards place de la Madeleine; it sits in between the twin buildings designed by Louis XV's chief architect, Ange-Jacques Gabriel, that now house the Hôtel de Crillon and **Hôtel de la Marine** (p63). The Greek-inspired **Église de la Madeleine** has an imposing façade of Corinthian columns.

5 Department Stores
From place de la Madeleine continue north along rue Tronche to bd Haussmann. You'll know you've arrived when you spot the golden and mosaic *coupoles* (cupolas) of **Printemps**. Next door is another department store **Galeries Lafayette**. Both *grands magasins* (p64) also have grand terraces where you can take in the view.

6 Gilded Opera House
From here, head down rue Halévy to reach the magnificent **Palais Garnier** (p59). If you don't mind paying to sit where the likes of Victor Hugo, Ernest Hemingway and Émile Zola once mused, you can finish with a coffee on the terrace of the historic Café de la Paix.

EXPERIENCES

Meander the Champs-Élysées
STREET

MAP: ❶ P56 C3

Often called the most beautiful avenue in the world, the **Avenue des Champs-Élysées** is now largely avoided by Parisians, other than those who work in the area, but its worldwide fame often makes it a bucket-list sight for tourists. It has a reputation for shopping, though keep in mind you can find most of the same stores back home. Beyond this, the avenue has beautiful architecture and a richer history than the high-street shops would lead you to believe. If you're in the area it's worth the stroll. Avoid the international chains and go for something French: the historic **Guerlain** store is particularly beautiful, you can pick up beauty products from cult French brand **Biologique Recherche**, or stop by a brach of the department store **Galeries Lafayette**. Another tip is to skip the overpriced touristy restaurants, and just stop somewhere for coffee.

Soak up the Grandeur of the Petit Palais
ART MUSEUM

MAP: ❷ P56 E4

Built for the 1900 Exposition Universelle, the **Petit Palais** *(petitpalais.paris.fr; permanent collection free/temporary exhibitions from €12)* is home to the Paris municipality's Museum of Fine Arts. This architectural stunner combines classical elements (like columns and mouldings) with art nouveau design, including a gold ironwork entrance and floral motifs in the curved staircase. The courtyard garden is a particularly lovely spot to stop for a coffee from the museum's cafe.

Notable works include *Les Halles* by Léon Lhermitte; *The Sleepers* by Gustave Courbet, a commission from a Turkish diplomat who then kept it hidden behind a curtain due to its racy subject matter; and the recently restored *Portrait de l'Artiste en Costume Oriental* (Self-Portrait in Oriental Attire) by Rembrandt, who added the dog later to his only full-length self-portrait to hide his legs, as he wasn't happy with the final result. Excellent guided tours are available with an English-speaking guide.

Learn to Cook the French Way at Le Cordon Bleu
COOKING SCHOOL

MAP: ❸ P56 F4

The world-famous **Le Cordon Bleu** *(cordonbleu.edu/paris-hoteldelamarine; from €35)* cooking school now has a day school for culinary enthusiasts who want to learn how to whip up their own French cuisine at home. It's hidden away in an 18th-century apartment in the Hôtel de la Marine, which makes a beautiful setting with the original 1743 parquet flooring, coving and curved windows overlooking the place de la Concorde.

It brings to mind the film *Sabrina* when Audrey Hepburn's character was learning to cook at the Cordon Bleu with an Eiffel Tower backdrop. There's a mix of savoury and sweet masterclasses where you'll get hands-on, 30-minute demonstrations, classes for children and more.

Gape at Gilded Rooms at Hôtel de la Marine   MONUMENT-MUSEUM
MAP: **4** P56 **F4**

The beautiful **Hôtel de la Marine** *(hotel-de-la-marine.paris; from €9)* museum tells the story of the building's former life as La Garde-Meuble de la Couronne ('Royal Furniture Depository' in English) – responsible for conserving the crown's collection of furniture and objets d'art. Some of the most important events in French history took place here, including the signing of Marie Antoinette's death warrant (she was executed just outside on place de la Concorde) and the signing of the bill to abolish slavery in France. The superb audioguides provide commentary on each room, once the gilded apartments of La Garde-Meuble's last high official. A separate part of the building houses the Al Thani Foundation, a non-profit organisation that showcases incredible works of art from antiquity to the modern day. Two annual temporary exhibitions are staged in collaboration with world-class institutions such as London's Victoria and Albert Museum.

GRAND PALAIS
Erected for the 1900 Exposition Universelle (World Fair), the glass-roofed **Grand Palais** (MAP: **5** P56 **D4**) reopened in 2025 after a painstaking restoration that returned it to its original art nouveau splendour. The four-year project enlarged the exhibition space and capacity, while adding a buzzy brasserie, called the Grand Café, with one of the prettiest terraces in Paris. Bedecked in cast iron and glass, the soaring *nef* (nave) hosts major events, art shows and even DJ-led soirées throughout the year. In the winter, there's a massive ice skating rink set up – considered the world's largest such temporary rink – with glittering disco balls adding to the party vibes.

Sashay La Galerie Dior   FASHION MUSEUM
MAP: **6** P56 **C4**

Sitting next to Dior's huge flagship boutique, **La Galerie Dior** *(galerie dior.com; adult/concession €14/10)* is a fabulous fashion museum that takes you through the history of the famed French brand. The visit starts on the museum's immaculate white curved staircase, a popular photo spot, which highlights the colourful backdrop of 1874 miniature Dior creations. From here you'll wander into an enchanted garden and

PONT ALEXANDRE III

Another monument built for the 1900 Exposition Universelle, along with the Petit Palais and Grand Palais, the gilded gold **Pont Alexandre III** (MAP: ❼ P56 **D5**) is one of the city's art nouveau masterpieces and Paris' most emblematic bridge. Named after Tsar Alexander III, who finalised the Franco-Russian alliance in 1892, it was Alexander's son Nicholas II who laid the bridge's foundation stone in 1896. Its opulent design features four imposing columns, two at each end, topped with golden bronze sculptures of winged horses that represent Arts, Sciences, Commerce and Industry, accompanied by a series of sculpted fantastical creatures such as nymphs, cherubs and sea monsters. The opulent backdrop and Eiffel Tower view make it a popular spot for photos.

---

through a mini atelier where Dior's artisans can be found showcasing their savoir-faire before finishing the grand tour with the pièce de résistance, a room full of glittering Dior ballgowns. The exhibition changes twice a year so the delicate dresses can return to storage, and to tempt you back to see more of Dior's incredible archives. Book tickets in advance to avoid the long queues outside. Exit through the gift shop, or revive yourself at Café Dior before you leave – it comes with Dior prices, *bien sûr*, but it's a great spot for people-watching.

Browse les Grands Magasins DEPARTMENT STORES

In true Paris style, the city's *grands magasins* (department stores) are more than simply a shopping destination, they're also historical monuments and architectural feats of their time. The 9th *arrondissement* is home to two of the grandest, the flagships of **Galeries Lafayette Haussmann** (MAP: ❽ P56 **H2**; *haussmann.galerieslafayette.com*) and **Printemps** (MAP: ❾ P56 **H2**; *printemps.com*), which sit nearly side by side on bd Haussmann. Both specialise in high-end luxury, but there's pretty much something for everyone.

If you're not here to shop, they're worth a visit for the architecture alone. The stained-glass art nouveau *coupole* at Galeries Lafayette Haussmann has show-stopping Christmas installations, and Printemps has its own *coupoles* to match. Printemps offers tours booked through the Cultival website, while Galeries Lafayette also offers fashion shows and cooking classes. Avoid going on weekends if you want to dodge the crowds. A drink from one of the panoramic terraces admittedly costs more than what you'd pay on the ground, but worth the splurge for the view.

LISTINGS

Best Places for...

€ Budget €€ Midrange €€€ Top End

See p56 for map of locations

Eating

Classic French

Bouillon Chartier €
10 H3
Expect to queue for an hour (or more) but the classic dishes are great value. *11.30am-midnight*

Brasserie Baroche €€
11 C3
A perfect spot for people-watching with a slice of the signature *pâté en croute*. *7am-12.30am Mon-Sat*

Fine Dining

Pavyllon €€€
12 E4
Yannick Alléno's *haute cuisine;* the set lunch menu offers a more affordable taste. *noon-2.30pm & 7-10.30pm*

Le George at Four Seasons Hotel George V €€€
13 B4
Sustainable, Mediterranean-inspired cuisine with one Michelin star. *12.30-2.30pm & 7-10.30pm*

Afternoon Tea

La Galerie at Hôtel Plaza Athénée €€€
14 C4
World Pastry Champion Angelo Musa puts a contemporary twist on classic French cakes. *2-7pm*

Café Antonia at Le Bristol €€€
15 E3
An elegant experience at the palace hotel famed for its gastronomy, or in the lush garden in summer. *3.30-6pm*

Drinking

Hotel Bars

Les Ambassadeurs at Hôtel de Crillon
16 F4
One of Paris' most palatial hotels of course has an equally opulent bar. *5pm-1am*

CopperBay at Hotel Lancaster
17 B3
The cool 10e *arrondissement* cocktail bar CopperBay has opened up a third outpost. *5pm-1.30am*

Coffee Shops

Café Nuances
18 B4
Brothers Charles and Raphaël Corrot are sourcing and roasting some of the best coffee beans in Paris. *8am-7pm*

Shopping

Gourmet Shops

Caviar Kaspia
19 F3
Flagship for historic caviar brand on place de la Madeleine. There's a 1920s dining room upstairs. *10am-1am Mon-Sat*

La Maison de la Truffe
See **19** F3
Also on the foodie-loved place de la Madeleine, this shop's truffle-infused range runs from affordable crisps to the splurge-worthy whole truffles. *10am-10.30pm Mon-Sat*

★ WORTH A TRIP

Bois de Boulogne

On the western edge of Paris, the Bois de Boulogne was once a royal hunting preserve. Now it welcomes one and all for verdant strolls, rowing boat rides, an array of formal gardens and greenhouses, plus a famous art foundation, amusement park and the clay courts of Roland Garros.

PLANNING TIP
Vélib' bike-share stations are near most park entrances, but not within the park itself. Be warned that the area can be a distinctly adult playground, with sex workers cruising along allée de Longchamp and allée de la Reine Marguerite.

Scan this QR code for opening hours and information about individual attractions.

Playground for All
The 845-hectare Bois de Boulogne was originally part of the forest of Vouvray. At times it was the home of castles and a convent, at other times a haunt of brigands and a site of robberies and battles. The park's current incarnation was the work of Baron Haussmann, inspired by London's Hyde Park in the 19th century. Myriad sights include **Lac Inférieur** where you can rent a rowing boat, and 15km of cycle paths.

Fondation Louis Vuitton
This striking contemporary-art centre was designed by Frank Gehry. The soaring glass-panelled building hosts stellar temporary shows. A shuttle runs between the Arc de Triomphe and the museum during opening hours.

Jardin d'Acclimatation
Inaugurated by Emperor Napoléon III as France's first leisure park, the Jardin d'Acclimatation is a long-time family favourite offering a host of attractions including a petting zoo and trampolines. Fully renovated in 2018, it's still delightfully old school, with rides like the Enchanted River (1928).

TARAS VERKHOVYNETS/SHUTTERSTOCK

Parc de Bagatelle
Few parks are as romantic as this one (pictured above), punctuated with waterfalls, rose garden and a Chinese-style pagoda. The restored château was built as the result of a 1775 wager between Marie Antoinette and her brother-in-law, the Count of Artois.

Villa Windsor
Home to Charles de Gaulle after WWII, this mansion was where the Duke and Duchess of Windsor lived after Edward VIII abdicated the British throne.

Le Pré Catelan
The **Jardin Shakespeare** is lush with plants mentioned in his plays. Watch for summer performances in the open-air theatre. The restaurant, also called Le Pré Catelan, is helmed by Frédéric Anton to the tune of three Michelin stars.

Jardin des Serres d'Auteuil
It's worth the pilgrimage to the Bois' southeastern end for the impressive conservatories (1898). Browse a luxuriant collection of rare tropical plants; you'll find an aviary and carp-filled pool in the palmarium.

QUICK BREAK
There's a food truck outside the Fondation Louis Vuitton exit, in the Jardin d'Acclimatation. Or buy picnic supplies outside the park and bring them – amenities are limited inside.

See p84 for eating, drinking and shopping listings

Researched by Fabienne Fong Yan

Explore
Louvre & Les Halles

In the vibrant historical heart of Paris, the Louvre takes centre stage. Once the residence of kings, it's now the world's most visited museum. This quarter, crammed with historical landmarks, perfectly embodies Paris' urban evolution through the ages. While Baron Haussmann's urban planning largely defines the district's present-day layout – with vast squares and high-end venues – its essence is also found in its narrow cobblestone streets and well-preserved 19th-century covered passages. Les Halles and its surroundings – once described as 'the belly of Paris' by French writer Émile Zola – remain a vibrant hub of movement and commerce.

Getting Around

Walking
The area doesn't cover much ground but offers many cultural attractions, activities and food venues. It's easiest and best explored on foot.

Metro
Châtelet is Paris' most central hub for metro and suburban train lines. Other convenient stations include Palais Royal–Musée du Louvre (line 7) and Sentier (line 3).

Cycling
Cycling is becoming increasingly convenient in the area, with restrictions on car traffic and an increase in bike lanes. Rental bike stations are common around the main landmarks.

★
THE BEST

ART PALACE Musée du Louvre (p72)

GARDEN OASIS Jardin du Palais Royal (p80)

MARKET STREET Rue Montorgueil (p82)

JAPANESE EATS Rue Ste-Anne (p82)

MONET WATER LILIES Musée de l'Orangerie (p81)

Entrance of the Jardin du Palais Royal (p80)
VIVIAN SONG/SHUTTERSTOCK

★ **TOP EXPERIENCE**

Musée du Louvre

The Musée du Louvre is undeniably Paris' pièce de résistance, boasting 35,000 works of art on display, including iconic masterpieces, spread across four floors. Glancing at each piece for one minute would take 24 days without sleeping. Plan carefully to fully experience the world's largest art museum!

MAP P70 **E5**

PLANNING TIP
Book your ticket online in advance. Wear comfortable shoes, as you will be walking through 403 halls and nearly 15km of corridors!

Scan this QR code to check for special rates and room closures.

First Time at the Louvre?

Entering the museum for the first time can be intimidating. The key to approaching the vast collections of the Louvre is to consider them from two significant perspectives: Western art spanning from the Middle Ages to the mid-19th century, and the art and crafts of five ancient civilisations that preceded and influenced it. Simultaneously, immerse yourself in the museum's architecture shaped by multiple sovereigns. To navigate the museum, just remember that there are three wings: Sully (East) and the parallel Richelieu (North) and Denon (South).

The Louvre can be both awe-inspiring and overwhelming. Maybe the best way to visit it is to allow yourself to choose, explore and be pleasantly surprised. Don't worry about seeing every masterpiece – enjoy the journey itself.

Guided by Ancient Civilisations

The antiquities department showcases pieces dating from the Neolithic period to the decline of the Roman Empire. Exploring chronologically the treasures of ancient civilisations will primarily lead you through the ground floor, with additional areas dedicated to Egyptian antiquities on Level 1. Begin your journey in the **Richelieu Wing**, exploring

VIOLA DOLAS/SHUTTERSTOCK

Mesopotamian art (from what is considered the earliest human civilisation). Continue to the **Sully Wing** to descend into the Sphinx' Crypt and uncover Egyptian art. Proceed to the **Denon Wing** to see Greek, Etruscan and Roman art.

Gardens of Sculptures

Sculpture enthusiasts should not miss the Cour Marly and Cour Puget, on Level -1 of the Richelieu Wing. These indoor courtyards bathed in natural light house French masterpieces created under Louis XIV. The **Cour Marly** provides an atmospheric setting reminiscent of its original location in one of the king's residences. Interestingly, in an arrangement that may seem counterintuitive, ascending to the upper level will transport you back in time to medieval French sculpture. Moving through the Richelieu Wing

QUICK BREAK
Inside the museum, the **Café Mollien** offers a splendid terrace view of the Carrousel du Louvre. The **Café Richelieu** is run by the Angelina team: sample its famous hot chocolate!

Louvre

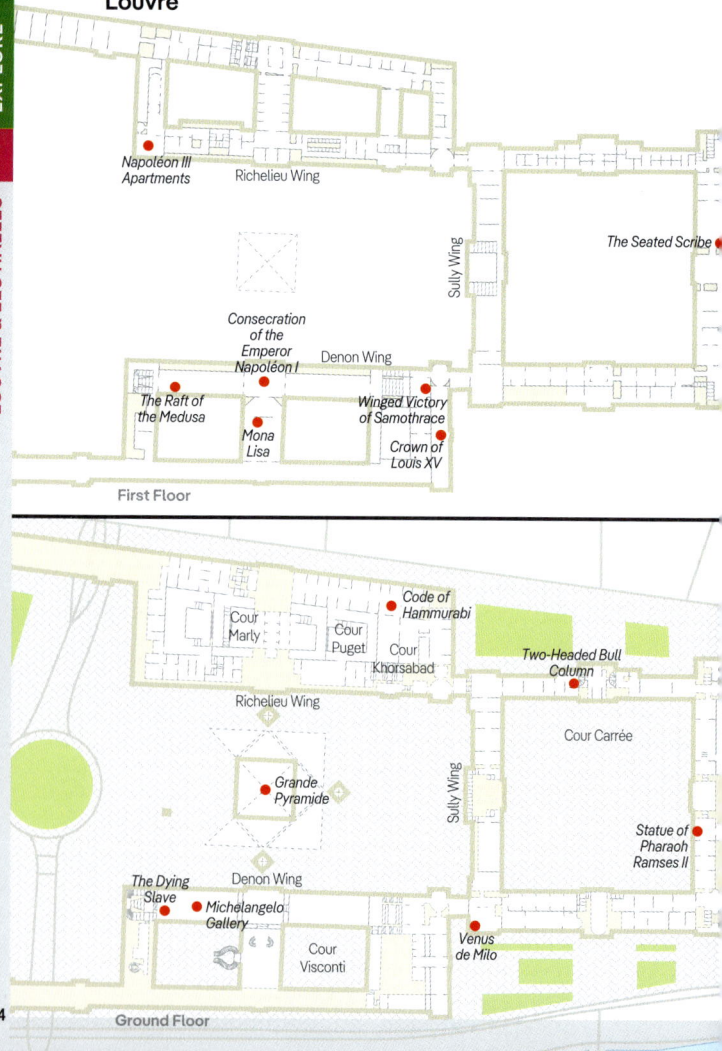

on the ground floor, you'll then encounter more sculptures from the 17th to the 19th centuries.

A European Tour of Masterpieces

The top floors showcase European paintings and decorative arts from the Middle Ages to the mid-19th century. Many visitors explore these floors towards the end of their visit, following the sequential order of the rooms. If you're a painting enthusiast, it's advisable to prioritise these floors! They are must-visit areas for iconic artworks like the *Mona Lisa,* as well as monumental paintings such as *The Wedding Feast at Cana* and *The Raft of the Medusa*. In addition, don't miss the impressive **Great Gallery**, the historic **Salon Carré** (the precursor to exhibition salons) and the opulent **Galerie d'Apollon**, adorned with stunning murals and golden embellishments, and home to the French royal jewels.

Around the Louvre, Around the World

Like no ordinary museum, the Louvre takes you on a journey to different eras and continents. Don't miss the **Napoléon III Apartments**, almost untouched for nearly 150 years, at the end of the Richelieu Wing on Level 1. For a broader cultural experience, explore the small section dedicated to American, African, Asian and Oceanic arts, situated in a remote part of the Denon Wing (access through Level 1).

Louvre Itineraries

There are different ways to experience the museum, whether you have particular artworks in mind or prefer to discover freely. Here are some itinerary ideas to make the most of your time.

ANTIQUE MYSTERY

The oldest piece is the **Aïn Ghazal statue** (Room 303, Sully Wing), unearthed in the 1980s in Jordan, its subject still a mystery: man, child, god? In comparison, the *Winged Victory of Samothrace* and the *Venus de Milo* date back to the 3rd and 1st century BCE – more than 8000 years separate them from the enigmatic statue!

FROM FORTRESS TO MUSEUM
Initially built as a 12th-century stronghold by King Philippe Auguste, the Louvre remained untouched for three centuries. But from 1546 onwards, no fewer than 20 phases of destruction and reconstruction took place! The Louvre became a museum after the French Revolution. IM Pei's Great Pyramid was erected in 1989. More changes are expected by 2030 to welcome the annual eight million visitors.

A Couple of Hours for the Essentials

If you're short on time, you can approach the Louvre by focusing on some iconic pieces. Start face-to-face with the **Great Sphinx of Tanis**, and explore the **Egyptian Antiquities** in the Sully Wing. On Level 1, view the **Seated Scribe** (Room 635), then proceed to the lavishly decorated **Rooms 600–622**, showcasing the 18th-century royal court lifestyle.

Head to the ground level using the central staircase and head directly to Room 345 to admire the **Venus de Milo**. From here, make your way up again via the magnificent staircase, where the **Winged Victory of Samothrace** awaits you.

Once on Level 1 again, continue your journey through the Denon Wing. Take a glance at the golden **Galerie d'Apollon** (Room 705) before immersing yourself in the painting galleries. Start with the **Salon Carré** (Room 708), which leads to the impressive **Great Gallery**, featuring masterpieces by renowned Italian artists, including Leonardo da Vinci's **Mona Lisa** (Room 711), at least until it is moved to a dedicated room, as part of the museum renovation plans.

If you have extra time, visit the **Cour Marly** and **Cour Puget** in the Richelieu Wing to bask in the light through the glass roof and marvel at their imposing sculptures, including the Marly horses.

Half a Day at the Louvre

With additional time, you can further explore the magnificent Renaissance sections of the Sully and Denon wings: discover the **Greek and Roman Antiquities** displayed across the Ballroom and the Salle du Manège. These rooms showcase the imported style from Italy, with notable features like the gate supported by the Cariatides, originally designed for hosting musicians. Can you imagine that Molière himself performed in front of King Louis XIV in this very space?

Ascend the grand Mollien staircase to Level 1, where you'll find the Red Galleries housing masterpieces by French artists, including Delacroix' *Liberty Leading the People* (Room 700).

To end your visit with a spectacular experience, head to **Cour Khorsabad** (Room 229 in the Richelieu Wing) and admire the monumental vestiges of the Assyrian city and palace of King Sargon II at Dur-Sharrukin (now Khorsabad).

The Full Louvre

Are you up for a more extensive exploration? If you entered from the Carousel's entrance, you might have seen some of the medieval remains, dating back to 1190 when King Philippe-Auguste decided to build the Louvre fortress around Paris. Descend beneath the Cour Carrée to witness the surviving elements of the **original moats and drawbridge**.

Then, make a jump in time and walk up to the impressive **Napoléon III Apartments** in the Richelieu Wing (Rooms 535–49) for a taste of lavish Second Empire style.

Last but not least, art enthusiasts shouldn't miss the top floor of the Sully Wing, which showcases two centuries of **European and French masterpieces**. If you're more into **decorative arts**, you will prefer to spend time wandering the Richelieu Wing galleries on Level 1.

Alternatively, discover a small collection of **artworks from Asia, Africa, Oceania and the Americas** in a more intimate section (Pavillon des Sessions, Rooms 424–33). Note that these regions are better represented in other dedicated museums in Paris, like the Musée du Quai Branly.

LOUVRE WITH KIDS

If you're visiting with children, you can take a break at the Studio (Richelieu Wing, Level -1), which provides creative materials for them to enjoy.

LAVISH LOUVRE

If you think you've seen the Galerie d'Apollon elsewhere, it's because it served as a model for the Hall of Mirrors in Versailles (p206). Louis XIV, the 'Roi Soleil', had this gallery made by the greatest painters, gilders and sculptors.

WALKING TOUR

Walk the Covered Passages

The area's covered galleries were inspired by those at the Palais Royal, where shops and cabarets thrived in the 18th century. Landlords soon started constructing their own *passages couverts,* which offered the novel experience of shopping indoors, sheltered from bad weather. This tour is recommended on weekdays as passages in residential areas may be closed on weekends.

START	END	LENGTH
Palais Royal	Passage des Panoramas	2km; 1 hour

1 Atmospheric Arcade

The northern gallery of the Palais Royal, called the Galerie Beaujolais, houses a few luxury shops. It's connected to **passage du Perron**, which used to be a meeting place for speculators due to its proximity to the stock exchange. Exit north and look for stairs on your right.

2 Historic Rivalry

Check out **Olympia Le-Tan**, famous for her original 'book clutch' concept. Exiting the passage, you'll be right across from Galerie Vivienne. Its owner bought and rebuilt passage des Deux Pavillons, directing people from Palais Royal into his gallery, much to the annoyance of his rival, the owner of Galerie Colbert next door. Don't be tricked by this rivalry. Walk a few steps left and enter Galerie Colbert.

3 Art Nouveau Lunch

At the heart of Galerie Colbert's rotunda stands a statue depicting the nymph Eurydice being bitten by a snake. You can stop and have lunch at **Le Grand Colbert** and admire its art nouveau decor. Head left onto rue des Petits Champs, then right towards the entrance of passage Choiseul.

4 Stationery Magic

Restored in 2007, the passage Choiseul is one of the longest in Paris and used to have strong associations with literature and theatre. This heritage is still evident at **Lavrut**, a magnificent stationery store. Old upscale shops coexist with newer cafes and concept stores. Exit at the north end of passage Choiseul. Enjoy square Louvois and its ornamental fountain as you head to 6 rue Vivienne.

5 Gorgeous Galerie

One of the city's most stunning covered galleries, **Galerie Vivienne** transports you to another world. It's bathed in light and adorned with a mosaic floor, beautifully decorated shopfronts and illuminated windows. Treat yourself to coffee and cake at Le Valentin Vivienne, appreciate the fine fabrics at Wolff and Descourtis, discover vintage postcards at Librairie Jousseaume and find a gift at the pretty Si tu Veux toy store.

6 Vintage Shop Signs

Leave through the rue de la Banque exit towards Palais Brongniart. Make a detour to the charming place des Petits-Pères before continuing to 7 rue St-Marc. Just opposite, the **passage des Panoramas** – interconnected with other galleries – exudes picturesque charm with vintage shop signs. Pop by **Culottées Panoramas** (p86) for a quick takeaway item or settle in at **Caffè Stern**, housed in a former engraving workshop.

EXPLORE

LOUVRE & LES HALLES

EXPERIENCES

Stroll in the Palais Royal GARDEN
MAP: ① P70 E4

A serene haven adored by locals, the **Jardin du Palais Royal** *(domaine-palais-royal.fr)* is tucked between the Louvre and the bustling av de l'Opéra. There's something mesmerising about strolling beneath its manicured trees and arcaded galleries – their depth and symmetry creating an illusion of infinity. Built in 1624 by Cardinal de Richelieu, Louis XIII's Prime Minister, Palais Royal has long been at the heart of Paris' political and cultural life. Its galleries date back to the late 18th century, when they were home to shops, cabarets and residences. Some landmarks have endured the test of time. Beneath the Galerie de Beaujolais, for instance, a 200-year-old iconic restaurant still stands: Napoléon Bonaparte and his wife Joséphine used to lunch at Le Grand Véfour. The contemporary artworks displayed in the southern part of the garden are like an open-air museum.

Wander Through the Jardin des Tuileries GARDEN
MAP: ② P70 B4

It's the sense of infinite perspective that first meets the eye when walking into the Jardin des Tuileries. We owe its design to royal gardener André Le Nôtre, hence some resemblance with Versailles. Structured like a traditional French garden, the first part made of flowerbeds is best enjoyed from the windows of the Louvre. In the middle, lines of perfectly trimmed trees offer some shade to joggers. Contemporary and classical sculptures play hide-and-seek in the garden's alleyways. During summer and winter holidays, the garden hosts one of the most popular Parisian fairs, with dozens of rides and food stalls. A 70m-high big wheel offers a chance for a bird's-eye view of Paris on clear days!

Explore Art Beyond the Louvre MUSEUMS & GALLERIES

Art enthusiasts should not miss Musée de l'Orangerie and the Jeu

---

 PARIS 2024 CAULDRON

In 2024 the rise of the flying Olympic cauldron was a spectacular rendezvous in Paris' sky. Watching the hot-air balloon cradling the Olympic Flame soar every evening had become a ritual, and looking for the best viewing spots, a real sport! We admired not only the cauldron's original design, but also the perfect illusion of fire created by electricity and vapour. In welcome news, the city announced that it would be back every summer until the opening of the 2028 Los Angeles Games. Admire it from the Jardin du Carrousel and from rue du 29 Juillet, on the Tuileries' northern side.

de Paume, both in the Jardin des Tuileries, as well as Musée des Arts Décoratifs in the Louvre's northern wing.

The **Musée de l'Orangerie** (MAP: ③ P70 **A4**; *musee-orangerie.fr; adult/child €12.50/8.50*) provides a unique immersive experience into Monet's water lilies. Housed in specially designed oval rooms, the immense canvases completely draw the viewer in. Arriving early usually allows for a more tranquil viewing. The **Jeu de Paume** (MAP: ④ P70 **A3**; *jeudepaume.org; adult/child €12/free*) stands in contrast with its impressionist counterpart: it primarily focuses on contemporary photography and new media. Last but not least, the **Musée des Arts Décoratifs** (*madparis.fr; adult/under 26 yr €15/free*) provides a rich testament to the French *art de vivre* (art of living) and history of decorative arts. Its collection pays tribute to craftspeople who have brought beauty and functionality into our daily lives – from furniture making to jewellery. Design lovers will enjoy the museum shop.

Gape at the Treasures of the National Library   LIBRARY MUSEUM

MAP: ⑤ P70 **E2**

Initiated by Cardinal de Richelieu, the **Musée de la BNF** (*Bibliothèque Nationale de France; bnf.fr/en/the-bnf-museum; €24*) also houses the Depot Légal (legal depot), where every published work in France is registered – a staggering 40 million documents. Not just books; we're talking manuscripts, photographs and even theatrical costumes: each catalogued piece must serve a purpose in advancing human knowledge.

To make this extensive archive more accessible, the Richelieu site was ingeniously transformed into a museum. In **Galerie Mazarin**, a remarkable corridor boasting an Italian-style painted ceiling, 900 objects from antiquity to modern times, rare manuscripts and maps, and religious artefacts are exhibited and changed every four months. It's like a constantly changing mini-Louvre! Note that the national library is also renowned for its breathtaking reading rooms: the **Oval Room** (*bnf.fr/en/richelieu*), open to the public, and the beautiful **Salle Labrouste**, for researchers only. You can still catch a glimpse of the latter as long as you don't disturb the readers.

CENTRE POMPIDOU

Until 2030 Centre Pompidou will be closed to the public. The renovation addresses safety, accessibility and sustainability issues – but also aims at rethinking the space. By the end of 2026, a gallery curated by Centre Pompidou, dedicated to creation and conservation, will be opened in Massy, a 40-minute train ride from Paris.

Eat & Shop Like in Japan
LITTLE TOKYO

Just a stone's throw away from the Palais Royal, Paris' Japanese quarter has thrived on **rue Ste-Anne** and the surrounding streets since the 1980s, forming today a vibrant neighbourhood beloved by Parisians who appreciate Japanese, and more recently Korean, cultures. Foodies will love wandering around, trying a *matcha melonpan* (bun) from **Aki Boulangerie** (MAP: ❻ P70 **D3**; *akiparis.fr*) or the *anko dorayaki* (red-bean paste-filled pancake) from **Tomo** (MAP: ❼ P70 **E3**; *patisserietomo.fr*), one of the area's first Japanese tearooms. Although these two have been around a long time, the area is now home to all sorts of food concepts imported from Japan: from the traditional seafood omelette (*okonomiyaki*) to matcha-only tearooms.

If you're more into finding souvenirs, stop by **Nishikidori – Le Comptoir des Poivres** (MAP: ❽ P70 **E3**; *nishikidori.com*), a high-end delicatessen shop specialising in pepper, and **Maison Wa** (*maisonwa.com*) next door, where you'll find a tasteful selection of Japanese ceramics and decoration. **Book Off** (MAP: ❾ P70 **D2**; *lingonbook.fr*) is one of the largest bookshops dedicated to Japan, where you're sure to find any manga you like.

Go Food Shopping on Rue Montorgueil
MARKET STREET

Vintage shop signs recall rue Montorgueil's past as the supply lane to Les Halles' food market. Now a busy pedestrian market street, its establishments have an old story to tell. Don't miss the oldest bakery in Paris, **Stohrer** (MAP: ❿ P70 **G3**; *stohrer.fr*) – open since 1730 – renowned for its rum baba, and the chocolate at **À La Mère de Famille** (MAP: ⓫ P70 **H3**; *lameredefamille.com*). Cheese lovers can pop next door to **La Fermette** (*la-fermette-paris.com*), while the tastiest *saucissons* (dry sausages) can be found a few steps further along at **Cul de Cochon** (*culdecochon.com*).

Au Rocher de Cancale (*instagram.com/aurocherdecancale*) has been serving oysters since the 1800s, and **L'Escargot Montorgueil** (*escargotmontorgueil.com*) specialises in buttered snails. For a hearty meal, order a pig's trotter at the iconic brasserie **Au Pied de Cochon** (MAP: ⓬ P70 **G4**; *pieddecochon.com*), open overnight. During the heyday of Les Halles, it made its name serving affordable meals to late-night workers, using less noble, but still tasty, parts of the pig. On Thursdays and Sundays, get your groceries from the market around Église St-Eustache.

Admire Contemporary Art at the Bourse de Commerce
GALLERY

MAP: ⓭ P70 **F4**

The circular walls, the glass roof and the dome ceiling, all create a vertiginous impression at the **Bourse de Commerce** (*pinaultcollection.com*; *adult/child €15/*

free). It's hard to imagine that this place was once a bustling hub for commercial trades or even a wheat warehouse. It is now a contemporary art gallery showcasing the collection of its patron, French billionaire François Pinault. But beyond his already impressive collection, the Bourse du Commerce welcomes well-established and emerging contemporary artists alike to create temporary exhibitions in situ. The central room is usually dedicated to an installation, while more traditional exhibitions are hosted on the floors above.

When visiting this unique space, have a look at the compelling circular mural, depicting international trade during an era of colonial expansion: it deserves both an admiring and a critical eye. Daily guided tours in English are available (no additional charge), providing insightful commentary on the site's heritage.

Listen to Jazz on Rue des Lombards
JAZZ CLUBS

Whether you're an ardent jazz enthusiast or simply seeking an evening of soul-stirring melodies, the jazz bars along rue des Lombards are your gateway to an unforgettable night out. At **Sunset/Sunside** (MAP: 14 P70 **H5**; *sunset-sunside.com; €20, prices can vary)*, get a taste of two clubs in one. Sunset highlights acoustic and traditional jazz styles, while Sunside showcases more contemporary jazz and improvisation. Head next door to **Le Baiser Salé** *(lebaisersale.com; prices vary)* to listen to contemporary or fusion jazz, with Afro-Caribbean influences. For a contrasting ambience, head to the spacious and sophisticated atmosphere of **Duc des Lombards** (MAP: 15 P70 **H6**; *ducdeslombards.com; €29–41)*, where you can savour the sounds of classical jazz, swing or even Latin jazz with two concerts per night.

 THE NEW FONDATION CARTIER

At the time of research, **Fondation Cartier pour l'Art Contemporain** was about to move into new premises on place du Palais Royal. The new location is rather iconic: a Haussmannian landmark, formerly the Louvre des Antiquaires – a 1970s antique department store. Jean Nouvel, who had already designed the much-admired former building, has remained the Fondation's architect and worked on the long-awaited renovation of the new building's interior. The contemporary art exhibitions commissioned by the Fondation will take place on three levels. This new addition reinforces the artistic footprint in the area, already hosting the most famous Parisian museums and galleries.

LISTINGS

Best Places for...

€ Budget €€ Midrange €€€ Top End

See p70 for map of locations

Eating

Picks near Palais Royal

Daroco €€
 E3

Pair a Neapolitan pizza with a glass of wine under the mirror ceiling of this rather chic Italian restaurant, in the romantic covered passage Galerie Vivienne. *noon-3pm & 7-11.30pm Tue-Sat, to 11pm Sun & Mon*

Jantchi €€
17 E3

Whether you're into *bulgogi*, kimchi soup or traditional *yukkaejang* (vermicelli soup), you will find your favourite dish at this Korean restaurant housed in an old classic building. *noon-2.45pm & 6.30-10.15pm Mon-Fri, 11.45am-10.30pm Sat*

Eats Thyme €€
18 F4

A Lebanese restaurant with vegan, vegetarian and meat options, with plenty of side choices. Don't miss the *manoush* flatbread. *11am-10.30pm Mon-Sat, to 4.30pm Sun*

Comme un Bouillon €
19 D2

A small establishment serving French popular classics, including the traditional *steak-frites* and *oeufs mayonnaise*, hidden in a street near the Palais Garnier. *11.45am-10pm Mon-Fri, noon-10pm Sat*

Picks near the Louvre

Matin des Oliviers €€
20 D4

A great spot for a tasty Mediterranean brunch or snack break near the Louvre. Choose from Turkish eggs to revisited avocado toast. *9am-6pm Mon-Thu, to 8pm Fri, 8am-8pm Sat & Sun*

Boutique Yam'Tcha €€
21 F5

Take a regenerating break at this Hong Kongese tearoom offering soft *bao* buns with original fillings – Stilton and cherry jelly anyone? *noon-7pm Tue, Thu & Sat, to 4pm Wed, noon-6pm & 7-10pm Fri*

Au Petit Bar €
 C3

This quaint tiny bar still serving traditional Parisian ham-and-butter baguette sandwiches is a surprisingly rare (and delicious!), very affordable find in this high-end area. *7am-9.30pm Mon-Sat*

19 SAINT ROCH €€€
23 C3

Near the Tuileries, this creative restaurant offers refined French dishes with seasonal products, designed by a chef who's worked in high-level kitchens. *12.15-2pm & 7-11pm Tue-Fri*

Picks near Montorgueil

La Tour Montlhéry – Chez Denise €€
 G5

A favourite among locals, this traditional restaurant serves classic and regional dishes. Go for meaty meals, and don't miss *foie de veau* or *andouillette!* *noon-12.30am*

Le Petit Bouillon Pharamond €
 H4

Try all the French classics in this old-style house, from bœuf bourguignon to duck confit. Then pick from the dozens of desserts on the menu. *11.45am-midnight*

Les Dessous de la Robe €€
 G6

By day, have an affordable three-course meal paired with an excellent wine from its *cave* (wine cellar); by night, enjoy a tapas-style dinner. *noon-2.30pm & 7-10.30pm Tue-Sat, 7-10.30pm Mon*

Postiche Bistrot €€
 G4

A beloved bistro among locals for dinner, offering occasionally audacious French dishes, with a well-curated wine selection. *6.30-10.30pm Mon-Fri, noon-3.30pm & 6.30-10.30pm Sat*

Best Vegetarian

BrEAThe €€
 G3

Creative vegan kitchen serving a great variety of sushi and Japanese-style dishes. Try the 'Discovery' plate to share and pair with a sesame latte. *noon-2.30pm & 6.30-10pm Mon-Sat, from 11.30am Sun*

Kitchen Izakaya €€
29 H4

Don't be afraid to order three to four small plates among the refined 'tapas-style' options at this charming canteen, tucked behind rue Montorgueil. *noon-3pm & 7-11pm Tue-Sat, noon-2.30pm Mon*

Maslow €€
30 G6

A large, welcoming vegetarian restaurant by the river, advocating for hearty, creative meals and slow living. Pair one cocktail, with or without alcohol, with your meal. *noon-11pm Mon-Sat, 11.15am-9pm Sun*

Eric & Lydie €–€€
31 H4

In this hybrid place in passage du Grand Cerf, locals often go for the vegetarian bento box (meat options can be available). For a snack, try the cakes! *11.30am-7pm Wed-Fri, to 6pm Sat, from 1pm Tue*

Japanese Food

Kodawari Ramen Tsukiji €
32 E4

One of the most popular ramen venues in the quarter, not only for its original immersive fish-market decor, but also for its fusion recipes. *11.45am-11pm*

Udon Jubey €
 D3

Sit at the counter or in the underground vault to enjoy light udon noodles served in extra creamy broth or cold refreshing dishes, ideal for hot summer days. *11.30am-9.45pm*

Michi €€
 E2

Here, the chef serves high-quality delicate sushi, in the style of tiny Tokyoite venues. You can sit at the counter to admire his skills. *noon-2pm & 7-10pm Tue-Sat*

Chez Miki €€
 E2

An elegant Japanese canteen offering small bites to share as well as more hearty rice bowls topped with grilled or freshly sliced fish. *noon-2.30pm & 6-10pm Thu-Mon*

Drinking

Hotel Bars

Bar Hemingway
36 C2

American writer Ernest Hemingway frequented this bar during his time

Bar Hemingway (p85)

in Paris. Within the Ritz Hotel, it's renowned for its vintage decor reflecting the style of the 1920s and 1930s. *5pm-midnight*

Bar 228
37 B3

In the prestigious Le Meurice hotel, this Philippe Starck–designed bar is primarily known for its extensive selection of premium spirits, wines and skilfully prepared cocktails. *noon-1am*

Bar 8
38 B3

Offering a sophisticated and contemporary atmosphere at the Mandarin Oriental, where guests can enjoy original cocktails crafted at the central oval marble bar. *noon-midnight Sun-Wed, to 1am Thu-Sat*

ROOF
39 G4

The best thing about the Madame Rêve hotel bar, besides its large outdoor terrace, is, of course, its wonderful panoramic view over Paris, best enjoyed on summer days. *4pm-1am*

Montgueil Mixers

Dernier Bar avant la Fin du Monde
40 G6

Fantasy and science-fiction fans will enjoy grabbing a drink at this themed bar, where pop culture references bring all the fun. *3pm-midnight Mon-Thu, to 2am Fri, 11.30am-2am Sat, 11.30am-midnight Sun*

Le Cœur Fou
41 G3

A small bar mainly frequented by locals who like to enjoy its summer terrace. Its simplicity makes it the perfect apéritif spot. *4pm-2am*

Experimental Cocktail Club
42 H3

A bar with a speakeasy vibe and skilled mixologists, offering a sophisticated experience for cocktail enthusiasts and connoisseurs. *7pm-2am Mon-Thu, to 4am Fri & Sat, from 8pm Sun*

Golden Promise Whisky Bar
43 H4

Comfortably seated in a stone vault, learn about whisky with expert bar staff and taste some of the 400 bottles at this specialised bar. *6pm-1am Tue-Thu, to 2am Fri & Sat*

Coffee Shops

Culottées Panoramas
44 F1

Hidden in passage des Panoramas, this small coffee shop is perfect to take a break from the crowds, sipping your latte or filter coffee. Also serves food. *9am-4pm Mon-Fri, 10am-5pm Sat & Sun*

Café Joyeux Opéra
45 D2
This coffee-shop chain employs individuals with disabilities, offering them meaningful employment and a chance to connect with others. Try their blend in passage Choiseul. *9am-6pm Mon-Fri, 11am-7pm Sat*

Shopping

Curiosity Cabinets

Les Drapeaux de France – Noxa
46 E4
Located on place Colette, this unique workshop has been specialising in the art of miniature soldiers and figurines since 1949. *10am-7pm Mon-Sat, 11am-6pm Sun*

Rickshaw
47 H4
In passage du Grand Cerf, this charming store abounds in Indian-style decorative objects, tableware, furniture… and just small curiosities. *11am-7pm Mon-Sat*

Athanase
48 E3
Inside the Galerie Vivienne, this gallery-cum-bookshop is a treasure trove of etchings and ancient maps. Entering this shop is like entering the mind of an old-time explorer. *10.30am-7pm*

Design & Nature
49 F3
Discover the fascinating and delicate art of taxidermy in this gallery specialising in naturalised animals and entomology. *10am-7pm Mon-Fri, 11am-7pm Sat*

Iconic Addresses

La Samaritaine
50 F6
First opened in 1869, this department store revolutionised shopping by offering a wide range of goods under one single roof. It's always held a special place in Parisian hearts, with its iconic façade overlooking the Seine. Reopened in 2021 after a massive restoration. *10am-8pm*

Merci #2
51 E4
Paris-themed books, fruit-shaped candles, designer accessories and homewares you didn't know you needed – this Parisian concept brand has it all. *10.30am-7.30pm Mon-Wed, 10am-8pm Thu-Sun*

Concept Stores

Brigitte Tanaka
52 D3
One French and one Japanese designer teamed up to create a tiny shop (worth the detour by itself) where you will find only delicately embroidered organza bags, all inspired by Paris. *11am-2pm & 3-7pm Mon-Sat*

Au Nain Bleu
53 C4
A traditional toy shop with a beautiful selection of quality plush toys, including several made-in-France teddy bears. *11am-7pm Mon-Sat*

Kure Bazaar
54 D4
Following a French manicure at its relaxing beauty salon facing av de l'Opéra, don't leave without your selection of nail polish in a Paris-themed box. *9.30am-8pm*

Junku
55 D3
It's a little bit more than a mere Japanese bookstore. People interested in this culture will love shopping for stationery, a few tableware items, small toys and accessories. *10am-7pm Mon-Sat*

Explore
Montmartre & Northern Paris

Researched by Rooksana Hossenally

Perched on a hill in the 18e *arrondissement,* Montmartre has long stood apart, first as a rural village, then as a bohemian stomping ground for artists like Picasso and Toulouse-Lautrec. Its winding streets, once home to windmills and cabarets, drew creatives seeking inspiration and escape from central Paris. Meanwhile, the surrounding northern neighbourhoods evolved as working-class enclaves, shaped by waves of immigration and cultural fusion. Over time, gentrification, artistic revival and a renewed interest in authentic, local experiences have transformed the area. Today, this corner of Paris blends grit and charm, and is the most exciting place to get under the surface of the city.

Getting Around

 Metro

Your best bet is taking line 2 (Anvers, Barbès-Rochechouart), line 4 (Château Rouge, Porte de Clignancourt) or line 12 (Abbesses, Jules Joffrin), covering Montmartre and beyond.

 **Walking**

Essential here, as it's the only way to soak up Montmartre's hills, hidden stairways and cobblestone lanes. Wear good shoes and bring a rain jacket.

 **Bus & Tram**

Offers a slower, scenic ride: try bus 85 or 31 for local hops, or tram T3b to reach the St-Ouen flea market and La Villette with ease.

Basilique du Sacré-Cœur (p93)
DAN BRECKWOLDT/SHUTTERSTOCK

THE BEST

PARIS PANORAMAS Basilique du Sacré-Cœur (p93)

ANTIQUES MARKET Marché aux Puces de St-Ouen (p94)

RECORD STORE Yoyaku (p101)

WALK Canal St-Martin (p102)

KIDS' MUSEUM Cité des Sciences et de l'Industrie (p103)

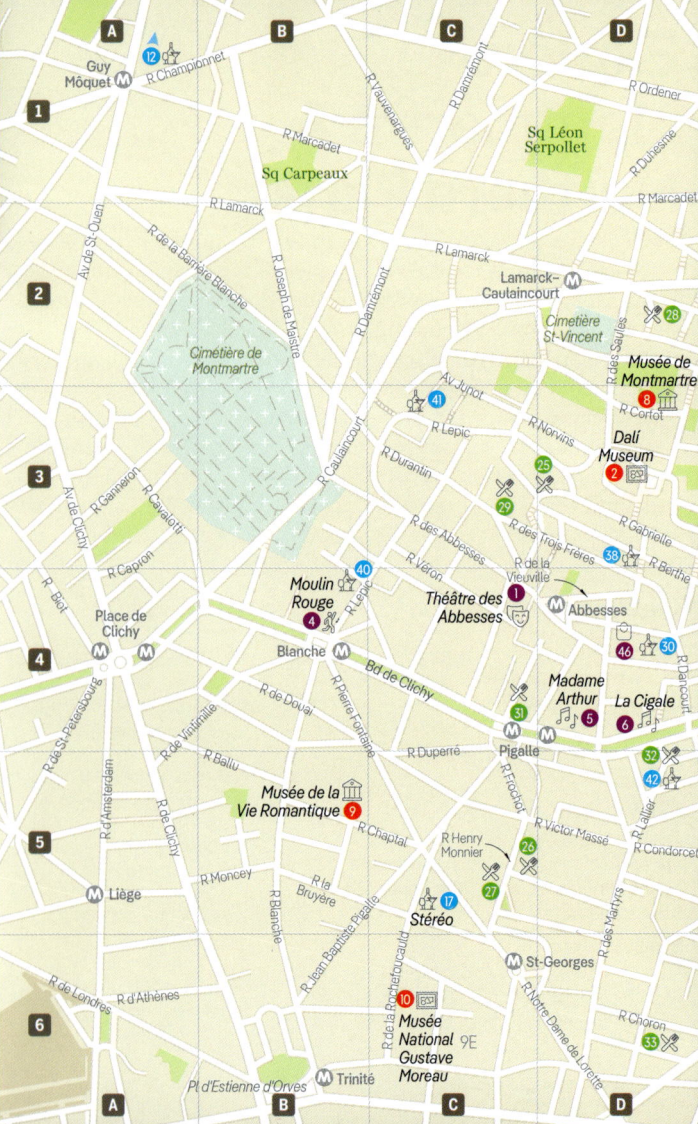

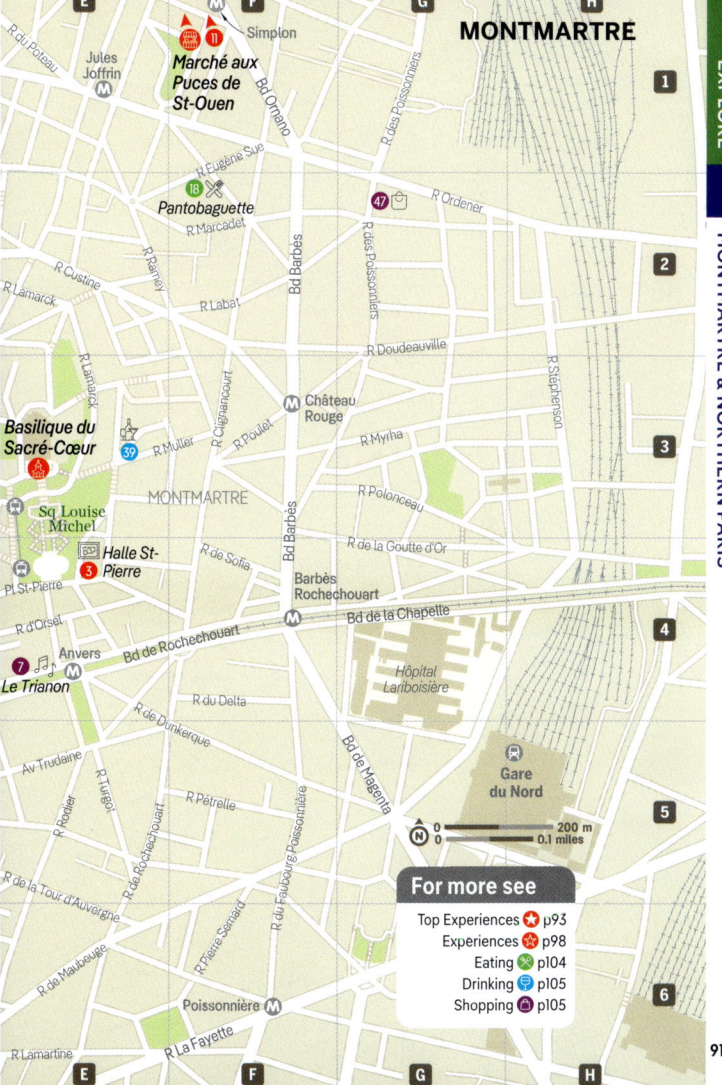

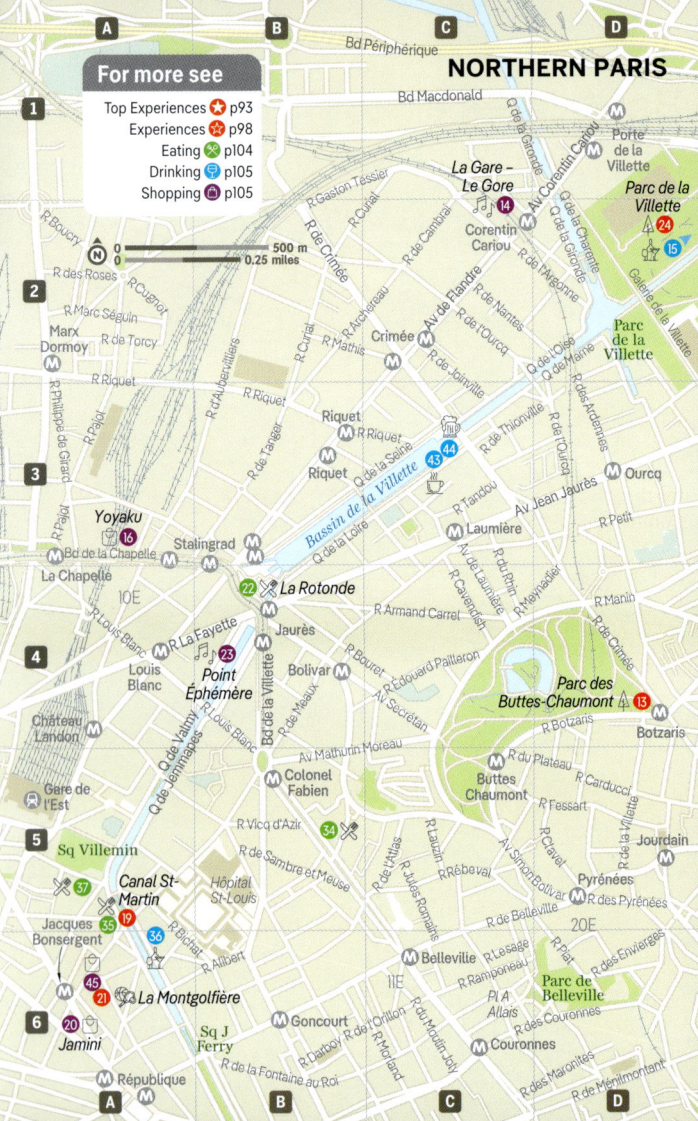

★ TOP EXPERIENCE

Basilique du Sacré-Cœur

Rising above Montmartre, the Basilique du Sacré-Cœur is more than a landmark; it's a vantage point, a sanctuary, a Parisian rite of passage, and one of the city's most visited landmarks. From its gleaming domes to one of the world's largest mosaics, it stuns with grandeur.

Behind the History

Perched at the highest point in Paris, Montmartre officially became part of the city in 1860. The Basilique du Sacré-Cœur, whose luminous white dome hovers above Paris like a celestial apparition, was built later, rising as close to the heavens as possible to atone for the city's sins, particularly those under the Paris Commune, a radical socialist government behind the bloody 1871 insurrections, making it a politically charged monument many locals disagree with.

A Staggering Mosaic

Designed in a striking Roman-Byzantine style, the basilica took five architects over four decades to complete (1875–1919). Its brilliant white façade comes from calcite-rich stone that naturally cleans itself with rain. Inside, the apse features *Christ in Majesty,* one of the world's largest mosaics, while the Blessed Sacrament, positioned above the high altar, remains the heart of the basilica's spiritual devotion.

Sweeping City Views

The north-facing campanile houses the 19-tonne Savoyarde bell, cast in Annecy in 1895 to honour Savoy's union with France. Climb the 300 steps to the dome for breathtaking views. The basilica's perpetual adoration prayer cycle, which began in 1885, continues uninterrupted, and on Sundays the grand organ resonates through the space during Mass and vespers.

MAP P90 **E3**

PLANNING TIP
Arrive early to avoid the crowds; as it's a sunset spot, it gets overcrowded around then. Visit on weekdays to avoid the crowds.

Scan this QR code for information on Mass and opening hours.

★ **TOP EXPERIENCE**

Les Puces de St-Ouen

Founded in 1885, the **Marché aux Puces de St-Ouen** is the world's largest antiques market, located just beyond Paris' northern edge. Spanning 12 distinct markets, it's a treasure trove of antiques, vintage furniture, rare collectibles and fashion. Whether you're a serious collector or a curious wanderer, the maze-like alleys offer endless inspiration.

MAP P90 **F1**

PLANNING TIP
Sunday morning is the best time to visit. Vendors are all open, the crowds are manageable, and there's a lively local buzz.

Scan this QR code for opening hours and other practicalities.

A Storied Legacy of Treasure Hunting

Just beyond Paris' northern edge, Les Puces unfolds like a village within a village, equal parts treasure trove and time capsule. What began as an informal sprawl of ragpickers selling secondhand wares has evolved into the largest antiques market in the world, a labyrinthine network of more than a dozen markets spread across 7 hectares. On weekends, some 180,000 visitors descend upon its narrow alleys, hunting for everything from gilded mirrors and art deco light fixtures to vinyl records and timeworn furniture. With its mix of museum-grade galleries and showrooms, dusty bric-a-brac stalls and discreet ateliers, it's a window into the layered, eclectic soul of Paris.

A Maze of Markets

The allure of Les Puces lies in the diversity and distinct rhythm of each market. **Marché Vernaison**, the oldest, is a warren of open-air lanes lined with vintage postcards, embroidered linens and costume jewellery. **Marché Paul Bert Serpette**, the crown jewel, draws a discerning crowd of interior designers who come for 20th-century design icons, museum-worthy antiques and impeccably curated vignettes. Inside the vaulted glass pavilion of **Marché Dauphine**, the atmosphere is more

GABRIEL12/SHUTTERSTOCK

freewheeling; think vinyl records, retro cameras, tribal artefacts and the occasional taxidermied bird. **L'Entrepôt** is one of the smallest markets but it's mighty and has a bunch of old zinc-top brasserie bars and spiral staircases from houses all over the country. The joy, of course, is in the serendipity.

A Weekend Ritual of Culture, Food & People-Watching

A visit here is as much about ambience as it is about the hunt. Open Fridays, Saturdays, Sundays and Mondays, the market comes alive with a mix of locals, designers, tourists and curious *flâneurs*. Live music often spills out of cafes, while dealers chat with regulars over espresso and wine. The flea market isn't just a shopping destination, it's a cultural experience of everyday Parisian life, regardless of whether you're buying or just browsing. In fact, **La Chope des Puces**, an old bistro that puts on jazz concerts, is an ode to the unique spirit of this sprawling village.

QUICK BREAK
Join the locals savouring couscous at **Le Coq d'Or** on rue des Rosiers, or enjoy a bargain bistro meal at nearby **Le Bouillon du Coq**, opened by Michelin-starred chef Thierry Marx.

👣 WALKING TOUR

Walk Mythic Montmartre

Montmartre is a big village brimming with history at every turn. The long-time haunt of artists and bohemians, the area oozes atmosphere. Discover the main sights and hidden secrets, while delving into its legends and lore, with this walking tour.

START	END	LENGTH
Pigalle Metro	Halle St-Pierre	2.5 km; 1½ hours

❶ Love Rules

Start at the Pigalle metro station and walk up rue Houdon to reach rue des Abbesses, with its shops and cafes. Duck into the tiny gated park to admire the **Mur des Je t'aime**, a wall mural composed of 'I Love Yous' in 250 world languages. Avoid the steep stairs by taking paved rue de la Vieuville, which turns into rue des Trois Frères.

❷ Artists & Musicians

At rue Androuet you'll pass **Au Marché de la Butte**, featured in the film *Amélie,* and then continue to place Émile Goudeau and **Le Bateau-Lavoir** artist studios, where artists like Picasso once lived. Take rue d'Orchampt, passing the former home of Dalida, the glamorous chanteuse who sold more than 10 million albums. (She's buried in nearby Cimetière de Montmartre.)

❸ Pink Sensation

Then walk to rue de l'Abreuvoir, one of the most scenic streets in the city. Pass by ivy-clad houses and **La Maison Rose** restaurant, likely the most Instagrammed building in Paris, and probably built in the mid-1800s. Its pink walls came later and were inspired by a trip the then-owner Laure Germaine Pichot took to Barcelona. She was also Picasso's lover and muse.

❹ City Vineyard

Take time to admire the bucolic vineyard of the **Clos Montmartre**, a unique sight in Paris. Every October, during the Fête des Vendanges (the grape harvest celebration), the whole area comes alive with parties and a parade. Artist Pierre-Auguste Renoir lived next door in what is now the charming small Musée de Montmartre.

❺ Buzzing Square

Continue on to rue St-Vincent to Parc de la Turlure, for a magnificent view of the back of the Sacré-Cœur. Make a detour west to the **place du Tertre** to see the crowded square that still buzzes with artists sketching portraits and cafes like **Chez la Mère Catherine**, where the bistro was born. The area pulses with a nostalgic charm that recalls Montmartre's bohemian heyday.

❻ Art & Textiles

Back at Sacré-Cœur, walk left down the stairs through the square Louise Michel to the **Halle St-Pierre**, where you can see the basilica from the bottom of its pedestal. This gallery is housed in a glass-and-iron structure that once served as a market in Montmartre's textile district of St-Pierre.

EXPERIENCES

Discover Arty Hangouts in Montmartre
ART

Visitors are often busy admiring the standalone houses and quaint cafes that look like they are stuck in a time past, but look beyond and you'll see that Montmartre's arty side lives on in the form of street art–splashed walls, artist ateliers and galleries, as well as more formal venues like the **Théâtre des Abbesses** (MAP: ❶ P90 **C4**; *theatredelaville-paris.com/fr/lieux/les-abbesses*), which puts on plays and contemporary ballets. There is also a small **Dalí Museum** (MAP: ❷ P90 **D3**; *daliparis.com*) with more than 300 artworks. Don't miss the **Halle St-Pierre** (MAP: ❸ P90 **E4**; *hallesaintpierre.org*), an atmospheric art nouveau venue with contemporary art shows, a cafe and a book shop, surrounded by fabric markets. Try to time your visit with an event at the **Cité des Arts de Montmartre** *(citedesartsparis.net)* on rue Girardon, when the artists in residency at the cluster of ateliers hidden behind the stone wall in the leafy garden open their doors to the public and you get to explore this secret village.

Toast a Cocktail (with Cabaret) in Pigalle
NIGHTLIFE

Since the Belle Époque, Pigalle has been Paris' playground of after-dark pleasures. Its reputation truly took shape after WWII, when it became a hub for neon-lit sex shops, cabarets and smoky bars. While many of its infamous establishments are fading, Pigalle's spirit endures in legendary venues like the **Moulin Rouge** (MAP: ❹ P90 **B4**; *moulinrouge.fr; adult €103*), where since 1889 high-kicking dancers and extravagant sets bring the cancan to life in nightly shows at 9pm and 11pm. Cabaret **Madame Arthur** (MAP: ❺ P90 **D4**; *madamearthur.fr*) is a fun evening out with live music and gender-bending performances, keeping Pigalle's legacy of spectacle and seduction alive.

Beyond the show lights, Pigalle's warren of small spaces has always been central to its illicit charm, once home to shadowy dens, opium-fuelled escapades and whispered rendezvous. Today, these tight quarters have found a new life as cocktail bars where locals and visitors mingle over expertly crafted drinks. Spots like Sister Midnight (p105), **Dirty Dick**, **Minore** and **Classique** shake up inventive cocktails, blending Pigalle's hedonistic past with a squeakier-clean present.

Catch a Concert in Northern Paris
MUSIC

The area's concert venues have become key destinations for both emerging talent and established acts. **La Cigale** (MAP: ❻ P90 **D4**; *lacigale.fr*) hosts indie and alternative concerts, while **La Boule Noire** *(laboule-noire.fr)*, in the same complex, caters to underground genres. **Le Trianon** (MAP: 7 P90 E4; *letrianon.fr*) offers a blend of world music and rock, and **Elysée Montmartre** *(elyseemontmartre.com/fr)*, steps down the road, draws large crowds for rock and electronic shows. These venues feature artists from all over the world, showcasing an eclectic mix of sounds, from jazz and blues to electronic and experimental music. There are also a couple of notable clubs, including one of Paris' biggest venues, **La Machine du Moulin Rouge** *(lamachinedumoulinrouge.com)*, below the Moulin Rouge, and **Folies Pigalle** *(instagram.com/foliespigalle)* and the smaller newcomer **Mikado Dancing** *(orsohotels.com/hotel-rochechouart/mikado-dancing)*.

Explore Artist Ateliers & Villa Museums

MUSEUMS

In Montmartre, the **Musée de Montmartre** (MAP: 8 P90 D3; *museedemontmartre.fr; adult/child €15/free*) occupies a 17th-century building that once housed Renoir, immersing visitors in the area's vibrant artistic past. Down the hill in Pigalle, the **Musée de la Vie Romantique** (MAP: 9 P90 B5; *museevieromantique.paris.fr*) offers a glimpse into the life of Dutch painter Ary Scheffer and his illustrious guests, including Dickens and Chopin. Nearby, the **Musée National Gustave Moreau** (MAP: 10 P90 C6), housed in the symbolist painter's former home, invites visitors to explore his evocative works and charming studio via a creaky wooden spiral staircase. Beyond these iconic spots, other northern Paris museums such as **Musée Jacquemart-André** *(musee-jacquemart-andre.com)*, **Musée Nissim de Camondo** *(madparis.fr/Musee-Nissim-de-Camondo-125)*, **Musée Cernuschi** *(cernuschi.paris.fr)* and **Musée Jean-Jacques Henner**

THE PETITE CEINTURE

The 35km Petite Ceinture (Little Belt) railway, constructed some 150 years ago to encircle the city, ceased operations decades ago. Forbidden to access, it soon became overgrown with vegetation, and home to social recluses and *cataphiles* (from 'catacombs'), urban explorers who emerge from the underground tunnels occupying former quarries. In recent years, the city has begun regenerating the railway and opening sections as walking paths and parks. A number of its abandoned train stations have been turned into bars, such as **La REcyclerie** (MAP: 11 P90 F1) and **Le Hasard Ludique** (MAP: 12 P90 A1), that offer food, drinks, concerts and events all year round.

(musee-henner.fr) are worth a visit for art lovers.

Have a Picnic in Parc des Buttes-Chaumont
PARK

MAP: 13 P92 D4

With its undulating terrain, **Parc des Buttes-Chaumont** offers excellent picnic areas, highly appreciated by locals in summer. We can spend entire afternoons lying down on the steep grassy slopes with drinks, sandwiches and card games.

Yet this charming backdrop hides a more sombre story. A former landfill and then a gypsum quarry, it was finally abandoned in 1860, leaving the area neglected and prone to crime. It was only under Napoléon III that it was transformed to become today's peaceful hilly refuge. With a bit of stamina, don't hesitate to climb the artificial hill standing in the middle of the lake: you'll discover characteristic elements of English gardens, including bridges, grottoes and a replica of a Greek ruin, Sybille's Temple.

Soak up the Energy of the City Outskirts
CULTURE HUBS

MAP: 14 P92 C2

As Paris sprawls outward, so does its creativity, as abandoned train stations, factories and wastelands are reborn as cultural playgrounds.. Repurposed SNCF buildings like **La Gare – Le Gore** *(instagram.com/la_gare_le_gore)* jazz club with a basement club, **La Station – Gare des Mines** (for experimental music) in Aubervilliers and eco-cultural hub **La Cité Fertile** in Pantin have brought new energy to forgotten corners. Massive art incubators like **POUSH** in Aubervilliers and the **Fiminco Foundation** in Romainville now house international artists. Even former universities and factories, like **Césure** in the Latin Quarter and an old airship hangar in Meudon, are now cultural spaces, blending performance, community and creativity.

Dance all Night at Mia Mao
NIGHTCLUB

MAP: 15 P92 D2

After a sleepy spell, Paris' nightlife is roaring back to life, especially its electronic music scene. New clubs are opening at a dizzying pace, from the cavernous 3000-sq-metre **Mia Mao** *(mia mao.fr)* in La Villette to gritty, genre-blending nights at **Essaim** *(instagram.com/essaimparis)* near Gare du Nord. Over in place de Clichy, **La Fête** *(instagram.com/paris.lafete)* is drawing stylish crowds, while **Fawa Wafa** *(fawa-wafa.org),* tucked under a 19e-*arrondissement* flyover (formerly Le Péripate), offers a raw, DIY energy. Across the city, underground parties and pop-up sets are multiplying, with lineups spanning house, techno, Afrobeat and experimental sounds. It's a good time to be a night owl in Paris, if you can keep up.

Browse Vinyl at Top Record Stores SHOPPING

Vinyl is having a serious moment in Paris, and the city's revival is best felt in its old and new generation of record shops. **Yoyaku** (MAP: 16 P92 A3) in La Chapelle is one of Paris' top independent record stores, known for its tightly curated selection of vinyl spanning house, techno, minimal, electro and acid. It also distributes music for over 500 labels and 500 shops worldwide. In 2020 the team opened **Chapelle XIV**, a sleek cultural space in the 20e *arrondissement* that blends a record shop, cafe, gallery and creative workshop under one roof. Open daily, it's a great spot to browse records or catch an art show. **Dizonord**, just north of Montmartre, is a playful, eclectic space offering new and secondhand vinyl, books, tapes and kid-friendly events. Over by Canal St-Martin, **Record Station** is a crate-digger's dream, packed with original pressings and imports spanning soul, funk, punk, jazz, reggae and more. There are lots of other spots across the city; check out the Instagram account @grooovz.paris for a map and news.

Lounge at a Listening Bar NIGHTLIFE

The concept of listening bars, originally popularised in Japan,

AFRICA CONNECTION

Paris' African heritage is complex, runs deep and is rooted in its former colonies – Senegal, Mali, Ivory Coast, Algeria and the Democratic Republic of Congo were once part of the French colonial empire – especially in neighbourhoods like Château Rouge and La Goutte d'Or in Barbès. These areas pulse with life, from the scent of grilled meat and *bissap* juice to the colourful stalls of Marché Dejean selling spices, fabrics and beauty products from across the continent. Institutions like the Musée Dapper (now closed) have spotlighted African art and thought. Music venues such as **Le 360** and **New Morning** showcase musical talent from all over Africa.

has inspired the opening of new bars that play vinyl records. Gone are the days of music merely as background noise, as bars put listening to music on vinyl back in the spotlight. Favourite bars in the north of Paris include wine bar **Stéréo** (MAP: 17 P90 C5; *stereoparis. com*) near Pigalle and tapas bar **Pantobaguette** (MAP: 18 P90 F2; *pantobaguette.fr*) close to Montmartre. Elsewhere in town, check out Le Discobar, Montezuma Café, Bambino, Fréquence and original vinyl bar Les Disquaires (p131), among others.

BATIGNOLLES VILLAGE

Tucked into Paris' 17e *arrondissement*, Batignolles is a tranquil pocket of the city where leafy squares such as place Dr Félix Lobligeois, parks like the modern Parc Clichy-Batignolles–Martin Luther King, with a bar and food counters packed with locals in summer, and a village-like rhythm offer a welcome pause from the urban buzz. With few tourists, it's a favourite for Parisians craving space to breathe. The Eiffel Tower was assembled nearby, and today the neighbourhood still echoes with creative energy; pottery studios abound, many offering hands-on workshops.

Discover the Charms of Canal St-Martin   CANAL

A short walk from Gare de l'Est, **Canal St-Martin** (MAP: 19 P92 **A5**) offers a slower, stylish side of Paris. The tree-lined waterway, spanned by iron footbridges, comes to life in warmer months when locals settle along the banks with wine, snacks and portable speakers. It's the kind of place where picnics stretch into impromptu dinners at a nearby restaurant. This locally loved area is packed with creative boutiques, trendy bars and restaurants. Browse the beautiful Indian homeware at **Jamini** (MAP: 20 P92 **A6**; *jaminidesign.com*), the carefully curated homeware at **La Trésorerie** *(latresorerie.fr)* over the road, and the treasures at nearby thrift store **Thanx God I'm a VIP.** *(thanxgod.com)*, where you might be able to dig out a Dior jacket at a bargain price. If you're here to work and you want to work out, then the glass-roof **La Montgolfière** (MAP: 21 P92 **A6**; *lamontgolfiereclub.com*), inside an old hot-air-balloon workshop, should be your go-to. Pop into bookshop **Artazart** *(artazart.com)* to leaf through the fantastic books and design magazines from all over the globe.

Cruise the Canals of Paris   BOAT

As well as a cruise along the Seine, it's also possible to explore northern Paris on a canal cruise. Make a booking to explore the Canal St-Martin and Parc de la Villette and watch the locals sitting canalside enjoying drinks, and pass through swing bridges and banks covered in street art. Several companies offer cruises, such as **Canauxrama** *(canauxrama.com)* in Jaurès, **Paris Canal Croisières** *(pariscanal.com)* from Porte de Pantin, and **Akwa Experience** *(akwa-experience.com/en)* from whom you can hire a self-drive boat with a group of people and putter along the Canal de l'Ourcq, bookended by Jaurès and La Villette.

Revel in the Creative Edge of Paris
NIGHTLIFE

This last pocket of Paris, just before the *périphérique* (ring road) spills into the suburbs, is an eldorado for night owls and culture seekers. Along the canal between Stalingrad and Jaurès, iconic venues like **La Rotonde** (MAP: 22 P92 **B4**), housed in a grand 18th-century rotunda, and **Point Ephémère** (MAP: 23 P92 **B4**; *point ephemere.org*), a hub for alternative music and visual arts, pulse with activity year-round. Keep walking towards Riquet and you'll find **Le 104** *(104.fr)*, a multidisciplinary space that's part gallery, part community centre and part dance-floor for the city's youth. By night, venues like **Le Zénith** *(le-zenith.com)*, **Le Trabendo** *(letrabendo.net)* and **Cabaret Sauvage** *(cabaretsauvage.com)* take over, offering everything from indie gigs to global club nights. On the water, **La Péniche Cinéma** *(penichecinema.com)*, a floating club-bar, and the **Grande Halle de la Villette** *(lavillette. com)*, a former abattoir turned events hall, complete the vibrant scene.

Explore the Parc de la Villette
PARK & MUSEUM

MAP: 24 P92 **D2**

Spanning 55 hectares in northeast Paris, **Parc de la Villette** *(lavillette. com)* is a bold blend of modern design and cultural ambition. Created by architect Bernard Tschumi, it hosts exhibitions, performances and workshops year-round. With over 20 themed gardens and open lawns, it's also a space for play, sport and relaxation. Highlights include the eco-friendly Jardins Passagers and a small urban farm for children. If you're there in summer, then plan an evening at the **Cinéma en Plein air**, an annual open-air film festival, a beloved summer tradition; bring a blanket and some snacks. **Festival 100%** in spring is also worth popping by for the cutting-edge performances, installations and art by emerging talents. A centrepiece is the **Cité des Sciences et de l'Industrie** *(cite-sciences.fr)*, one of Paris' best museums for immersive, kid-friendly learning. Don't miss the recently reopened and refurbished **La Géode** *(lageode.fr)*, a huge mirrored dome and 3D cinema that catches the sky in its curves.

LISTINGS

Best Places for...

€ Budget €€ Midrange €€€ Top End

See p90 & p92 for maps of locations

Eating

Bistro Vibes

Le Bon, La Butte €€
MAP P90 25 D3

A cosy bistro serving French staples like tender steak and new potatoes with a contemporary twist in laid-back surroundings. *dinner Tue-Thu, lunch & dinner Fri-Sun*

Buvette Gastrothèque €€
MAP P90 26 C5

A great spot inside an old bistro with easy bites like croque monsieur and shepherd's pie made with fresh produce. *hours vary*

Magnolia €€
MAP P90 27 C5

A light-filled French bistro with a nod to the 1970s and French staples with a twist, made with seasonal produce. *lunch & dinner Thu & Fri, dinner Tue, Wed & Sat*

Montmartre Faves

Aléa €€
MAP P90 28 D2

Terrific, simple market-led cuisine in a light-filled spot locals love. Three-course lunch *menu* for under €30 during the week. *lunch & dinner Wed-Sat, lunch Sun*

La Part des Anges €€
MAP P90 29 C3

A true laid-back local spot off the radar for its exposed stone walls and great classics like *magret de canard*. *dinner Tue-Fri, lunch & dinner Sat*

Le Progrès €€
MAP P90 30 D4

A typical Parisian cafe open all day for coffee and wine, and the day's specials, as well as snails and steak tartare à la carte. *9am-2am*

Pigalle Picks

Bouillon Pigalle €
MAP P90 31 C4

Terrific value, this *bouillon*, or traditional spot selling classics on the cheap, is one of several in the city not to miss for escargot and *steak-frites*. *noon-midnight Sun-Thu, from 11.30am Fri & Sat*

Maggie €€
MAP P90 32 D5

This vintage-style dining space with vestiges of its days as a 1920s dancing hall serves traditional French food. Don't miss the rooftop bar. *7-10pm Tue-Sat*

Caillebotte €€€
MAP P90 33 D6

A local neobistro favourite with an unbeatably priced weekday lunch *menu* in contemporary surroundings. *12.30-3pm & 7.30-11.30pm Mon-Sat*

Trendy Canal

Le Canon d'Achille €€
MAP P92 34 B5

Natural wines and Mediterranean-inspired small plates shine at this intimate spot with a relaxed, neighbourhood vibe. *noon-2pm & 5-11pm Mon-Fri, 5pm-midnight Sat*

Early June €€
MAP P92 35 A5

A globally minded, chef-in-residence concept where each visit offers a new, creative tasting menu in a cosy, minimalist setting. *6pm-midnight Wed-Sun*

Comptoir Général €€
MAP P92 36 A6

Tropical cocktails, Afro-Caribbean snacks and an overgrown, eclectic decor make this canal-side bar feel like an urban jungle. *hours vary*

Les Enfants Perdus €€
MAP P92 37 A5

A romantic neobistro with vintage charm, serving refined French fare and one of the best brunches in the area. *noon-2.30pm & 7-10.30pm*

Drinking

After-Dark Montmartre

Le Tagada
MAP P90 38 D3

This family-run bar is named after a red 1970s strawberry-flavoured sweet and is good for pre-dinner drinks in a laid-back atmosphere. *5pm-2am Tue-Sat*

Au Soleil de la Butte
MAP P90 39 E3

The perfect spot to keep the night going. There's a small bar at ground level, but the real action is downstairs on the basement dance floor. *8am-2am*

Le Café des Deux Moulins
MAP P90 40 B4

Featured in the film *Amélie*, you've got to hang out at least once at a typical Parisian cafe for a glass of wine against the retro backdrop. *9am-2am*

Creative Cocktails

Le Très Particulier
MAP P90 41 C3

Known for its cocktails, this bar is hidden in the garden of a small, fancy Montmartre hotel that's a must for its picturesque setting. *6pm-2am Mon-Sat, 4pm-midnight Sun*

Sister Midnight
MAP P90 42 D5

Expertly crafted cocktails with seasonal ingredients, plus drag and burlesque shows on Saturdays make this an inclusive Pigalle favourite. *6pm-1am Tue-Thu, to 2am Fri & Sat*

On the Water

Le Pavillon des Canaux
MAP P92 43 C3

A whimsical cafe-bar styled like a cosy home next to the Bassin de la Villette. Enjoy coffee in the 'bathtub' or work from the 'bedroom'. *hours vary*

Paname Brewing Company
MAP P92 44 C3

This canal-side micro-brewery attracts a lively crowd with its house-made beers and expansive deck overlooking the water. *11am-1am*

Shopping

Unique Finds

Macon & Lesquoy
MAP P92 45 A6

The art of embroidery is celebrated in brooches, badges and original creations at this boutique near the Canal St-Martin. *hours vary*

Flash Vintage
MAP P90 46 D4

Compact, funky vintage-clothing boutique with a focus on 1970s and '80s apparel and accessories. *11am-8pm*

La Laiterie de Paris
MAP P90 47 G2

Pierre Coulon, the first cheesemaker in Paris, sources milk from small dairies in Normandy and Brittany to create a delicious selection. *hours vary*

Explore
Le Marais

Researched by Rowan Twine

The 4e *arrondissement* is the only district in Paris that escaped the Haussmannian redesign of Paris, with almost all of its narrow streets and occasionally crooked buildings from the pre-Revolutionary era intact. Today, Le Marais also offers a plethora of activities. Admire stunning 17th- and 18th-century *hôtels particuliers* (mansions), many of which house museums. Enjoy falafel in a historically Jewish district, then stretch your budget in trendy boutiques, designer stores and art galleries. An LGBTIQ+-friendly attitude welcomes the community to rainbow-hued bars and clubs. Le Marais invites exploration of its winding lanes and never fails to satisfy.

Getting Around

Walking
Le Marais is best explored on foot to navigate the crowds, browse boutiques and admire the architecture.

Bicycle
Flying down the rue Rivoli bike lanes is a great way to access Le Marais, but weekend crowds can be frustrating, so it's easiest to save the bike for larger streets.

Metro
For the lower Marais, the best stop is St-Paul, but it can get crowded on weekends. Metro stations Filles du Calvaire and Arts et Métiers are both good alternatives.

★
THE BEST

HISTORIC SQUARE Place des Vosges (p114)

ART GALLERY Galerie Emmanuel Perrotin (p119)

GOURMET MARKET Le Marché des Enfants Rouges (p117)

SURPRISE-FILLED MUSEUM Musée Carnavalet (p114)

STREET ART Invader (p116)

Legay Choc (p118)
ELENA DIJOUR/SHUTTERSTOCK

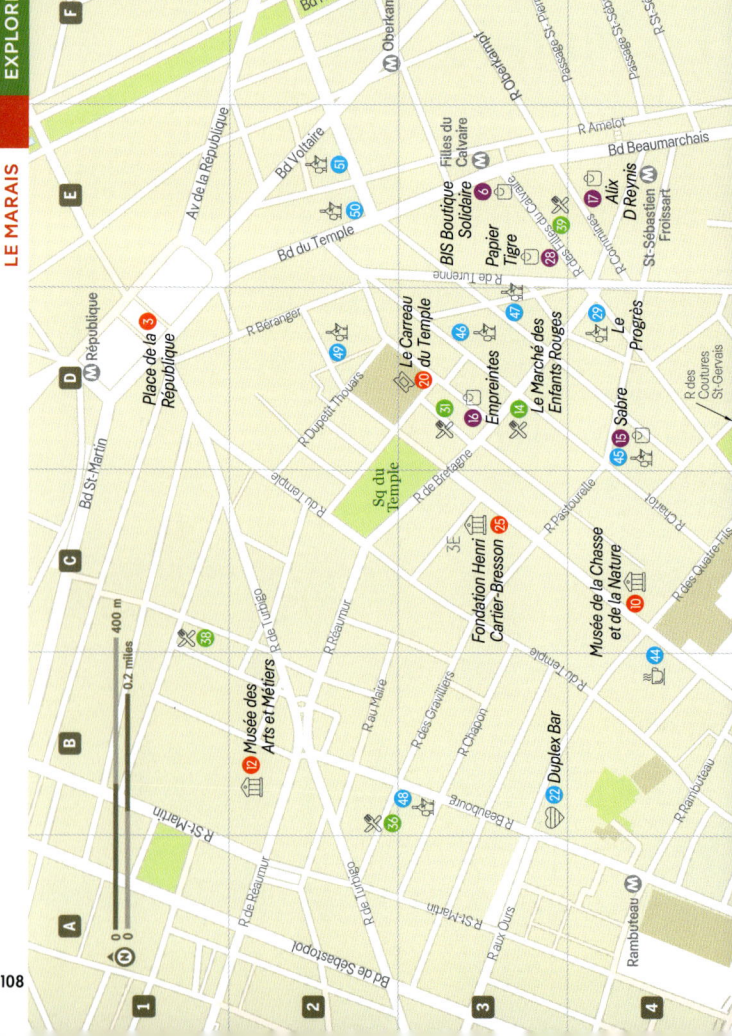

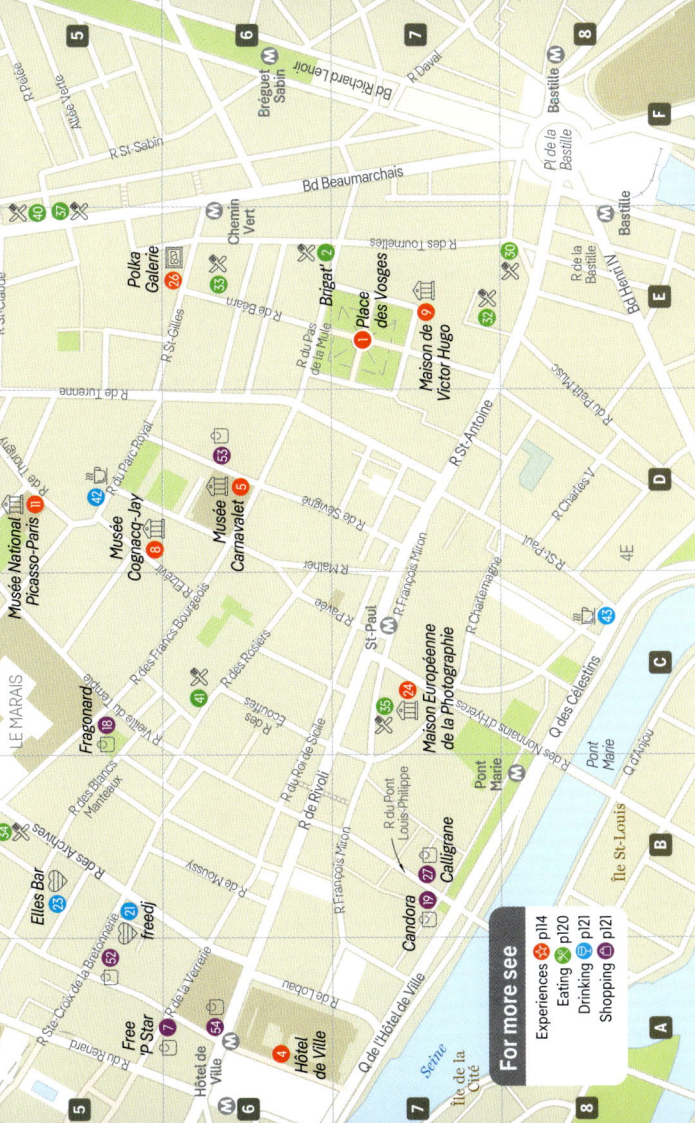

WALKING TOUR

Walk Through Time in Le Marais

One of the few areas untouched by Baron Haussmann's reconstructions, Le Marais contains layers of history dating to the Middle Ages. Its evolutions from marsh to aristocratic hub to insalubrious shambles are still peeking out between its present-day luxury. Navigate through bustling streets to discover the tranquillity of 17th-century mansions and hidden courtyards.

START	END	LENGTH
Rue François Miron	Nicolas Flamel's House	3km; 3 hours

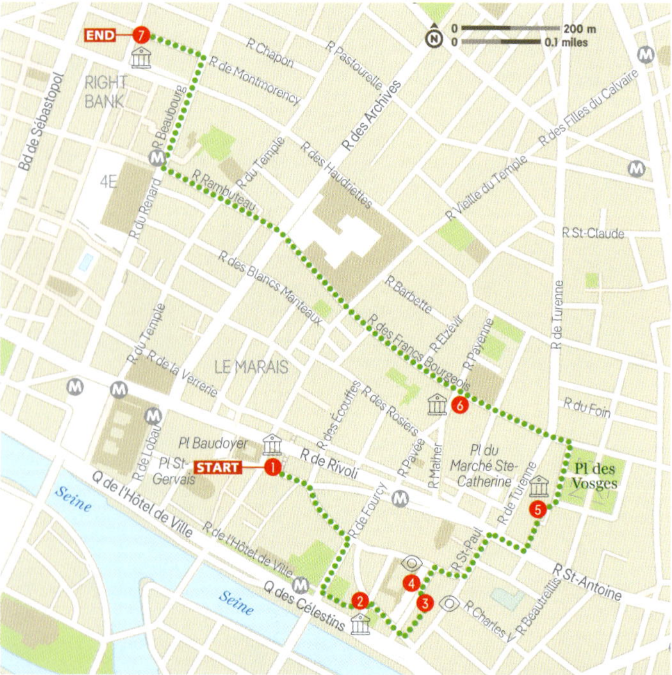

1 Medieval Magic

Walk to rue François Miron to find two of the city's oldest houses at Nos 11 and 13. They date from the 14th century, although their current appearances include 16th-century additions. No 46 is the **Association pour la Sauvegarde et la Mise en Valeur du Paris Historique**: visit to tour their medieval cellar.

2 Gothic Glory

Head east along rue de Jouy, then south along rue des Nonnains-d'Hyères before walking east on rue de l'Hôtel de Ville until you reach **Hôtel de Sens**. This remarkable Gothic mansion from the 15th century was once a residence for the town of Sens' archbishops. History remembers the execution of one of Queen Margot's suitors, which she supposedly witnessed from a window of the mansion.

3 Cobbled Courtyards

Take rue de l'Ave Maria and reach the entrance to **Village St-Paul's courtyards**. This densely packed neighbourhood was once home to the domestic servants who accompanied wealthy local families. As you walk through, try to picture the women washing clothes and live chickens clucking in the courtyards that now house fashionable boutiques and restaurants.

4 Hidden Medieval Vestiges

Exit through rue des Jardins St-Paul. You'll find yourself across from the largest remnants of the **Enceinte de Philippe Auguste** (King Philippe Auguste's Wall), a defensive fortification built at the end of the 12th century to protect Paris from potential attacks. Head north to rue St-Antoine and enter the courtyard of Hôtel de Sully.

5 Hôtel Hopping

Built in 1624, the magnificent **Hôtel de Sully** represents the characteristic *hôtels particuliers* of Le Marais during its fashionable era and features a passageway leading to place des Vosges. From there, head north along its western side. At the corner, turn west onto rue Francs-Bourgeois and continue to reach the entrance of the Hôtel de Lamoignon courtyard.

6 Paris' First Public Library

In 1759 the last resident of **Hôtel de Lamoignon** bequeathed 14,000 books to the city of Paris upon his death. Four years later, this *hôtel particulier* became Paris' first public library, open to all. Today, it houses the Historical Library of Paris.

7 Legends & Lore

Continue along rue Francs-Bourgeois towards metro Rambuteau, then turn right onto rue Beaubourg and look for rue de Montmorency. Tucked away, the elaborately carved **Maison de Nicolas Flamel** is believed to be the oldest house in the city (1407). It was built by the scribe (and supposed alchemist associated with the Philosopher's Stone).

WALKING TOUR

Explore Jewish Traditions

Le Marais has been home to Jewish communities since the Middle Ages. This walking tour guides you through significant sites where their heritage in Le Marais is still visible, as well as places of Holocaust remembrance, inseparable from the area's history.

START	END	LENGTH
Musée d'Art et d'Histoire du Judaïsme	Mémorial de la Shoah	1.4km; 2½ hours

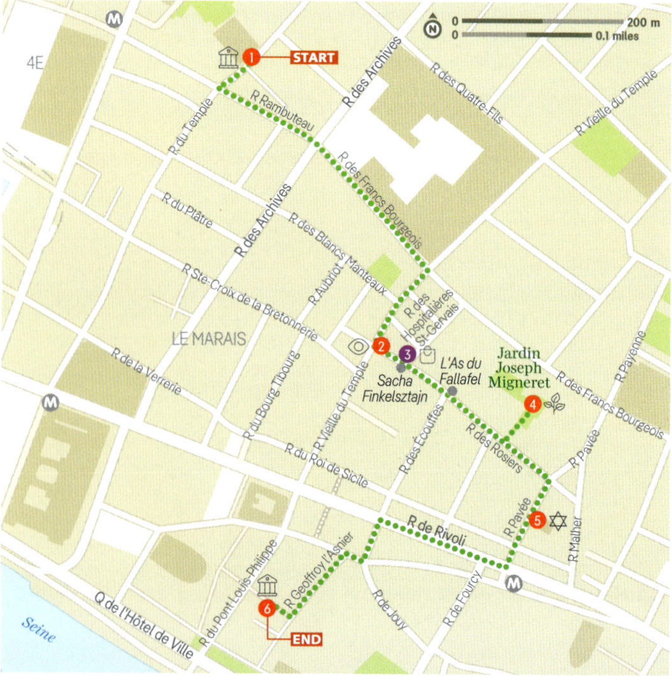

1 Jewish History & Customs

Start at the **Musée d'Art et d'Histoire du Judaïsme**, housed in the historic Hôtel de St-Aignan, one of the most impressive *hôtels particuliers* in Le Marais. Established in 1948 by Holocaust survivors, this institution showcases a diverse collection of artworks, encompassing European and Maghreb communities. Visit the side room that showcases the beautifully varied styles of *menorahs* found across the continents.

2 Foodie Street

Cross rue des Archives and head to **rue des Rosiers**, renowned for its culinary delights and cultural importance. Stop at **Sacha Finkelsztajn's** little yellow bakery to indulge in mouth-watering apple strudels, Polish cheesecakes and braided bagels. Along the street, look up to see the signage that is all that remains of the St-Paul hammam, the neighbourhood *schvitz* (bathhouse).

3 Book Break

At 52 rue des Rosiers, visit **Librairie du Temple**, a bookshop dedicated to Jewish books and culture. You'll also find arty postcards, decorative and religious objects. For a quick bite along the way, grab a perfectly soft-but-crisp falafel from the institution that is **L'As du Fallafel**.

4 Secret Garden

Take a peek at **Joseph Migneret Garden**. Named after a professor who played a vital role in rescuing Jewish children during WWII, this hidden garden is a peaceful sanctuary.

5 Art Nouveau Synagogue

Continue to rue Pavée, where you'll find a striking **synagogue** designed by Hector Guimard, famous for his art nouveau metro station entrances. He created it as a tribute to his Jewish wife. You're now at the former location of the Pletzel ('small square' in Yiddish). After experiencing the intersection of art and faith, continue to the allée des Justes de France, a narrow street that hosts open-air exhibitions that shed light on different aspects of Jewish history.

6 Holocaust Memorial

Conclude your tour at the **Mémorial de la Shoah**. The memorial itself comprises a museum and document centre dedicated to the Shoah, a Hebrew word meaning 'catastrophe' and synonymous in France with the Holocaust. It's a solemn and contemplative setting, including the **Mur des Noms**, inscribed with the names of 76,000 deported Jews, and the Tomb of the Unknown Jewish Martyr in the crypt.

EXPERIENCES

Relax in the Royal Place des Vosges   SQUARE

Place des Vosges (MAP: ❶ P108 **E7**) has truly stood the test of time. The vision of King Henry IV, who wanted a grand square in Paris, this iconic landmark was constructed in 1605 and has remained a social hub and one of the most elegant squares in the city throughout the centuries.

Today, visitors and locals alike still converge upon the spacious lawns beneath the shade of trees. The square is ideal for picnicking, so consider stopping into **Brigat'** (MAP: ❷ P108 **E6**; *brigat.paris*) to buy tiramisu patisserie to enjoy on the grass. Later, stroll the arcades to admire art galleries and *hôtels particuliers,* including the former residence of writer Victor Hugo, or have coffee at one of the traditional French restaurants nestled under the arcades.

Admire Lively Place de la République   SQUARE

MAP: ❸ P108 **D1**

Place de la République has become one of Paris' most renowned squares, largely due to the years of social unrest that have marked recent decades in France. Symbolising democracy and the collective spirit of the people, the square serves as a gathering point for demonstrations and marches, with groups often gathering around the statue of Marianne in the centre. Criss-crossed by commuters during the week, at the weekend this expansive square becomes a space frequented by skateboarders, dancing clubs, street performers and locals who come together to socialise and participate in civic activities.

Visit the Hôtel de Ville   CITY HALL

MAP: ❹ P108 **A6**

The intricate neoclassical façade of Paris' town hall can evoke a sense of awe. The **Hôtel de Ville** features numerous statues representing notable figures from Paris' history, including politicians, scientists, artists and industry pioneers, as well as allegories of the arts.

The esplanade, now known as place de la Libération, was called place de Grève until President Charles de Gaulle delivered his 'liberation of Paris' speech at the Hôtel de Ville in 1944. It now regularly welcomes cultural events and street performers, but these kinds of shows replaced another – for five centuries it had been the site where criminals were executed.

Journey Through Paris' History at Musée Carnavalet   MUSEUM

MAP: ❺ P108 **D6**

At the **Musée Carnavalet** *(carnavalet.paris.fr; free),* you're first welcomed by a grand hall adorned with old shop signs, reminders of Paris' vibrant commercial life throughout the centuries. As you wander through the museum's spacious rooms, you'll encounter artworks, artefacts and historical finds that recount the layered history of Paris.

The city is showcased in all its forms and across all eras through numerous scale models, paintings, architectural remnants and modern masterpieces. Murals, entire shops and even a hotel ballroom were all moved to the Hôtel Carnavalet to testify to their enduring magnificence. Our favourite floor is dedicated to the French Revolution and includes a pair of guillotine earrings, complete with dangling severed heads.

Go Vintage Shopping in the Fashion Capital SHOPPING

Every year Paris Fashion Week brings hordes of stylishly attired attendees to Le Marais, but the cost of buying a new Parisian wardrobe can add up quickly. Fortunately, Le Marais boasts a range of vintage and secondhand boutiques to suit all manner of budgets and styles. Wander in and out of boutiques along rue Turenne or head straight to these favourites.

Less curated and more affordable are **BIS Boutique Solidaire** (MAP: 6 P108 **E3**; *bisboutiquesolidaire.fr*) and the boutiques of **Free 'P Star** (MAP: 7 P108 **A6**; *instagram.com/freepstar_officiel*) on rue Verrière; **Bobby** (*bobbyparis.com*) stocks more current styles; **Système Solaire** (*systeme-solere.*

BEST MANSION MUSEUMS
Discover a variety of topics while exploring magnificent former *hôtels particuliers*.

Musée Cognacq-Jay
MAP: 8 P108 **D5**
Housed in the Hôtel Donon are the collections of Ernest Cognacq and Marie-Louise Jay, founders of La Samaritaine department store.

Maison de Victor Hugo
MAP: 9 P108 **E7**
The residence (from 1832 to 1848) of this icon of French literature showcases his personal belongings, manuscripts and memorabilia.

Musée de la Chasse et de la Nature
MAP: 10 P108 **C4**
This unusual museum explores the historical relationship of humans and animals with a focus on the hunt.

Musée National Picasso-Paris
MAP: 11 P108 **D5**
Dating to the 17th century, the Hôtel Salé's classic architecture contrasts with 5000 artworks by Picasso.

com) and the **Room** (*theroom.fr*) focus on luxury items with matching prices; finally, **BRUT** (*brut-clothing.com*) offers military deadstock and reworked original designs.

Be Inspired by Human Invention at Musée des Arts et Métiers MUSEUM
MAP: 12 P108 B2

The immersive collection of the **Musée des Arts et Métiers** *(arts-et-metiers.net; adult/child €12/free)* includes scientific instruments, mechanical devices, vehicles, communication equipment and much more. It features iconic inventions such as Blaise Pascal's Pascaline (an early mechanical calculator), the original model of the Statue of Liberty designed by Bartholdi, Foucault's pendulum (with daily demonstrations at noon and 5pm), and even a reconstruction of the laboratory of chemist Antoine Lavoisier. There is also a disconcerting darkened room dedicated to mechanical moving dolls and toys, which includes videos of their movements complete with discordant music. Additionally, the museum offers educational opportunities for children through regular workshops that familiarise them with the spirit of invention and pioneering innovation. Visit on a weekday morning to enjoy having the museum largely to yourself.

Go Flashing Street Art in Le Marais STREET ART
MAP: 13 P108 F3

Invader is a French street artist known internationally for his pixelated mosaic creations and there is a particularly dense concentration of them in Le Marais. Track which ones you've spotted by downloading his free app, **Flash Invaders**, and photographing or 'flashing' them as you explore. Pay attention to building façades as you wander, starting your collection with his *Cheshire Cat*. Immortalise the experience by creating your own Invader-inspired T-shirt to wear home with **Les Imprimeuses** *(lesimprimeuses.com; per person €50)* – their child-friendly workshop is a fun and memorable family activity.

PARISIAN POP-UP MARKETS

The food markets, *brocantes* (flea markets) and *vide-greniers* (garage sales) of Paris offer a wide range of products, from vegetables to antique mirrors. *Brocantes* tend to have higher-quality items, while *vide-greniers* can be more of a mix. They often reflect the tastes of their *arrondissement,* so expect more high-quality goods in Le Marais, especially around rue de Bretagne. You can find fresh-food markets along the bd Beaumarchais and in place Baudoyer. The dates and locations for all markets are listed online and most happen at weekends. Arrive early and bring cash, and take your time strolling between stalls to admire the goods on offer.

Brunch from the Stalls at Marché des Enfants Rouges

MARKET

MAP: 14 P108 D3

Le Marché des Enfants Rouges *(closed Monday),* dating back to the 17th century, still exudes plenty of charm after undergoing renovations in the 1990s. It has become a vibrant gathering place for both locals and visitors. The market is home to a diverse array of food stalls and small eateries. Whether you're passing by or looking to sit down, take a moment to immerse yourself in the lively atmosphere and explore the generous, typically French market stalls offering fresh food, fruit, flowers, cheese and charcuterie. As the market is open on Sundays, one of the best experiences is to indulge in brunch at one of the numerous local or international food stalls surrounding the market. You can enjoy vegetarian delights at **Au Coin Bio** *(aucoinbio-restaurant.fr),* order a Japanese bento at **Chez Taeko** or tuck into Levantine pitas at **Chez Jeanphi** *(instagram.com/chez_jeanphi).* You can do a culinary world tour!

Buy the Best Products Made in France

SHOPPING

Dining has always been an important part of French culture, which is why creating your own set of cutlery at **Sabre** (MAP: 15 P108 D4; *sabre.fr*) is a perfect way to bring Paris home to your table. **Empreintes** (MAP: 16 P108 D3; *empreintes-paris.com*) showcases some of the best French designers, with a focus on artisanal decorative objects, jewellery and home goods. **Alix D Reynis** (MAP: 17 P108 E4; *alixdreynis.com*) designs elegant ranges of porcelain goods that are handmade in Limoges. For traditional cubes of green Marseille soap, try **Marius Fabre** *(marius-fabre.com).* Finally, if you need something to fit all your goodies, stop into **RSVP** *(rsvp-paris.com)* to pick out a handmade leather bag, or **Praline** *(pralineparis.com)* for bags stitched in Paris using sofa material from Strasbourg.

Discover the Art of Perfumery

SHOPPING

Le Marais is drenched in perfumeries; walking along rue de Francs Bourgeois from rue Turenne you'll be enveloped in clouds of fragrance wafting out of boutiques. There are renowned brands like **Fragonard** (MAP: 18 P108 C5; *fragonard.com*), niche houses such as **Frederic Malle** *(fredericmalle.fr)* and perfume concept store **Liquides Bar à Parfums** *(liquides-parfums.com).* For an immersive and personalised experience, join a workshop at **Candora** (MAP: 19 P108 B7; *candora-fragrance.com; from €98*): here you can learn about the history of perfumery and create your own individual scent.

IN THE TEMPLARS' FOOTSTEPS
Street names like rue du Temple, rue Vieille-du-Temple and rue du Trésor in Le Marais hint at the Templars' presence here. While their treasure remains a mystery, the Templars' historical influence is undeniable. In the 12th century they were granted lands by the king, transforming the marshy area into what it is today. The Templar enclosure and dungeon are long gone, leaving only a blue trace on the ground outlining their previous location near the town hall of the 3e *arrondissement*. **Le Carreau du Temple** (MAP: 20 P108 **D3**), once a market for various household and fashion goods, now hosts a range of cultural and sporting events.

Celebrate with All Communities & Orientations   PROUD MARAIS

Le Marais has maintained its reputation as a stronghold of the LGBTIQ+ community, although rising property prices in the past decade have led to the displacement of emblematic establishments. Nonetheless, the inclusive identity of the area remains, and it celebrates Pride all year long.

The gay-friendly vibe is concentrated around rue Ste-Croix de la Bretonnerie, the southern part of rue du Temple, and place des Émeutes de Stonewall. Day or night, everyone is welcome at the surrounding restaurants, with **Tata Burger** *(instagram.com/tataburger_restaurant)* offering suggestive burgers and **Legay Choc** *(instagram.com/legaychoc)* phallic sweet treats.

The excitement begins when night falls; **freedj** (MAP: 21 P108 **B5**; *freedj.fr*), **Cox** *(cox.fr)* around the corner, nearby **Les Souffleurs** *(instagram.com/lessouffleuses)* and **Duplex Bar** (MAP: 22 P108 **B3**; *instagram.com/duplex_bar_paris*) are vibrant bars that attract a diverse crowd. **Elles Bar** (MAP: 23 P108 **B5**; *instagram.com/elles_bar_paris*) provides a venue for lesbians. Slightly further away on rue St-Martin are feminist venue **La Mutinerie** *(lamutinerie.eu)* and **Les Aimant·e·s** *(instagram.com/barlesaimantes),* both open daily.

Explore Art in Le Marais   GALLERIES

The **Maison Européenne de la Photographie** (MAP: 24 P108 **C7**; *MEP; mep-fr.org; adult/child €13/free*) is dedicated to contemporary photography – temporary exhibitions feature cutting-edge international photographers. In a different vein, the **Fondation Henri Cartier-Bresson** (MAP: 25 P108 **C3**; *henricartierbresson.org; adult/child €10/6)* preserves the work of the renowned French photographer, considered a pioneer of modern photojournalism. The foundation exhibits highlights from the archives and work by contemporary photographers. Finally, **Polka Galerie** (MAP: 26 P108 E6; *polkagalerie.com*) exhibits and sells fine-art photography, both by established contemporary artists and emerging photographers.

The artistic exploration of Le Marais would not be complete without its numerous art galleries. **Lafayette Anticipations** *(lafayetteanticipations.com)* offers a hybrid experience, with cultural events, temporary exhibitions of contemporary designers, a trendy bookshop and a cafe. **Galerie Emmanuel Perrotin** *(perrotin.com)*, which exhibits international artists in its spacious gallery, runs cultural events and sells art-inspired items. The area also supports art communities, with buzzing venues like **MAIF Social Club** *(maifsocialclub.fr; free)* running a programme of exhibitions, workshops, a cafe and an ethical concept store.

Shop for Stunning Stationery in Le Marais   SHOPPING

France has a storied history of writing; from novelists to Marie Antoinette's coded letters in the **Musée des Archives Nationales** *(archives-nationales.culture.gouv.fr)*. For stationery to inspire your own writing, **Calligrane** (MAP: 27 P108 B7; *calligrane.fr*) is a homage to all things paper, offering tastefully curated objects and stationery. Be sure to ease open the drawers to uncover more beautiful items. Steps away in **Mélodies Graphique** *(melodies-graphiques.com)* you'll find gilded, baroque-inspired collections of cards, books and stamps. **Papier Tigre** (MAP: 28 P108 E3; *papiertigre.fr*) is a colourful modern French brand that designs many products just across the street from the boutique.

Sit & Absorb Parisian Life in Le Marais   PEOPLE-WATCHING

Le Marais is a place to see and be seen, and by far the best way to do this is while sipping a glass of wine or a cup of coffee. For these more traditional spots, be sure to have cash, as many have minimum spends for cards. It can be competitive getting a seat under the striped awnings of **Le Progrès** (MAP: 29 P108 D4; *leprogresmarais.fr*), so arrive for your morning coffee and settle in. **Le Saint-Gervais** *(lesaintgervais.fr)* is an afternoon suntrap and is conveniently around the corner from the **Musée National Picasso-Paris** *(museepicassoparis.fr)*. For the evening, funky **Café La Perle** *(cafelaperle.com)* is a fashion and artsy hotspot. While you're here look across the street for the regularly changing murals by Le Mur.

LISTINGS

Best Places for...

€ Budget €€ Midrange €€€ Top End

See p108 for map of locations

Eating

Modern French

Brutus €€
30 E8
Enjoy *galettes* (buckwheat crêpes) and artisanal cider on a sun-soaked *terrasse*. Leave room for the chocolate hazelnut *galette*. *hours vary*

Bistrot Instinct €€€
31 D3
Creative seasonal menus from Chef Maximilian Wollek, his *œuf mayonnaise* is a permanent fixture. *noon-2pm & 6.30-9.30pm Mon-Sat*

Capitaine €€€
32 E7
This cosy modern brasserie has a regularly changing menu with a seafood focus. *noon-2pm & 7.30-10.30pm Wed-Sat, 7.30-10.30pm Tue*

Quick Bites

Notre Café Marais €
33 E6
Bright cafe with terrace. Serves simple, classic fare while employing and supporting people with Down syndrome. *8.30am-3pm Tue-Fri*

Carré Pain de Mie €€
34 B5
Combining the best of Japan and France, these cloud-like sandwiches include fillings like *tonkotsu* and croque monsieur. *10am-8pm*

La Collective Parisienne €
35 C7
Social-enterprise cafe. Wholesome seasonal lunches from a four-item menu plus a dessert. *noon-3pm Mon-Fri*

Vegetarian

Kitchen €€
36 B2
Friendly *cantine*-style cafe with a juice bar serving hearty organic dishes such as rice bowls with roasted veggies. *8am-2.30pm Mon-Fri, 8am-3.30pm Sat & Sun*

Land&Monkeys €
37 E5
Vegans can now enjoy French classics from this fully plant-based *boulangerie* (bakery), like quiche Lorraine and *jambon-beurre* baguettes. *7.30am-7.30pm*

Chez Eating €€
38 C1
Owner Yi Ting runs this one-woman show, creating East Asian dishes bursting with flavour. *noon-3pm Mon, Tue & Thu-Sat*

Sweet Treats

Petite Île Boulangerie €
39 E3
This *boulangerie* excels at sweet treats with black sesame. *8am-6pm Tue-Sat, 9am-2.30pm Sun*

Moon Croissant €€
40 E5
These croissant specialists use the finest ingredients, creating delicious explosions of buttery flakes and fillings. *7.30am-5pm Wed-Sun*

Yann Couvreur €€
41 C6
The renowned French pastry chef's Marais store features his best creations, such as vanilla *millefeuilles*. *10am-8pm*

Drinking

Specialist Coffee

Causeries
 D5
A delicate oasis of Danish coffee and natural wine with a gentle vinyl soundtrack. *hours vary*

Artesano
43 C8
Arturo Valentino roasts his Mexican coffee every week for this cafe filled with sun, music, photography and rich coffee. *9am-1.30pm & 2.30-5.30pm*

Ha Noi 1988 Flowers & Archives
44 B4
Discover salted-cream or egg-yolk coffee at this florally perfumed Vietnamese cafe and flower shop. *10am-7pm*

Hidden Bars

Sotto
 D4
This cellar-like bar hidden underneath Italian restaurant Carboni's is the ideal spot for a fruity cocktail and a tiramisu. *7pm-2am*

Little Red Door
 D3
Speakeasy with talented mixologists, through a small, discreet entrance. Expect queues. *5pm-1.30am*

Candelaria
47 D3
Hidden cocktail bar accessed through a taco restaurant; one of Paris' original speakeasies. *4pm-2am*

Spootnik Bar
 B3
If a futuristic cosmonaut met an audiophile in Berlin, they'd open this delicious cocktail bar. *7pm-2am Tue-Sat*

Wine Bars

Le Barav
 D2
The perfect neighbourhood bar for great prices and an excellent playlist. If the terrace is full, get your name on the waitlist. *5pm-midnight Tue-Sat*

Martin
 E2
This terrace is always full of conversation and cigarette smoke; small plates and a lengthy natural-wine list. *4pm-2am Tue-Sat*

Terra Bar à Vins
See B3
Modern wine bar where well-dressed patrons enjoy a bite to eat in minimalist surroundings. *7pm-1am Tue-Sat*

Delicatessen Place
 E2
Get comfy in this wine bar decorated straight from a vintage market. *5-10pm*

Shopping

Concept stores

Fleux
52 A5
Several shops on rue des Francs-Bourgeois, with a range of decorations and fashion objects. *10.45am-8.30pm Mon-Sat, 10.30am-8.45pm Sun*

L'Éclaireur Sévigné
 D6
A discreet but spacious store with contemporary, high-tech-inspired decor, where renowned *haute couture* houses present their creations. *11am-7pm Mon-Sat*

Le BHV Marais
54 A6
Faithful to its heritage as a Parisian *grand magasin* (department store), offering a comprehensive range of products from fashion to DIY tools. *10am-8pm, Mon-Sat, 11am-7pm Sun*

See p136 for eating, drinking and shopping listings

Explore
Bastille & Eastern Paris

Researched by Peter Yeung & Fabienne Fong Yan

This lesser-known, more typically local area, which spans parts of the 11e, 12e and 20e *arrondissements,* has key historical sites and a compelling industrial heritage to complement an increasingly cool, youthful scene. Near Bastille, craft workshops that bustled in the 19th and early 20th centuries are today home to vibrant arts venues, hipster cafes, independent shops and creative restaurants. Going east, the landscape transforms into the Bois de Vincennes (p138), one of Paris' green lungs. These neighbourhoods are distinct but most retain a village-like charm thanks to their history as *faubourgs* (small boroughs), representing a different, more relaxed and lived-in side of Paris.

Getting Around

 Walking
This is the best way to explore and it's eminently possible thanks to the area's density and surfeit of green paths.

Bicycle
The area is well served by the municipal Vélib' bikes and there are many cycling lanes, even if busier streets near Bastille are trickier to navigate.

 Metro
Lines 1 and 8 will likely be the most helpful if you want to save time and energy (or if the weather isn't great).

★

THE BEST

GREEN SPACE Cimetière du Père Lachaise (p126)

MARKET Marché d'Aligre (p132)

PROMENADE Coulée Verte René-Dumont (p130)

HISTORIC SQUARE Place de la Bastille (p130)

SWIM The Seine (p134)

Coulée Verte René-Dumont (p130)
PICSART_AH/SHUTTERSTOCK

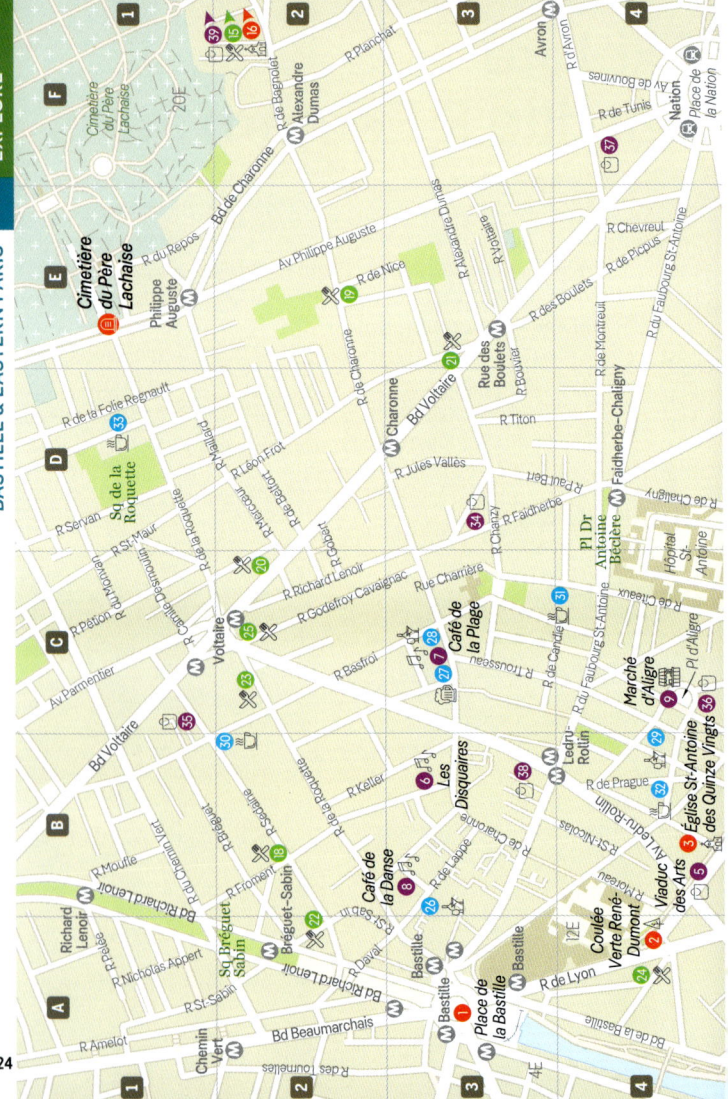

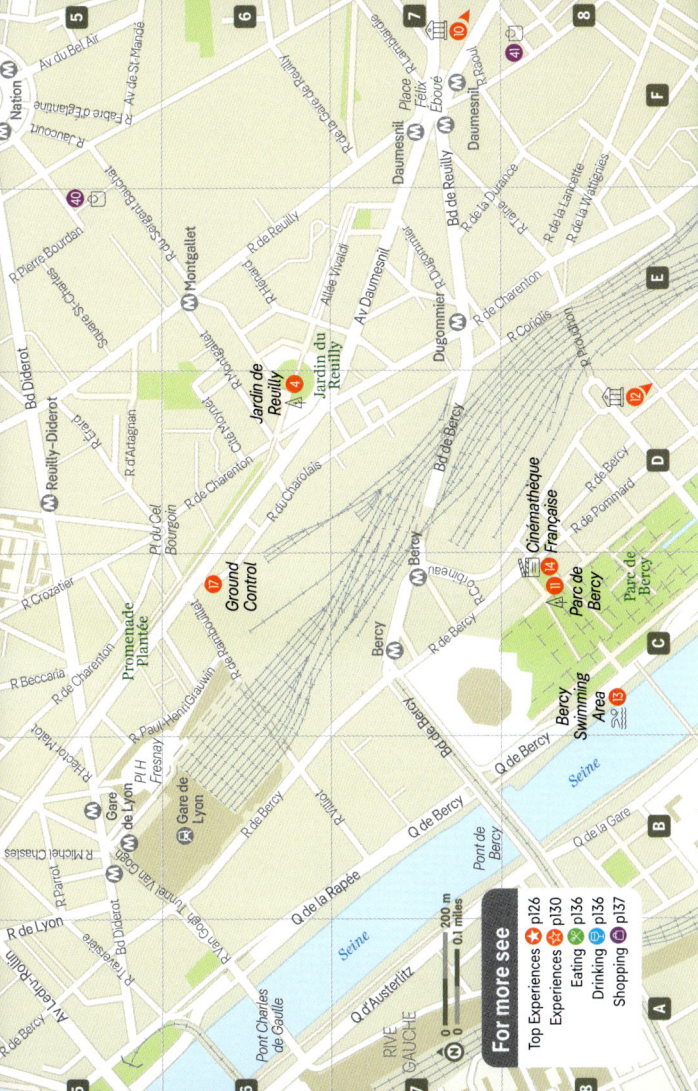

★ TOP EXPERIENCE

Cimetière du Père Lachaise

Opened in 1804, the world's most visited cemetery is a resting place for the renowned, its 43 hectares holding more than 70,000 ornate tombs. A stroll here is akin to exploring a verdant sculpture garden in one of Paris' biggest green spaces – a bastion of biodiversity.

MAP P124 **E1**

PLANNING TIP
Wear comfortable shoes: the cemetery is vast, with uneven terrain and stairs. Be prepared for walking and stay hydrated.

An Eternal English Garden
When it was built, Père Lachaise was intended as a response to local neighbourhood graveyards being full – at the time, it was ground-breaking for Parisians to be buried outside the *quartier* in which they'd lived. For its design, architect Alexandre-Théodore Brongniart took inspiration from English gardens, with winding paths and a significant portion dedicated to nature.

The Creation of a Legend
Overlooked at the time of its inauguration, the cemetery faced challenges due to its location far from the city. To enhance its appeal, the city of Paris relocated the graves of famous figures like Molière and La Fontaine (Division 25), and had an impressive sepulchre erected for the mythical medieval lovers Héloïse and Abélard (Division 7). Over time, politicians, scientists, artists and writers followed, solidifying Père Lachaise's reputation.

Funerary Art for Posterity
The entire site is recognised for its heritage, with all funerary steles dating to before 1900 listed as Historical Monuments. Among them, the Wall of the Federates; Godde's chapel on the former Jesuit house site; bd Ménilmontant's monumental

Scan this QR code for opening hours and a map.

PASCALE GUERET/SHUTTERSTOCK

gate; the Monument to the Dead and 10 sepulchres including Héloïse and Abélard, Molière and La Fontaine, and Oscar Wilde (Division 89).

Rituals & Superstitions

Père Lachaise has superstitions associated with its iconic graves. Couples renew their vows in front of Héloïse and Abélard's tomb, seeking eternal love. Oscar Wilde's tomb has long been the object of passionate kisses believed to bring luck in love. Journalist Victor Noir's effigy (Division 92) is central to erotic morbid fertility rituals. Laying hands at the dolmen of medium Allan Kardec (Division 44) is believed to grant wishes. Lastly, the ritual offerings left on Jim Morrison's grave (Division 6) perpetuate a cult (mainly based on alcohol).

QUICK BREAK
Nearby rue St-Maur is packed with great restaurants, including these on-trend, Asian-accented picks: **Le Servan** (run by two sisters from the Philippines), **SENsation** and **Double Dragon**.

WALKING TOUR

Walk the Artisans' Courts

As far back as the 15th century there's been a proud tradition of artisanship among Faubourg St-Antoine's inhabitants, including woodworkers, furniture makers and potters, with their workshops lining the area's picturesque, tranquil courtyards and passages. A stroll here will immerse you in the historic atmosphere, even if the area is quickly modernising.

START	END	LENGTH
Cour Damoye	Passage du Chantier	1.5km; 1 hour

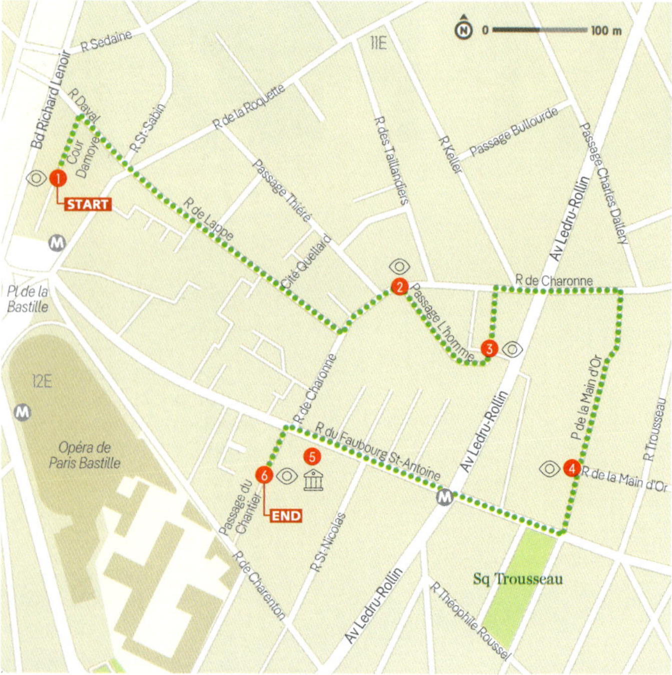

1 Secret Passage

Start at **Cour Damoye**, a site founded by an ironmonger that was previously home to ragpickers and scrap dealers, but is now a courtyard filled with charming townhouses whose large glass façades you can peek through. Take the time to peruse some of the modern independent businesses now here, including a fun coffee-roasting workshop.

2 Nostalgia in Heaps

Exit via rue Daval and head along frantic rue de Lappe, known for its buzzing bars and rowdy nightlife, for a few minutes. Dating to the 17th century, this street was once home to cabinetmakers, followed by metalworkers. Turn left onto rue de Charonne then into **passage L'homme**, surrounded by nostalgic, peeling storefronts, a cute antique games shop and a furniture shop with the sign of a chair hanging out front.

3 Street Art & Jewellery

Follow the street's curve onto **passage Josset**, past colourful street murals, then perhaps stop to admire the gorgeous jewellery at Les Fleurs boutique. Get caffeinated at Passager, which also serves breakfast and lunch items, including bagel sandwiches, before turning right onto busy rue de Charonne.

4 Hidden Sculpture

Continue to **passage de la Main d'Or**, once again cobblestoned and calm, where you can check out engravings and sculptures (such as the niche above the doorway of No 18). Traverse the narrow passage on the southern end.

5 Industrial History

Turn right and walk to **74 rue du Faubourg St-Antoine**, formerly a 19th-century furniture factory, where you can admire the 32m brick chimney soaring above the neighbourhood. This is an incredible vestige of industrial history, illustrating the melange of artisanship and industry that marks Paris' past.

6 Marie Antoinette's Cabinets

Then make a final detour through **passage du Chantier**, a tunnel-like route still home to artisans. Former Queen of France Marie Antoinette bought cabinets and tables from Adam Weiswiler, whose renowned workshop was once located here. The passage still has its old shop signs hanging overhead, adding to the charm.

EXPERIENCES

Visit an Iconic Symbol of Liberty at Bastille   MONUMENT & SQUARE

MAP: ① P124 A3

On 14 July 1789, the inhabitants of the Faubourg St-Antoine, sick of prolonged food shortages due to an ongoing siege, stormed Bastille prison in search of weapons. But when the guards refused to surrender, the situation escalated. Rebels seized 250 barrels of gunpowder, freed prisoners and put military governor Bernard-René Jordan de Launay's head on a pike. This event was the first episode of the French Revolution.

The **place de la Bastille** is a powerful symbol of these events, but also broadly represents the freedom of the French people. At the centre of the square is the 52m-high **Colonne de Juillet**, a green-bronze column topped by a gilded winged Liberty. Revolutionaries from the uprising of 1830 are buried beneath.

This symbolic political history means that Bastille draws frequent protests, so if you're in the mood for marching, join in for a quintessential Parisian experience. Otherwise, there's usually a more relaxed atmosphere, so grab a coffee at one of the many surrounding cafe terraces and gaze at this iconic symbol.

Stroll the Coulée Verte René-Dumont   WALKING

One of Paris' most distinctive green pathways occupies the disused 19th-century Vincennes railway viaduct. Reborn in 1993 as the world's first elevated park, the 4.5km **Coulée Verte René-Dumont** (or 'Promenade Plantée'; MAP: ② P124 A4), connecting Vincennes to Bastille, inspired New York City's High Line. It's a surprising serene escape from the city streets – planted with a fragrant profusion of cherry trees, maples, rose trellises, bamboo corridors and lavender. Access along the first section near Bastille is via staircases (lifts here invariably don't work). Following the tracks to Vincennes, you'll take in a

---

   BASTILLE'S ANCIENT FORTRESS

Nothing remains of Bastille's fortress, which was originally constructed in the 14th century to defend the eastern flank of Paris against the English during the Hundred Years' War. By 1417 the royal castle became a state prison, housing inmates for centuries until it was destroyed during the 1789 Revolution. Today, only a small sign on a building near bd Henri IV indicates the boundaries of the former stronghold, once boasting eight towers and surrounded by a 24m-wide moat. Over the centuries, various urban designs have updated the place de la Bastille – Napoléon wanted an elephant-shaped fountain that was never realised.

Colonne de Juillet

variety of sights: the pointed spire of **Église St-Antoine des Quinze Vingts** (MAP: ③ P124 **B4**), Haussmannian buildings with Parisian zinc rooftops and intricate art nouveau façades, the pretty **Jardin de Reuilly** (MAP: ④ P124 **D6**), prime for a picnic and with sparkling water on tap, and then, at the gateway to Bois de Vincennes, murals in homage to legendary female French explorer Alexandra David-Néel.

Buy Direct from Skilled Artisans at Viaduc des Arts   SHOPPING

MAP: ⑤ P124 **B4**

The grand arches of the Bastille viaduct, constructed in the 19th century to support a railway line, are these days home to a rich variety of contemporary arts and crafts workshops, also known as the **Viaduc des Arts** (*leviaducdesarts.com/en*). About 40 artisans – including fashion designers, glassblowers, chocolate makers, shoesmiths and lute makers – inhabit the 1.5km viaduct along av Daumesnil. Glass façades let you peek in from the street, but you can enter most places to buy products, such as delicious jams made on-site by **Confiture Parisienne**, or stylish jewellery at **La Fabrique Nomade**, which employs refugees.

Listen to Live Music at Bastille   CONCERT

Bastille is a great place to see live music in a smaller, more intimate setting. **Les Disquaires** (MAP: ⑥

P124 **B3**; *lesdisquaires.com*) is a cafe-concert venue with an eclectic programme, largely focusing on rock and pop, before turning into a nightclub open until 5am on weekends. The Brazilian samba nights on Fridays at **Café de la Plage** (MAP: **7** P124 **C3**; *lecafedelaplage-paris.com*), which also holds *forró* dance classes, are a joy. Meanwhile, the 500-seat **Café de la Danse** (MAP: **8** P124 **B3**; *cafedeladanse.com*) welcomes mid-tier acts from around the world. Elsewhere, don't miss the Tuesday jazz nights at **Le POPUP du Label** (*popup.paris*), which hosts all kinds of emerging artists throughout the week, and **Supersonic** (*supersonic-club.fr*), another platform for young talent, with shows every day that often have free entry.

Hit up Marché d'Aligre on Market Day MARKET
MAP: **9** P124 **C4**

The vibrant **Marché d'Aligre** is without doubt one of the best of the more than 70 open-air fresh-produce markets in Paris. Built in 1843 and later named after local resident Étienne François d'Aligre, the first president of the Parliament of Paris, the market is split into three sections. The covered **Halle Beauvau** is home to permanent vendors of cheese, wine, olives and other produce. Meanwhile, the **outdoor market**, which runs along rue d'Aligre, features dozens of stalls with fresh fruit and vegetables, meat and fish, flowers and more, attracting early-morning grocery shoppers. Closed only on Mondays, it offers a perfect opportunity to experience the typical French way of shopping for fresh food. Lastly, the **flea-market section** is a gem, tracing its roots to a time when royal edicts allowed anyone to sell whatever they wanted on place d'Aligre. Beyond the market, Aligre forms a wider community, with many shop owners here established for decades, resisting gentrification. The area even hosts its own independent radio station, Aligre FM.

 FÊTE DE LA MUSIQUE

If you are in Paris on 21 June, the longest day of the year, get ready for the Fête de la Musique (Festival of Music). During this jovial annual celebration, which was launched in 1982 by the French government to encourage and support amateur music, the city's streets are filled all day and night with every kind of music genre imaginable. Concerts include big-hitter names, and are even held in unique venues like the Louvre, but one of the best ways to experience the festival is to just stroll around by foot in neighbourhoods like Bastille, encountering concerts by chance.

Learn About Colonialism & Immigration at Palais de la Porte Dorée
MUSEUM

MAP: 10 P124 F7

Set in a grandiose art deco building, the **Palais de la Porte Dorée** (Palace of the Golden Gate) is an underrated destination on the edge of Paris. Constructed for the Colonial Exhibition of 1931, a dark chapter in France's history during which racist stereotypes were perpetuated in a celebration of the French Empire, the building is nonetheless an architectural curio lined with massive columns, sprawling murals and glorious mosaics. Since 2007 the building has been home to the **Musée de l'Histoire de l'Immigration** *(histoire-immigration.fr/en; adult/child €12/free)*, a fascinating museum that covers the often painful history of immigration in France. Scant space is usually given to these stories in France, yet with the rise of the far right today they are more relevant than ever. The palace also hosts the diverting **Aquarium Tropical** *(combined entry with museum €15)*, home to 400 species, including small crocodiles, seahorses and stingrays. When your legs tire, pause at the airy cafe terrace.

See the Roses & Vineyards in Parc de Bercy
PARK

MAP: 11 P124 C8

Possibly the most underrated park in Paris, the **Parc de Bercy** houses a curious mishmash of styles. In the western area, large lawns are great for picnicking. The central area, **Jardin Yitzhak Rabin**, includes a pretty rose garden, while the central zone, full of little secluded areas to escape, also contains the **Maison du Jardinage**, an educational place in a plant-filled house where gardening experts give advice, and the newly opened **Maison de l'Animal**, an events space dedicated to urban biodiversity. To the east, across some footbridges, is the **Romantic garden** with fish-filled ponds.

The park is linked with wine-making: during the 19th century it was the site of enormous wine warehouses, when Paris was the world's largest hub for the wine trade. This vinicultural history, dating as far back as the Middle Ages, persisted until the 1950s when bottling on vineyards was preferred. Even today it endures through the park's 400 grapevines, still harvested annually, and you can see the train tracks that were once used to transport wine.

Play on a Merry-Go-Round at Musée des Arts Forains
MUSEUM

MAP: 12 P124 D8

Set within the impressive former wine warehouses of Bercy, the 11,400-sq-metre **Musée des Arts Forains** *(arts-forains.com/en; adult/child €18/12)* makes for a very jolly, interactive journey across the largest space dedicated to fun-fair objects in the world. The brisk, 1½-hour tours, which must be booked in advance daily, traverse wonder-filled spaces with mechanical opera singers, image-warping mirrors and a pedal-powered carousel. The objects, largely from the late 19th and early 20th centuries, come from the private collection of actor and antiques dealer Jean-Paul Favand. Note that tours in English only run during the summer when demand is high, but large groups might consider a private booking. Even so, non-French speakers can easily enjoy standard tours – it's a visual experience and guides provide notes in English. In December, the museum hosts the **Festival du Merveilleux**, a 10-day event of dance, opera, hypnosis and more.

Go for a Dip in the Seine   SWIMMING
MAP: 13 P124 C8

In 1900, during the first edition of the Olympic Games in Paris, swimming races took place in the Seine River. Decades of industrialisation polluted the waters until a nadir was reached in the 1970s. After a mass clean-up operation, including the construction of water-treatment plants and rain-water-storage basins, swimming was possible once again for the 2024 Games. Since the summer of 2025, the public has also been able to bathe in the iconic river, including at the **Bercy swimming area** by the Simone de Beauvoir footbridge. The area is supervised, marked with buoys, and equipped with showers and lockers.

Delve into Film Culture at Cinémathèque Française   MUSEUM
MAP: 14 P124 C8

The French have a profound affinity for cinema, also known as the seventh art form, with many Gallic directors leaving an indelible mark on the history of filmmaking – Agnès Varda, Jean-Luc Godard, Jacques Audiard and Alice Guy, to name a few. In Paris, home to over 70 cinemas including many independent venues, and nearly 400 screens – the most of any city in the world – going to the movies

FISH IN THE SEINE

Thousands of years ago, and even up to the Middle Ages, Paris was a city of marine life. The Seine, which is over 14,000 years old, teemed with eels and salmon. But by the 1970s there were only three fish species left in the 777km river, which spans northern France and cuts through the capital, as industrial and residential pollution decimated biodiversity. However, after decades of urban water policies alongside community efforts, things are going swimmingly: there are now nearly 40 species that have been officially registered, with more turning up all the time.

GROUND CONTROL

Located in a former mail-sorting hall, **Ground Control** (MAP: 17 P124 **C6**) *groundcontrolparis.com*) is a sprawling 6000-sq-metre culture and events space. While this isn't a place of great tradition and charm, it's modern and lively, filled with repurposed train station decor and colourful murals. There's a packed schedule, including dance and yoga classes, sports screenings, DJ sets and even an urban agriculture awareness workshop run by a local nonprofit (one of several that are based here). It's a great place to grab a drink with snacks from the many food stands, particularly during the summer at the large outdoor terrace.

---

is an unmissable experience. It's no surprise, then, that there's an entire complex dedicated to cinema culture. In the Parc de Bercy, the **Cinémathèque Française** – founded in 1936 and moved here in 2005 – offers a diverse programme of world cinema, with screenings often introduced by film experts or directors themselves, alongside debates and workshops. The informative 800-sq-metre **museum** *(cinematheque.fr; adult/child €10/5),* opened in 2021, recounts the birth of filmmaking in 1895 and offers a captivating journey through decades of cinema, showcasing vintage equipment and technologies in a way that's accessible for veteran cinephiles and young kids alike.

Experience a Slice of Village Life on Rue St-Blaise STREET

If you're tired of the at-times intense bustle of Paris, head to **rue St-Blaise**, whose cobblestoned street, old lamp posts, tranquil cafe terraces and quaint historic churches evoke the calm of a rural village in Provence. There's a good reason for this: the surrounding neighbourhood of Charonne was once a municipality separate from Paris that was home to factories for leather, matches, candles and hats – before being merged with the capital in 1860 by Napoléon III. These days, the unique pedestrianised area to the west of rue Vitruve is the perfect place to while away a few hours, sipping a *café allongé* and people-watching at one of the many cafes, such as **Les Rêveuses** (MAP: 15 P124 **F2**). It's worth taking a peek at the artist studios, from potters to woodworkers, that line the street. Looking northwest, there is a postcard view of the **Église St-Germain de Charonne** (MAP: 16 P124 **F2**), dating back to at least the 12th century. A scene from the cult French movie *Les Tontons Flingueurs* (1963) was filmed here.

LISTINGS

Best Places for...

€ Budget   €€ Midrange   €€€ Top End

See p124 for map of locations

Eating

Bastille Bakeries

Boulangerie MieMie €
18 B2

Bold, top-tier baked goods include featherweight cream puffs and a mega 'anti-waste' croissant cake made with pastry scraps. *8am-8pm Tue-Sat, 8am-1pm Sun*

Boulangerie Manobaké €
19 E2

Rising star in the bakery scene with a charming mosaic interior and quality cinnamon rolls, apple tarts and carrot cake. *hours vary*

VG Pâtisserie €
20 C2

Delicious vegan croissants and *pains au chocolat* made using organic wheat grown 80km from Paris. Gluten-free options. *1-7pm Tue, 9am-7pm Wed-Sat, 9am-6pm Sun*

Pépite €
21 E3

TikTokers come for decadent black sesame–filled croissants; the broader selection is seriously good too. *7am-8pm Tue-Sun*

Bastille Restos

Café de l'Industrie €
22 A2

Fake rhino heads, plastic pink flamingos and portraits of film stars fill this fun, retro bistro delivering affordable classics. *8.30am-2am*

Chez Aline €
23 C2

Former butcher's shop selling fine lunch food, with *jambon beurre* baguettes and *oeufs mimosa* (devilled eggs) on its daily blackboard. *11.30am-3.30pm Mon-Fri*

Amarante €€
24 A4

A carnivore's delight, with pork and veal specialities sitting alongside classic bistro staples. Understated and buoyed by impeccable service. *12.30-1.30pm & 7.30-9.30pm Thu-Tue*

Aux Bons Crus €€
25 C2

Throwback in the style of a French *relais routier* (truck stop), with red-and-white chequered tablecloths; one for gourmands. *noon-2.30pm & 7.30-10.30pm*

Drinking

Cocktails & Craft Beer

Bar des Ferrailleurs
26 B3

Situated on lively nightlife alley rue de la Lappe, this bar has a cosy ambience and creative cocktails. *6pm-2am, from 5pm in summer*

Les Cuves de Fauve
27 C3

One of the best places in the city to drink craft beer, with original brews, from IPAs to stouts, concocted in their on-site microbrewery; 16 beers on tap. *hours vary*

Septime La Cave
 C3

Sister to the renowned restaurant, this wine shop and bar specialises in natural wine. Choose a bottle and pair it with small plates. *4-11pm*

Le Baron Rouge
 B4

Grab a spot on the edge of the wooden barrels for a perfect soirée of cheese, charcuterie, bread and wine. *hours vary*

Coffee Shops

Le Sedaine Bar
 B2

This charming locals' joint run by an elderly couple is refreshingly uncool and husband Marc makes a memorable cappuccino. *6.30am-8pm Mon-Sat*

Mokochaya
 C4

Probably Paris' most hyped cafe, this Japanese-influenced space is beautiful and inventive, with offerings from speciality hot drinks to famous cookies. *8.30am-6pm Tue-Fri, 11am-3.30pm Sat*

La Tropicale Glacier
32 B4

Best known for its creative ice-cream flavours, this airy spot also serves all kinds of coffee. *10am-6pm Tue-Fri, to 7pm Sat & Sun*

Klover Coffee Showroom
 D1

This new minimalist space is a destination for coffee nerds and the Korean owner roasts the speciality beans himself. *hours vary*

Shopping

Gourmet Goods

Le Parti du Thé
34 D3

This wonderful tea shop, established in Paris for more than two decades, works directly with small-scale producers across the world. *hours vary*

Ursa Major Chocolats
35 C1

This exquisite chocolatier is run by three sisters known for their planet-inspired creations. *10am-1.30pm & 2.30-7.30pm Tue-Fri, 10am-7.30pm Sat*

Graineterie du Marché
36 C4

Around Marché d'Aligre, this unique shop sells all kinds of seeds, herbs and spices, and is possibly one of the few remaining stores of its kind in Paris. *hours vary*

L'Auguste Cave
 F4

This wine shop offers an excellent array of natural wines to take home (along with friendly advice if you're unsure). *hours vary*

Unique Finds

Plastic Soul Records
38 B3

The oldest and perhaps most charming record store in Paris, situated on av Ledru-Rollin. Friendly staff give recommendations. *hours vary*

Chapellerie De Punta en Blanco
39 F2

A unique hat shop offering a wide selection of handmade headwear, notably original Panama hats. *noon-7pm Tue-Sat*

Un Jour, une Vieillerie
40 E5

A treasure trove of retro collectibles full of Proustian nostalgia, sourced in France and antique malls in the US, near Nation. *12.30-6.30pm Wed-Sat*

Tucked Friperie
41 F8

This thrift store, whose mission is to make luxury accessible, offers a curated selection of trendy clothes and rare pieces. *1-8pm Wed-Sun*

★ WORTH A TRIP

Bois de Vincennes

The wonderful Bois de Vincennes is one of the capital's two 'green lungs' along with the Bois de Boulogne. Parisians flock to this 995-hectare forest for a breath of fresh air but also for the myriad things to see and do, from the racecourse to restorative nature walks.

PLANNING TIP
Phone signal can be weak. Bear this in mind when meeting friends and download maps on your phone. The forest is vast so consider a bicycle: Vélib' stations are scattered around.

Boating on the Lakes
Renting a rowing boat on a sunny day is a classic experience. Rent boats at **Lac Daumesnil** *(pictured right; per hour €15)* or the north edge of **Lac des Minimes** *(per hour €12)*. Boats seat up to four people. The isles at the lake's centre, Île de Reuilly and Île de Bercy, can be accessed by a footbridge. Don't miss the Greek-inspired Romantic Temple and the grotto below with waterfalls. Just south, **Kagyu-Dzong Buddhist temple** and towering **Great Pagoda**, open on weekends, make for a peaceful visit.

Fun-Packed Flower Park
Inaugurated in 1969, the 28-hectare **Parc Floral de Paris** is filled with botanical wonders, from bonsai gardens to tropical greenhouses *(adult/child €2.70/1.55)*. The site is jam-packed with family activities: 18-hole mini-golf, zip lines, escape game, children's theatre and a butterfly garden.

Château de Vincennes
To the north, the Château de Vincennes began in the 12th century as a hunting lodge before being transformed into a fortress, royal residence and prison. Entry to the courtyard is free; however, a **ticket** *(adult/child €13/free)* is required for the dungeon, one of Europe's tallest, and Sainte-Chapelle, a small version of its counterpart in central Paris.

Scan this QR code for seasonal opening hours and information on individual sites.

PETR KOVALENKOV/SHUTTERSTOCK

Parc Zoologique de Paris

The **Parc Zoologique de Paris** *(parczoologique deparis.fr/en; adult/child €22/17)* is a whole lot of fun. Divided into geographic zones such as Patagonia and Madagascar, this zoo contains more than 3000 animals and 250 species. There are daily feeding sessions with animals, including giraffes, sea lions, ostriches and baboons.

Jardin d'Agronomie Tropicale & École du Breuil

The lesser-known Jardin d'Agronomie Tropicale is filled with lush vegetation and remnants of the 1931 Colonial Exhibition, including a Cambodian stupa. École du Breuil, the horticulture school, is another delightful green space to visit, with a lotus garden and benches carved from tree trunks.

QUICK BREAK

There's a lovely *cantine* at the Jardin d'Agronomie Tropicale. Around the Lac des Minimes, snack at the **Confiserie du Lac** or at **Rosa Bonheur à l'Est**; live music until 1am on Friday and Saturday nights.

See p155 for eating, drinking and shopping listings

Explore
The Islands

Researched by
Alexis Averbuck

The Romans set up shop on these two inner-city islands and slowly the entire city radiated out. The larger of the two islands, Île de la Cité, is home to majestic Notre Dame, resplendent once again after its devastating 2019 fire, and Sainte-Chapelle, a symphony of kaleidoscopic 13th-century stained glass. It sits footsteps from today's functioning Palais de Justice and the dungeons in the French Revolution prison, Conciergerie. Cross Pont St-Louis to reach Île St-Louis, graced with charming boutiques and sun-bathed quays. In the evening from Pont Neuf, with its dramatic busts of ogres and kings, appreciate the lights sparkling on the length of the Seine.

Getting Around

Walking
The islands are easiest on foot, and the quays are a quick descent down stairs or ramps.

Metro & Bus
Cité (line 4) on Île de la Cité is the Islands' only metro station. St-Michel (line 4 and RER B and C) serves Notre Dame from the Left Bank, and Pont Marie (line 7) on the Right Bank is Île St-Louis' closest station. Buses serve the islands, too.

Boat
The hop-on, hop-off Batobus stops opposite Notre Dame on the Left Bank.

THE BEST

STAINED GLASS Sainte-Chapelle (p150)

CATHEDRAL Notre Dame (p144)

PALACE PRISON Conciergerie (p151)

PICNIC SPOT Seine quays (p154)

ANCIENT RUINS Crypte Archéologique (p147)

Île de la Cité
NICOELNINO/SHUTTERSTOCK

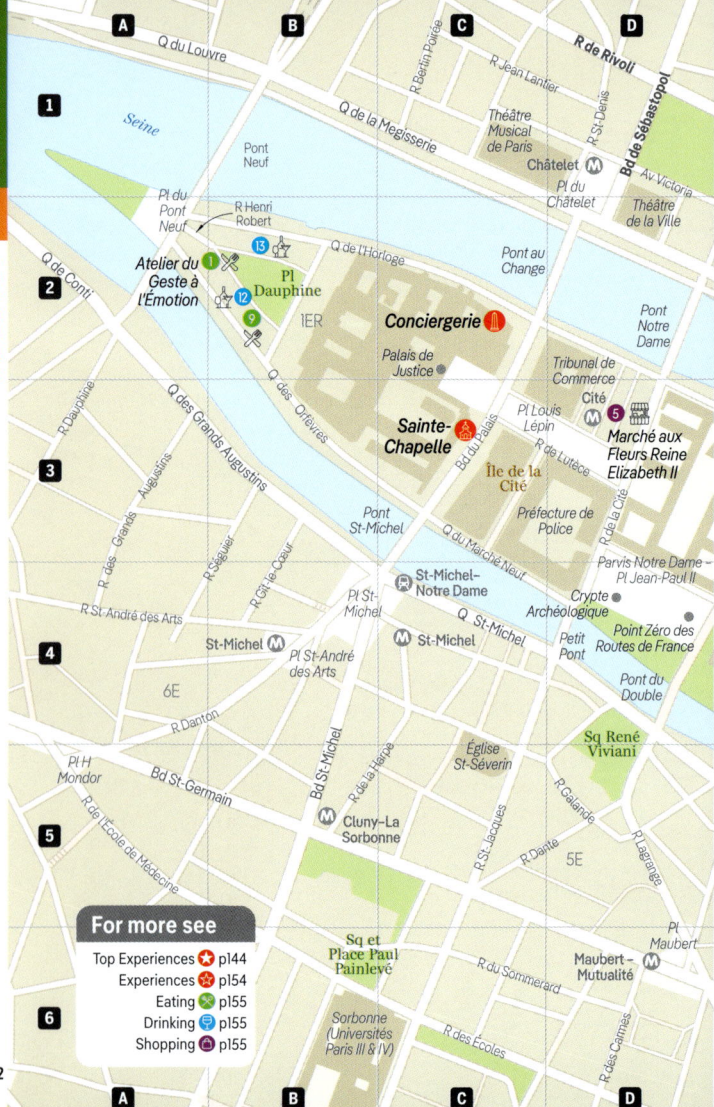

THE ISLANDS

Map of the Islands area of Paris, showing Île de la Cité and Île Saint-Louis along the Seine.

Key locations shown:
- Châtelet
- Hôtel de Ville
- Bazar de l'Hôtel de Ville (BHV)
- Pl de l'Hôtel de Ville
- Pl du Bourg Tibourg
- Pl Baudoyer
- Église St-Gervais - St-Protais
- Pl St-Gervais
- La Dame de Paris
- Café Leone
- Pont d'Arcole
- Pont Louis-Philippe
- Pl du Bataillon Français de l'ONU en Corée
- Sq A Schweitzer
- Pont Marie
- Cathédrale Notre Dame de Paris
- Sq Jean XXIII
- Sq de l'Île de France
- Pont de l'Archevêché
- Café Saint Régis
- Le Mâche-dru
- Aux Petits Cakes
- Île St-Louis
- Pont de la Tournelle
- Musée de la Sculpture en Plein Air
- Pont de Sully

Scale: 0–200 m / 0–0.1 miles

★ TOP EXPERIENCE

Notre Dame

Majestic and monumental, Paris' iconic French Gothic cathedral, reopened after the 2019 fire, has been restored to its original glory – its resplendent art and architecture, from bell towers to stained glass, shining like new. This is an actively working church and also the capital's most visited free sight.

MAP P142, **E4**

PLANNING TIP
Huge queues get longer through the day – arrive early or go late on Thursday night. Reserve tickets online or through the Notre Dame app from three days to two hours before arriving.

Scan this QR code to reserve tickets in advance.

Reigning Masterpiece

Cathédrale Notre Dame de Paris represents a generous history of building and rebuilding, long before the fire of 2019. It's constructed on the site occupied by a Gallo-Roman temple and was preceded by several earlier churches. The masterpiece we see today was begun in 1163 and largely completed by the early 14th century. It was badly damaged during the Revolution, prompting architect Eugène-Emmanuel Viollet-le-Duc to oversee extensive renovations between 1845 and 1864. That's when many of the magnificent, ornate flying buttresses that encircle the cathedral chancel and support its walls and roof were added. With the devastating 2019 fire, this French Gothic landmark, long considered the city's geographic and spiritual heart, went through a massive restoration and, amazingly, reopened its doors in December 2024. Because *everything* – including undamaged elements – was cleaned, the cathedral looks, literally, brand-new: stone a bright creamy-white, frescoes looking freshly painted and stained glass casting brilliant jewel tones across the walls.

Grand Plan & Fabulous Façade

Notre Dame is known for its sublime balance, though if you look closely you'll see all sorts of minor asymmetrical elements introduced to avoid

MISTERVLAD/SHUTTERSTOCK

monotony, in accordance with standard Gothic practice. These include the slightly different shapes of each of the three main portals, whose statues were once brightly coloured to make them more effective as a *Biblia pauperum* – a 'Bible of the poor' to help the illiterate faithful understand Old Testament stories, the Passion of the Christ and the lives of the saints.

Landmark Occasions

Historic events at Notre Dame abound. Henry VI of England was crowned here in 1431 as King of France. In 1558 Mary, Queen of Scots married the Dauphin Francis (later Francis II of France). At the unusual 1600 marriage of Marie de Médici to Henri of Navarre, he, as a Protestant who couldn't enter the church, stood outside. In 1804 Napoléon I was crowned by Pope Pius VII. And

QUICK BREAK
A few minutes from the cathedral, you'll find a cluster of eateries: Les Deux Colombes (p155; serving hearty classics), **Café Leone** (pizzas and pastas) and **La Dame de Paris** (top-notch pastries and sandwiches).

CATHEDRAL MUSIC

Music has always been a sacred part of Notre Dame's soul. Experience a Sunday Gregorian or polyphonic Mass or free organ recital. Or get a ticket for an **evening concert** *(musique-sacree-notredamedeparis.fr).*

Joan of Arc was beatified in 1909 and canonised in 1920.

Towers

A constant queue marks the entrance to the **Tours de Notre Dame** *(tours-notre-dame-de-paris.fr),* the cathedral's bell towers. Climb the 422 spiralling steps to the 69m top of the **South Tower** (pictured below; the one on the right as you face the church). On your way up, you'll pass through a room with displays on the cathedral's history before you reach the **Galerie des Chimères** (Gargoyles Gallery), where gargoyles grimace and grin. These grotesque statues divert rainwater from the roof to prevent masonry damage, with the water exiting through their elongated, open mouths. They also, purportedly, ward off evil spirits. Although they appear medieval, they were installed by Viollet-le-Duc in the 19th century.

JEROME LABOUYRIE/SHUTTERSTOCK

This route also brings you to Emmanuel, the cathedral's original 13-tonne bourdon bell (all of the cathedral's bells are named, as is the tradition). During the night of 24 August 1944, when the Île de la Cité was retaken by French, Allied and Resistance troops, the tolling of the Emmanuel announced Paris' approaching liberation. Emmanuel's peal purity apparently proceeds from the precious metals Parisian women threw into the pot when it was recast from copper and bronze in 1631.

Finish the climb at the top, where there's a spectacular view over Paris. You'll also have access to a terrace running between the two towers, allowing a view of the roof and spire. There's a 1000-visitor maximum per day, so book your timed-entry ticket in advance.

Rose Windows & Organ

Inside, behold the three masterpiece rose windows (pictured on p149) colouring the cathedral's vast 127m-long, 48m-wide interior. The 13m-wide southern window is the largest and depicts the theme of the Last Judgement. The window on the northern side of the transept remains virtually unchanged since the 13th century. Admire the 10m-wide window over the western façade, with the Virgin Mary in the centre, above the organ.

The organ is one of the largest in the world, with 8000 pipes (900 of which have historical classification), 115 stops, five 56-key manuals and a 32-key pedalboard.

Controversially, some of the stained glass in Notre Dame's southern chapels has been commissioned to be replaced by French artist Claire Tabouret, with an estimated installation of 2026. The idea is to take the originals, created by Viollet-le-Duc, and display them in a museum.

ANCIENT UNDERGROUND RUINS

Descend under the square in front of Notre Dame to the fascinating **Crypte Archéologique**, a 117m-long and 28m-wide cavity moodily displaying 4th-century Gallo-Roman ruins and other layers of Île de la Cité history. Cool computer simulations show the area as it was in Roman times, and exhibits delve into local Roman baths and artefacts from the cathedral's past.

SAVED BY THE HUNCHBACK

Damage inflicted during the French Revolution saw Notre Dame fall into ruin, and it was destined for demolition. Salvation came with the widespread popularity of Victor Hugo's 1831 novel *The Hunchback of Notre Dame,* which sparked a petition to save it. Much of the action – like when Quasimodo swings down a bell rope to save Esmeralda from the gallows – takes place there.

The Choir & Artwork

Don't miss the cathedral's grand wooden choir with its carved stalls and statues representing the Passion of the Christ. The exterior is ornately decorated with scenes from the Gospels.

Admire the 13 impressive paintings, called the **Mays**, in its nave chapels. From 1630 to 1707, city goldsmiths gave 76 of these as gifts commemorating one of the Acts of the Apostles. You'll also notice a collection of modern paintings and **tapestries**, including a Matisse, now hanging in place of a new collection of tapestries that's being woven.

Much of the art in the cathedral is now marked with clear signage in French, English and Spanish, making it easier to learn about each piece, sculpture or fresco.

Treasury

It is absolutely worth the fee *(adult/child €12/6)* to enter the *trésor* (treasury), which houses Notre Dame's dazzling sacred jewels and relics in the cathedral's southeastern transept. Check out the wonderful **Les Camées des Papes** (Papal cameos), sculpted with incredible finesse in shell and framed in silver. The 268 pieces depict every pope in miniature from St Pierre to Benoît XVI.

Crown of Thorns

The **Ste-Couronne** (Holy Crown), the wreath of thorns said to have been placed on Jesus' head before he was crucified, was given to Notre Dame in 1239 by the king St Louis (he acquired it from the Emperor of Constantinople). A gigantic golden reliquary in the axial chapel was made during the post-fire restoration to house the crown, a piece of the cross and a nail from the crucifixion. The crown is offered for viewing between 3pm and 5pm on the first Friday of the month and Fridays during Lent, plus 10am to 5pm on Good Friday.

AMITH NAG/SHUTTERSTOCK

Rebuilding Notre Dame

On the evening of 15 April 2019, a blaze broke out under the cathedral's roof. Firefighters were able to control the fire and ultimately save the church, but the damage was catastrophic. The restoration involved over 1000 artists and artisans and not only repaired fire-damaged elements, but cleaned and restored everything – pipe organ, 3000 sq metres of stained glass, paintings, copper sculptures, inside and out – to the untarnished condition of the era of Viollet-le-Duc. Even the oak beams (cut from over 2000 trees) have been hand-hewn using traditional axes. It all cost about €900 million (raised via donations).

CENTRE OF FRANCE

Notre Dame has always been the very heart of Paris – distances from Paris to every part of metropolitan France are measured from a bronze star embedded in the cathedral's front square.

★ TOP EXPERIENCE

Sainte-Chapelle

No sight is as dazzling as the Holy Chapel called Sainte-Chapelle, hidden like a precious gem in the original, 13th-century Palais de Justice (Law Courts) and Palais de la Cité (former royal residence). Paris' finest stained glass laces its sublime Gothic interior, best viewed on sunny days.

MAP P142 **C3**

PLANNING TIP
Tickets must be booked in advance for a time slot. Stir your soul at a classical music evening concert (buy tickets at fnac.com). There are entrance discounts on Wednesdays from April to September.

Scan this QR code for opening hours and to book tickets.

Ste-Couronne

Sainte-Chapelle was built in just six years and consecrated in 1248. It was conceived by French king Louis IX to house his collection of holy relics, including the famous **Crown of Thorns**, which he acquired in 1239 from the Emperor of Constantinople for a sum easily exceeding the amount it cost to build the chapel.

Enter through the lower chamber of the chapel and mount a spiral stair signposted 'Chapelle Haute' to reach the glorious upper chapel where royals worshipped. The relatively squat lower chamber supports the delicate masonry above, allowing for such a seemingly impossible array of windows.

'Reading' the Windows

Visitors are stunned by the 15 soaring stained-glass windows – 15m high in the nave, 13m in the apse – and monumental, 9m-wide rose window, which depict 1113 biblical scenes, from Genesis through to the Crown of Thorns reaching Paris. They are best read from left to right and top to bottom. Download the Sainte-Chapelle Windows app to study the windows in intricate detail. Or join a free one-hour guided tour in English (11am and 3pm; book your entrance ticket for half an hour before) or other speciality tours, or rent an audioguide (€3).

⭐ **TOP EXPERIENCE**

Conciergerie

A turreted wonder on the banks of the Seine, the Conciergerie is a vestige of the Palais de la Cité, the residence of French royals in the Middle Ages. It was later converted into a prison, where Marie Antoinette and thousands more lived out their final days.

Awaiting the Guillotine

During the Reign of Terror (1793–94), alleged enemies of the Revolution were incarcerated here before being brought before the Revolutionary Tribunal next door in the 13th-century **Palais de Justice** (still a working courthouse; enter for free).

As you walk through the halls and cells, recall that of the almost 2800 prisoners held in the Conciergerie's dungeons (in various 'classes' of cells, no less) before being sent to the guillotine, the star prisoner was Queen Marie Antoinette. Seek out the display of her personal items, like her camisole and cross. As the Revolution began to turn, radicals Danton and Robespierre were locked up at the Conciergerie and, finally, the judges of the tribunal themselves.

Treasure Hunt

Rent a HistoPad (tablet guide, €5) to explore in augmented reality and take part in an interactive, 3D treasure hunt. And check when you arrive: there are often free guided tours at 11am and 3pm.

Rotating exhibitions (like displays on Paris' culinary history or travel writing and advertising) fill the beautiful Rayonnant Gothic **Salle des Gens d'Armes**, Europe's largest surviving medieval hall.

MAP P142 **C2**

PLANNING TIP
Book a *billet jumelé* (joint ticket) online, covering both the Conciergerie and Sainte-Chapelle. Generally security queues are longer for the chapel, so head there first.

Scan this QR code for opening hours, tickets and practicalities.

WALKING TOUR

Walk the Islands

Paris' geographic, historic and spiritual heart lies here, in the Seine. The larger of the two islands, Île de la Cité, is home to Notre Dame. On this tour, slip away from the hubbub of the big sights and see the unexpected side of the islands.

START	END	LENGTH
Pont Neuf	Hôtel Lambert	2km; 2 hours

1 The Oldest Bridge
Step into island life Paris-style as the **Pont Neuf** hits the tip of Île de la Cité. The oldest bridge in Paris, it was inaugurated in 1607 when King Henri IV crossed it on a white stallion. An equestrian statue of the king, known as **Vert Galant** ('jolly rogue'), commemorates the occasion. Don't miss the *mascarons*, grotesque sculpted faces, decorating the bridge's seven arches.

2 By the Water
The emerald **square du Vert-Galant**, just down the stairs, occupies the tip of the island, like the prow of a ship in the Seine. It offers a bracing breath of fresh air, with stellar views, on the point where Hemingway and his pals used to fish.

3 Hidden Square
Amble over to hidden **place Dauphine**, built on a former marsh. This car-free square is one of the prettiest in Paris. Flanked by elegant buildings, it feels delightfully hidden. If you're lucky there'll be a heated game of pétanque underway beneath the trees.

4 Roman Ramparts
Make a beeline to lovely **rue des Ursins**, which was Paris' first dock. Keep an eye out for the crumbling remains of the Roman ramparts (at the junction of rue de Colombe), before ambling to the pocket park complete with lion's-head fountain. The mansion at 1 rue de Ursins is masquerading as medieval. It was actually built by Modernist architect Fernand Pouillon in 1958.

5 Street Musicians
Meander across **Pont St-Louis**, the bridge linking the two islands. (The Île St-Louis is named after the only sainted French king, Louis IX.) Catch a street jazz performance with dreamy Paris as your backdrop – the performers who routinely set up here add to the charm.

6 Famous Mansions
Find your own quiet stretch of shade-dappled quay to picnic or embrace history and architecture on **quai de Bourbon**. Read the plaques as you go, naming venerable residents: at No 19 artist Camille Claudel had her studio; 29 quai d'Anjou was where Ford Madox Ford founded the influential *Transatlantic Review* in 1924 with John Quinn, James Joyce and Ezra Pound.

7 Versailles Connection
Finish your tour of *hôtels particuliers* (mansions) with crowning-glory **Hôtel Lambert** (1 quai d'Anjou), built by King Louis XIV's architect Louis Le Vau – also responsible for Versailles. Now it's owned by telecom billionaire Xavier Niel, who plans to turn it into a cultural foundation. Nearby, seek a cool and contemplative retreat in French-baroque Église St-Louis en l'Île.

EXPERIENCES

Picnic on the Banks of the Seine
PICNIC

You can't miss the happy Parisians dotting the quays, relaxing, reading, romancing and, of course, picnicking. Join them! Outfit yourself at the islands' lovely purveyors – from luxe sandwiches at **Atelier du Geste à l'Émotion** (MAP: ❶ P142 **B2**) or **Le Mâche-dru** (MAP: ❷ P142 **G5**) to excellent breads at **Aux Petits Cakes** (MAP: ❸ P142 **H5**). On rue St-Louis en l'Île, you can buy *fromage* (cheese) from **La Ferme Saint-Aubin**, salami at **La Boucherie Gardil**, or a little of everything at the small grocery store or lovely **Fleuryan**. Pick up wine at **L'Etiquette**. Dessert? Choose chocolate from **Hadrien** or ice cream from **Berthillon**, *bien sûr!*

Lounge the Day Away in a Cafe
CAFES

MAP: ❹ P142 **F4**

When Parisians relax, they relax. A morning coffee, lingering lunch or pre-dinner drink can stretch on, and Paris' islands offer top chances to while the day away. For excellent people-watching, head to the point where Pont St-Louis meets the island of the same name. There, you'll find **Café Saint Régis** (*lesaintregis-paris.com*). Waiters in long white aprons, a ceramic-tiled interior and retro vintage decor make this buzzy spot a deliciously Parisian hangout any time of the day, from breakfast pastries, organic omelettes and mid-morning croque monsieurs (cheese and ham toasties) to Parisian classics – garlicky snails, onion soup, tartare – and late-night cocktails. Or pop across the street to **La Brasserie de l'Îsle Saint-Louis** (*labrasserie-isl.fr*) for its broad patio with ace views. From coffees to crisp glasses of Chablis you can graduate up to hearty *choucroute* (a decadent pile of sauerkraut topped with sausage and ham), perfect to set you up for a night out.

Stop & Smell the Roses at the Marché aux Fleurs
MARKET

MAP: ❺ P142 **D3**

As you stroll the Île de la Cité, look out for the sweet **Marché aux Fleurs Reine Elizabeth II**. Bang in the middle of the island, blooms have been sold at this quaint covered flower market since 1808, making it the oldest market of any kind in Paris. Browse blooming orchids, garden statuary and lavender sachets. A renovation is underway, in stages, through to 2028.

LISTINGS

Best Places for...

€ Budget   €€ Midrange   €€€ Top End

Eating

Living it Up

Poget & De Witte €€
6 F4
Oysters! With crisp Chablis or frothy Champagne. *11.45am-5pm Tue-Sun*

Le Sergent Recruteur €€€
7 G5
The islands' Michelin-starred treat, where plates look like art, and service is impeccable. *12.30-2.30pm Wed-Sat, 7.30-10.30pm Tue-Sat*

Île de la Cité Charm

Les Deux Colombes €€
8 E3
Tucked into a quiet corner of Île de la Cité with friendly service and hearty classics. *noon-3pm & 5.30-10pm Tue-Sun*

Restaurant Paul €€
9 B2
The best of the charming eateries on place Dauphine, with a good lunch-time prix-fixe menu. *noon-2.30pm & 7-10pm*

Drinking

Coffee Shops

Noir
10 G4
High-end coffee shop with delectable baked goods on rue St-Louis en l'Île. *8am-6pm Mon-Fri, from 9am Sat & Sun*

Minicafé
11 G5
Itsy-bitsy storefront with coffees, teas and matchas paired with gooey grand cookies. *10am-7pm Wed-Sun*

Wine Bars & Cavistes

Le Bar du Caveau
12 B2
The wine bar of the neighbouring restaurant. Enchanting spot for wine from France's flagship regions accompanied by light dishes. *noon-10pm*

Napa
13 B2
Crammed-to-bursting wine shop with a few tables on place Dauphine for a sip and a charcuterie platter. Great wine advice. *10am-8pm*

Shopping

Eclectic Keepsakes

Clair de Rêve
14 G5
Slide back in time at this toy store where stringed marionettes made of papier-mâché, leather and porcelain bob from the ceiling. It also sells wind-up toys and music boxes. *11am-1pm & 2-7pm Tue-Sat*

Librairie Ulysse
15 H5
Stuffed to the rafters with antiquarian and new travel guides, *National Geographic* back editions and maps. It was the world's first travel book-shop when it was opened in 1971 by the intrepid Catherine Domaine. *hours vary (ring the bell)*

See p142 for map of locations

Explore
Latin Quarter

*Researched by
Rooksana Hossenally*

The Latin Quarter, one of Paris' oldest and most storied neighbourhoods, grew around the Sorbonne University in the Middle Ages, becoming a hub of scholarship, debate and revolutionary ideas. Its name comes from the Latin once spoken in its medieval schools, echoes of which still shape the area's intellectual spirit. Spanning the 5e and 6e *arrondissements,* between the Jardin du Luxembourg and the Jardin des Plantes, it's crowned by the neoclassical Panthéon, resting place of France's great minds. Roman ruins, student bars and bohemian haunts coexist with arthouse cinemas, museums and cultural landmarks like the Grande Mosquée de Paris.

Getting Around

Metro & RER
The Latin Quarter has some good transport links like metro lines 10 (Cluny–La Sorbonne) and 4 (St-Michel), and RER B (Luxembourg).

Bus
Hopping on a bus, such as Bus 38 or 47, is a more scenic and less hurried way to see the city rather than below ground.

Cycling
As there are more and more cycling lanes, cycling has become more pleasant. For short hops or spontaneous detours, grab a Vélib' city rental bike from one of the many docking stations nearby.

★
THE BEST

ROMAN RUINS Arènes de Lutèce (p166)

GARDEN Jardin des Plantes (p161)

MONUMENT Panthéon (p160)

MARKET STREET Rue Mouffetard (p167)

BIJOU MUSEUM Musée de Cluny (p166)

Panoramic view of the Latin Quarter
DALIU/SHUTTERSTOCK

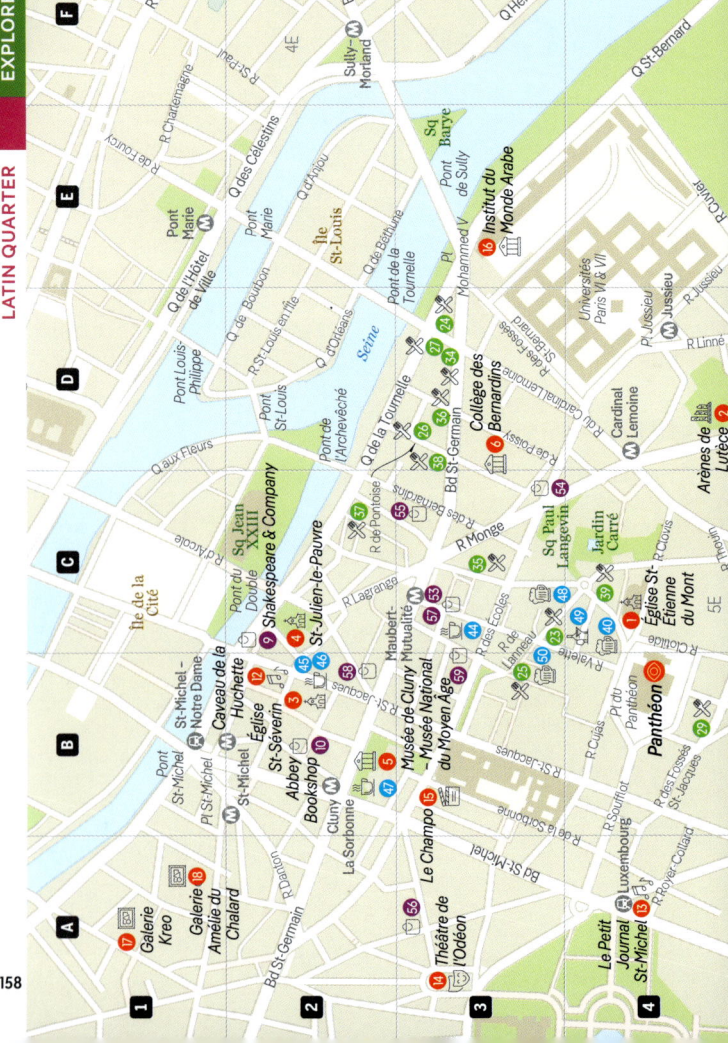

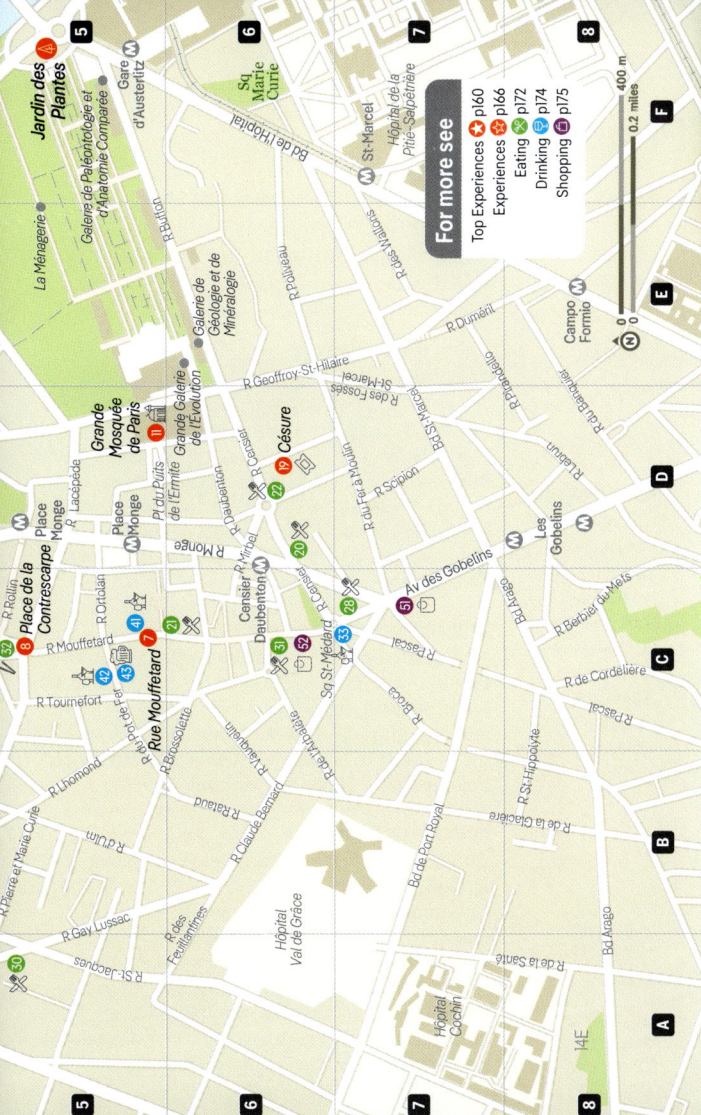

★ **TOP EXPERIENCE**

Panthéon

A symbol of national pride, this neoclassical marvel once held the title of Paris' tallest building. Today, it remains a prominent feature of the skyline, offering stunning city views from its dome, accessible by 203 steps. Inside, it's a mausoleum honouring France's greatest citizens.

MAP P158 **B4**

PLANNING TIP
Demand is high, particularly in summer (July and August), so book online as far in advance as possible. There are no cloakrooms or luggage storage facilities on-site.

Know the Backstory
The building was commissioned by Louis XV around 1750 as an abbey dedicated to Ste Geneviève, Paris' patron saint, in gratitude for his recovery from illness. It wasn't until 1790, a year after the French Revolution, that it opened, when it played a secular role as the temple of the nation and mausoleum for the remains of key figures. It did, however, revert back to religious purposes several times.

Where France's Greatest Citizens Rest
Two-time Nobel Prize–winner Marie Curie was the first woman to be interred based on achievement. In 2018 Auschwitz survivor, feminist icon and human-rights activist Simone Veil became the fifth woman to be interred. Other notable figures include Victor Hugo and Voltaire.

Foucault's Pendulum
Taking pride of place, Foucault's Pendulum is named after French physicist Léon Foucault. In 1851 he demonstrated the rotation of the Earth using laboratory apparatus rather than astronomical observations for the first time, by suspending the revolutionary device from the Panthéon's ceiling. The original pendulum is now housed at the Musée des Arts et Métiers (p116), while a working copy has been displayed at the Panthéon since 1995.

Scan this QR code for opening hours and to book tickets.

⭐ TOP EXPERIENCE

Jardin des Plantes

A garden oasis with a wealth of museums – and even a dinosaur or two – the 24-hectare botanical garden was originally created as a medicinal herb garden in 1626. There's plenty to see here, like the wealth of exotic plants inside four elegant greenhouses.

Gardens & Greenhouses

Wander through the **Jardin des Plantes** and you'll find more than just a botanical garden – it's a living museum. Paths wind past centuries-old trees, seasonal blooms and themed gardens, from medicinal plants to the tranquil Alpine Garden. Step into the soaring art deco greenhouses (the Grandes Serres) for a sensory journey through tropical rainforests and arid deserts. Inside, mist clings to lush leaves, orchids hang like jewels and the air is thick with green. Open year-round, the gardens are free to enter; greenhouses require a ticket. Arrive early for a quiet stroll, or linger at golden hour when the light feels cinematic.

Dinosaurs & Fossils

The spectacle is striking: a majestic herd of large terrestrial and aquatic vertebrates stretches out before you in one of Paris' most transportive museums. The **Galerie de Paléontologie et d'Anatomie Comparée** (pictured on p162) invites you to journey through 460 million years of evolution, with more than 2000 fossils – including 316 complete skeletons – on display. Marvel at the 25m-long diplodocus, a cast of a *Tyrannosaurus rex* skull, cynthiacetus the whale ancestor, and even *Sacabambaspis janvieri,* one of the oldest known vertebrates. Upstairs on the balcony, more than 5000 fossils trace the delicate imprints of

MAP P158, **F5**

PLANNING TIP
You need tickets for the museums and zoo. Go early to enjoy the gardens (free) at their most peaceful, ideally spring (end of March to mid-April), when cherry blossoms bloom.

Scan this QR code for opening hours and practicalities.

DELPIXEL/SHUTTERSTOCK

MOUNTAIN MAGIC

Don't miss the often overlooked **Alpine Garden**. Accessed via a tunnel (the garden itself is at a lower level), it's planted with 2000 species of mountain plants acclimated to central Paris.

ancient life – from insect wings to the petals of the first flowers. It's worth taking your time here, as there is so much to see.

Gallery of Evolution

They don't speak, but they tell the story of life itself. In the **Grande Galerie de l'Évolution**, over 7000 preserved specimens trace the astonishing diversity of the natural world. Opened in 1994 within a soaring 19th-century hall designed by Jules André, the space marries history and science under a luminous 1000-sq-metre glass roof. On the ground floor, skeletons of marine giants – the southern right whale, blue whale and sperm whale – greet visitors. Upper levels showcase land mammals and birds, with sweeping galleries offering views of the great 'procession of life' below. It's a theatrical, immersive celebration of Earth's biodiversity and evolution.

Gems & Minerals

The **Galerie de Géologie et de Minéralogie** dazzles with one of the world's oldest and most prestigious collections. Inside its elegant neoclassical hall, stretching 187m and framed by columned porticoes, visitors enter the spectacular 'Earth Treasures' room. Here, Martian meteorites, colossal crystals, rare rocks and luminous minerals reveal the extraordinary story of our planet and solar system. Named after mineralogy pioneer René Just Haüy, the gallery is both a scientific and visual marvel. As you explore, learn to distinguish sulphur from quartz and cooking salt, though they have different chemical formulas, the same composition can create two distinct minerals, depending on their crystal structure. Carbon, for example, appears both as a pencil lead and as a diamond!

Jardin des Plantes' Zoo

For a peaceful escape, visit **La Ménagerie** at the Jardin des Plantes, home to 500 animals across 150 species, many of which are endangered. One of the world's oldest zoos, it focuses on small and medium-sized species that thrive in its intimate enclosures. Wander through different habitats, from red pandas who stay in the trees to snow leopards perfectly adapted to snowy mountain environments, and witness the zoo's dedication to conservation and animal diversity. Designed for four- to six-year-olds and seven- to 12-year-olds, the Ménagerie's app lets children discover 15 species, including red pandas and Przewalski's horses, through fun challenges and quizzes.

HILLTOP MAZE
Explore the labyrinth planted on a small hill, crowned by a gazebo built in 1786. Below the maze is a soaring cedar of Lebanon classified as a 'remarkable tree'.

QUICK BREAK
Three **Louise** kiosks in the garden serve artisanal ice cream, crêpes and other treats. Queues are shorter at **Glaces Glazed**, an ice-cream brand with creative flavours, on nearby rue Geoffroy-St-Hilaire.

WALKING TOUR

Walk the Latin Quarter's Essentials

From its Roman-era amphitheatre to its medieval market street, there's no better neighbourhood for time travelling in Paris than the Latin Quarter. This compact tour will give you a glimpse of the area's incredible history and essential stops. If you can, allow more time to explore the museums along the way.

START	END	LENGTH
Place St-Michel	Grande Mosquée	4km; 2–3 hours

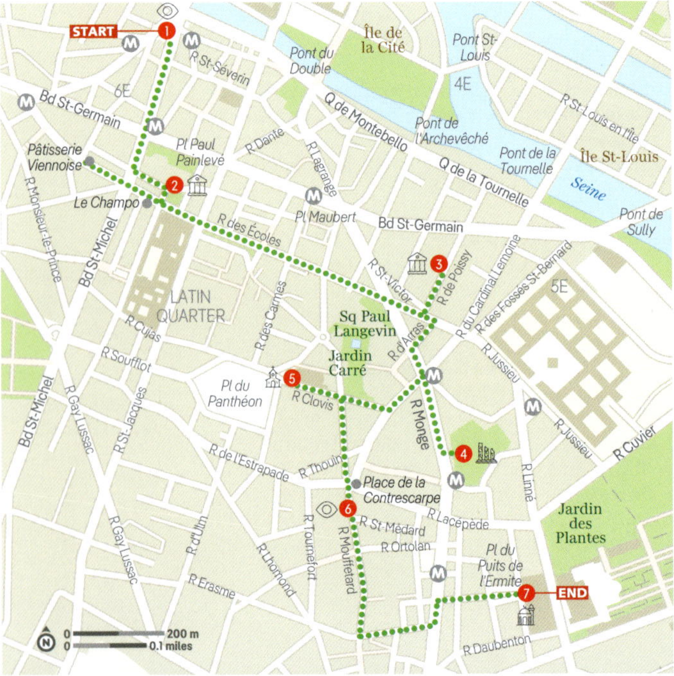

1 Iconic Fountain

Start at **place St-Michel**, braving the crowds for a glimpse of Notre Dame across the river. A historic entry point to the Left Bank, St-Michel is where Roman Lutetia once bridged the Seine to the Île de la Cité. A flourishing hub for scholars in the Middle Ages, today its grand boulevard is anchored by the 19th-century Fontaine St-Michel (fountain), depicting the archangel Michael defeating a dragon.

2 Must-See Museum

Walk up the boulevard in the direction of the Jardin du Luxembourg to reach the splendid **Musée de Cluny** (p166), housed inside a medieval mansion built atop Roman baths. If you have time to peruse the collections, head inside; otherwise you can admire the exterior: the contemporary entrance is juxtaposed with visible Gallo-Roman vestiges.

3 Medieval Magic

Pastry break! Make a detour to the near century-old **Pâtisserie Viennoise**, next to the grandiose Faculty of Medicine, before passing the art deco **Le Champo** (p170), one of a handful of arthouse cinemas in the area. Take rue des Écoles to the **Collège des Bernardins** (p167), a former 13th-century Cistercian college where cultural exhibits are staged inside a vaulted space.

4 Roman History

Stroll via rue Monge to reach the 2nd-century **Arènes de Lutèce** (p166). This Roman-era amphitheatre once staged gladiatorial combat (complete with wild animals) in front of thousands of spectators. Nowadays it's a tranquil spot, surrounded by greenery, where locals picnic and play ball games.

5 Jewel-Box Church

Head west on rue Clovis to see a section of the wall of Philippe II Augustus, the oldest city wall in Paris. Continue up the hill to see the **Église St-Étienne du Mont** (p166) and its marvellous facade, adjacent to the **Panthéon** (p160), the star of the Latin Quarter, where the great thinkers of France rest. Nearby is the Panthéon-Sorbonne University – one of the most famous buildings of the Sorbonne network.

6 Market Street

Head over to **place de la Contrescarpe** (p168) to soak up the cafe buzz and continue along **rue Mouffetard** (p167) for the medieval market-street vibes. The cobbled lane is lined with boutiques, eateries and – towards the bottom of the hill – market stalls.

7 Mint Tea at the Mosque

Finish close to the **Jardin des Plantes** (p161) at the **Grande Mosquée de Paris** (p169) for a steam bath and a bite to eat. If you've still got energy (and stamina), take a turn around the garden to gape at the botanical wonders, and maybe traverse the hilltop labyrinth, beforehand.

EXPERIENCES

Meet Paris' Patron Saint at Église St-Étienne du Mont CHURCH
MAP: ① P158 C4

The Latin Quarter was built on and around the gently sloping hill of Ste Geneviève. The star attraction on top of the hill is the Panthéon (p160), but don't miss the magnificent **Église St-Étienne du Mont** next to it. Built between 1492 and 1655, the church has a highly ornate façade that will make you gasp in amazement. The tomb of Ste Geneviève lies in a chapel in the nave's southeastern corner. The patron saint of Paris, she was born at Nanterre in 422 and is said to have turned away Attila the Hun from Paris in 451. A highly decorated reliquary near her tomb contains all that is left of her earthly remains: a finger bone. Fans of the Woody Allen film *Midnight in Paris* will recognise the stone steps on the northwestern corner as the place where Owen Wilson's character is collected by a vintage car and transported back to the 1920s.

Explore the Latin Quarter's Earliest Vestiges ROMAN RUINS
MAP: ② P158 D4

The Latin Quarter's impressive Roman and medieval roots can be seen throughout the neighbourhood. Top picks include the **Arènes de Lutèce**, a 2nd-century Roman amphitheatre that seated 10,000 people for gladiator fights. Found by accident in 1869 when rue Monge was under construction, it's now used by locals for playing football and boules. You'll also notice the remains of the Philippe II Augustus wall, the oldest city wall in Paris. Today, visible parts pass through buildings and car parks, including on rue Clovis, where the rubble and brick core are exposed

Tour the Latin Quarter's Lesser Visited Churches CHURCH

Meander away from Notre Dame to explore less visited churches. **Église St-Séverin** (MAP: ③ P158 B2; *saint-severin.com*), not far from St-Michel, is a Gothic church containing one of the oldest bells in Paris, cast in 1412. Also of note are the seven stained-glass windows depicting the seven sacraments, designed by Jean René Bazaine in 1970. One of the oldest churches in Paris is **St-Julien-le-Pauvre** (MAP: ④ P158 C2; *sjlp-paris.org*), where piano recitals (of Chopin, Liszt and others) are staged at least two evenings a week. You'll need a ticket to attend. When here, pay attention to the bas-relief, in a rowing boat, above the door. It's a medieval sculpture from the 14th century, cited as being the oldest in Paris.

Delve into the Middle Ages at the Remarkable Musée de Cluny MUSEUM
MAP: ⑤ P158 B2

The **Musée de Cluny – Musée National du Moyen Âge**

(musee-moyenage.fr; adult/child €13/free) showcases sublime treasures, from medieval statuary, stained glass and objets d'art to its celebrated series of tapestries, such as the famed *Lady and the Unicorn* (1500). The museum also incorporates the 15th-century mansion **Hôtel de Cluny** and the frigidarium (cold room) of a Roman-era bathhouse. Designed by architect Bernard Desmoulin, the contemporary entrance building houses the ticket office, bookshop, souvenir boutique and cloakroom. Following renovations, the museum now has enhanced explanatory panels and interactive displays. It is also possible to access the 1st-floor late-Gothic chapel, **La Chapelle de l'Hôtel de Cluny**, with rich carvings of Christ on the cross, 13 angels, and floral and foliage ornaments. Make time to visit the recently restored gardens, too. Not many visitors or locals know about them, making them feel like a secret. There's also a small cafe on-site that's a perfect pit stop in between sightseeing.

ISOGOOD_PATRICK/SHUTTERSTOCK

Lady and the Unicorn, **Musée de Cluny**

Catch an Art Exhibit in the Collège des Bernardins MEDIEVAL MONUMENT & MUSEUM

MAP: **6** P158 **D3**

Another architectural marvel in the area to put on your list is the **Collège des Bernardins** *(collegedesbernardins.fr; free)*. Dating back to 1248, this former Cistercian college originally served as the living quarters and place of study for novice monks. It's now an art gallery and Christian culture centre, with events ranging from lectures to film screenings and music performances. There's a stunning stone vaulted ceiling in the main hall. Some events take place here as part of the neighbourhood's **Festival Quartier du Livre**, a literary festival held in the first week of June.

Drink at a Cafe on Rue Mouffetard STREET

Dating to the Middle Ages, **rue Mouffetard** (MAP: **7** P158 **C5**) slopes down from the Panthéon and narrows to just 7m in places. Once named after the foul-smelling *mouffette* (skunk) due to the polluted Bièvre River, this cobbled street has seen centuries of change.

Though now lined with market stalls (except Mondays), casual eateries and tourist-friendly restaurants, it still retains echoes of its past. The 16th-century **Église St-Médard**, with its beautiful stained-glass windows, stands as one of the few historical landmarks that survived the Revolution and Haussmann's redesign of Paris.

An anchor is **place de la Contrescarpe** (MAP: ❽ P158 **C5**), once renowned for raucous goings-on (Hemingway described one of its watering holes as a cesspool). The area was a magnet for philosophers and writers drawn to its boisterous bars and dance halls. While the wild nights of Parisian bohemia have faded, the square is still lively with people-watching and cafe terrace culture. Today, visitors come for croque monsieurs and a dose of Left Bank nostalgia.

Browse the Latin Quarter's Beautiful Bookshops   BOOKSHOPS

French literary giants and expatriate authors found creative refuge in the city's cafes but also its bookshops, like the whimsical **Shakespeare & Company** (MAP: ❾ P158 **C2**; *shakespeareandcompany.com*), a hub for expats since 1919. Originally it stood at 12 rue de l'Odéon as a bookshop and library, and regulars included Ernest Hemingway and F Scott Fitzgerald. When WWII broke out, it was forced to close. In 1951 new owner George Whitman reopened the English-language bookshop in its current location at 37 rue de la Bûcherie, in a building that served as a monastery. More than 70 years later, it's still a must-visit spot for its bewitching atmosphere.

There's also the cosy, Canadian-run **Abbey Bookshop** (MAP: ❿ P158 **B2**; *abbeybookshop.org*), where towering stacks of books and regular readings invite lingering. Also worth making a note of is **Librairie Eyrolles** (*eyrolles.com*), a beloved Left Bank institution, known for its vast selection of art, design and photography books. And along the Seine, the *bouquinistes* continue to sell vintage books,

---

 THE BOUQUINISTES, THEN & NOW

Lining the top of the river banks at quai de la Tournelle, Pont Marie and quai du Louvre, green boxes open to reveal secondhand-book stalls operated by *bouquinistes* (book sellers). They're filled with out-of-print books, rare magazines, postcards and old posters, all waiting to be rediscovered. In the 16th century, itinerant peddlers sold their wares on Parisian bridges. Sometimes their subversive (for example, Protestant) materials would get them into trouble with the authorities. By 1859 the city had wised up: official licences were issued and eventually the permanent boxes were installed.

📖 LITERARY LUMINARIES

Expatriate writers from all over the world have long sought inspiration in Paris, including James Joyce, Ernest Hemingway and George Orwell, who all lived here. James Joyce's flat, at 71 rue du Cardinal Lemoine, is where he finished his novel *Ulysses*. Hemingway lived close by, at No 74. Conveniently for the party-loving novelist, his apartment was right above the Bal au Printemps dance hall. Nearby at 6 rue du Pot de Fer, George Orwell lived in a boarding house, noted as 'Hotel X' in his memoir *Down and Out in Paris and London*, before returning to London.

---

posters and magazines from green wooden stalls.

Soak Up the Calm of the Paris Mosque MOSQUE

MAP: ⓫ P158 **D5**

One of the biggest mosques in France and Paris' central mosque, the **Grande Mosquée de Paris** (*grandemosqueedeparis.fr*) has a striking Moorish-style minaret, which peeks out from behind smooth white walls as you approach along the street. Visit the interior to see the intricate tile work and calligraphy. There is also a **North African hammam** (steam bathhouse) with timings for women and men: a pretty courtyard **restaurant** (*la-mosquee.com*) that serves delicious couscous, tagines and meat skewers; and as well as a **tearoom** where staff serve sweet, fragrant mint tea and traditional cakes. There is also the possibility of smoking shisha in the front garden.

Savour the Latin Quarter's Jazz Bars JAZZ

In the years following WWI, the area pulsed with music in *bals* (evenings spent dancing) and bars, especially jazz, as crowds packed into the smoky cellars of **Caveau de la Huchette** (MAP: ⓬ P158 **B2**; *caveaudelahuchette.fr*) to hear Miles Davis and Sidney Bechet play into the night. The music spilled out into St-Germain des-Prés at candlelit spots like **Chez Papa** jazz club, which you'll find just up the road from the Café de Flore (p194). Another key spot not to miss is **Le Petit Journal** (MAP: ⓭ P158 **A4**; *parisjazzclub.net*) on bd St-Michel. It's here, in this old cafe with a capacity of over 100, that some of the jazz world's greats have performed for more than 50 years. Today, it's at the risk of closing its doors due to lack of funds. The passionate locals, some of whom play here regularly, are calling on the Ministry of Culture to help save it.

Explore Arty Odéon CINEMA

Named after the neoclassical Roman-inspired **Théâtre de l'Odéon** (MAP: 14 P158 A3), inaugurated in 1782), one of the most famous in the city for its classic and contemporary plays, the Odéon area is at the crossroads of St-Germain des Prés and St-Michel. The metro is marked by an Odéon cinema and there is a clutch of arthouse cinemas scattered across the Latin Quarter that are popular with figures in the film industry. The art deco **Le Champo** (MAP: 15 P158 B3; *cinema-lechampo.com*) opened in 1928 and is where director François Truffaut liked to go to see other directors' film retrospectives. Other notable independent cinemas include **Christine21** *(pariscinemaclub.com),* owned by Oscar-winning actress Isabelle Huppert and her son, and **Cinéma St-André des Arts**, on the street of the same name. **Studio Galande** *(studiogalande.fr)* is another one to have on your list, especially if you want to see *The Rocky Horror Picture Show*, which has been shown every Friday and Saturday evening for the last four decades.

Immerse in the Arab World at Institut du Monde Arabe MUSEUM

MAP: 16 P158 E3

At the southern end of the bd St-Germain, you'll find the **Institut du Monde Arabe** *(Arab World Institute or IMA; imarabe.org),* an unsung museum with a jaw-dropping design by the French architect Jean Nouvel. A metallic screen of moving geometric motifs was designed to look like a *mashrabiya,* a window of ornate latticework often found in Islamic architecture – the motifs are actually 240 light-sensitive shutters that automatically open and close to control the amount of light in the building. Founded by France and 18 Arab countries as a research hub, the IMA was established due to the perceived lack of representation for the Arab world in France. It seeks to provide a secular location for the promotion of Arab civilisation, art, knowledge and aesthetics. There's a

AMERICAN JAZZ LEGENDS

Ever since the end of WWI, France has offered American jazz musicians both a stage and a measure of respect they were often denied at home – along with basic civil rights. The Latin Quarter emerged after WWII as a sanctuary for jazz. In the 1940s and '50s, its smoky clubs welcomed talents like Bud Powell and Sidney Bechet, who found freedom and reverence in Paris' bohemian circles. Jean-Pierre Leloir's evocative book *Jazz Images* captures this deep French affection for the music and its makers. Paris wasn't paradise, but for many, it was a vital refuge and an inspiring one.

Institut du Monde Arabe

museum, library, auditorium, meeting rooms and a rooftop restaurant, **Dar Mima**, which whisks up food with influences from North African countries, such as fish tagine and couscous. The real selling point here is the view across the Paris rooftops.

Admire the Latin Quarter's Contemporary Art & Design GALLERY

Despite the area being one of the oldest in Paris, the Latin Quarter brims with contemporary arty findings. Drop in at the multiple gallery spaces of charismatic **Kamel Mennour** (*mennour.com/visit*). Starting out by selling artworks door-to-door, he founded his first gallery in 1999 and today represents 40 of the art world's biggest names, from Anish Kapoor to Alberto Giacometti.

For cutting-edge design, **Galerie Kreo** (MAP: 17 P158 A1; *galeriekreo.com*) is the go-to for clued-up designers and collectors. For artworks from emerging and more established artists, add **Galerie Amélie du Chalard** (MAP: 18 P158 A1; *amelieduchalard.com*), where the pieces are hung in a beautiful *hôtel particulier* (mansion) you'll wish you lived in. With so many students around, it's only natural that there should be more of a grassroots art scene too. Hybrid arts hub **Césure** (MAP: 19 P158 D6; *cesure.paris*) has recently opened its doors inside an old Sorbonne campus building, where dorms and common rooms have been turned into exhibition spaces, artist studios and residencies. Check the website for the schedule of events, from plays to parties.

LISTINGS

Best Places for...

€ Budget €€ Midrange €€€ Top End

See p158 for map of locations

Eating

Quick Bites

Pot O'Lait €
 D6
Try the tasty *galettes* (savoury buckwheat crêpes), generously filled with ingredients like goat's cheese and smoked salmon. *11.15am-2.30pm & 6.30-10pm Mon-Thu, 11.15am-2.30pm & 7-10.30pm Fri & Sat*

Dose €
21 C6
Get your caffeine hit with artisan-roasted craft coffee and follow with a lunch of homemade quiche on rue Mouffetard. *8am-6pm Tue-Fri, 9am-6pm Sat & Sun*

Cantine de Césure €
22 D6
Art hub Césure's canteen is a good-value, zero-waste spot with easy options like burgers and salads. *10am-11pm Tue-Sat*

Jozi Brunch €
23 C3
Easy plates of avocado toast and fruit pancakes served most of the day. *8am-4pm Mon-Fri, 9am-5.30pm Sat & Sun*

Fine Dining

La Tour d'Argent €€€
 D3
Overlooking Notre Dame from its perch on the Seine, storied La Tour d'Argent has served pressed duck and panoramic views since 1582, with a wine cellar of 450,000 bottles. *noon-2.15pm & 7-10.30pm Tue-Sat*

Le Coupe-Chou €€
25 B3
A centuries-old institution with an open fireplace, serving duck *magret* and other French classics. *7-10.30pm*

Baieta €€
 D3
Where one-star culinary sensation Julia Sedefdjian whisks up Niçoise creations like her take on bouillabaisse. *noon-2.15pm & 7-10.15pm Tue-Sat*

AT €€€
 D3
Switch things up from French food with Michelin-starred chef Atsushi Tanaka's contemporary-inspired dishes. *12.30-1.30pm & 7.30-8.30pm Tue-Sat*

Bistros

Calice €€
 C7
This retro bistro and wine bar near the bottom of rue Mouffetard serves reliable staples like meaty *pâté en croûte* as well as lighter fish dishes and fancy desserts. *noon-2pm & 7-10pm Tue-Sun*

Café de la Nouvelle Mairie €€
29 B4
Serving traditional bistro food done well, around the corner from the Panthéon on a fountained square with a breezy terrace in the warmer months. *8am-midnight Mon-Fri*

Les Papilles €€
 A5
A pocket-size old-school bistro, wine bar and *épicerie* (specialist

grocer) where bottles line the mahogany shelves all the way across, with excellent market-driven fare and natural wines to try. *noon-2pm & 6.30-10pm Tue-Sat*

Le Verre à Pied €
31 C6

One of the last remaining traditional bistros to have survived on busy market street rue Mouffetard, with bags of soul, which does a good *blanquette de veau* and roast beef washed down with wine. *9am-9pm Wed-Sat, 9.30am-4.30pm Sun*

Mouffetard Musts

Flocon €€
See **21** C6

One of the top dining spots in the area, Flocon reimagines bistro cuisine with a lighter, plant-forward twist, guided by seasonal ingredients and a strong commitment to sustainable values. *7-11pm Wed & Thu, noon-3pm & 7-11pm Fri-Sun*

OTTO by Eric Trochon €
 C5

Another spot worth noting on rue Mouffetard is this tiny canteen that does excellent Japanese-style big and small bites cooked over binchotan coal, and cocktails, backed by a Michelin-starred chef. *noon-2.30pm & 7-11pm Mon-Fri, noon-midnight Sat & Sun*

Cave La Bourgogne €
33 C7

On pretty square St-Médard, it's perfect for soaking up local vibes while sipping on a glass of red paired with classic cuisine. *7am-1am*

Food That Takes You on a Trip

Alliance €€€
34 D3

Between the Left Bank and bd St-Germain, this one-star restaurant pairs seasonal French cuisine with Japanese touches, offering dishes like Racan chicken with lobster roe in a serene, minimalist open-kitchen setting. *noon-3pm & 7.30-10.30pm Mon-Fri*

LAVA €€
35 C3

This fiery restaurant fuses a chef's love of open-flame cooking with a sommelier's flair, serving bold, spice-laced dishes and vibrant wines in a celebration of travel, *terroir* (land) and technique. *noon-2pm & 6.30-10pm Tue-Sat*

Kitchen Ter(re) €€
36 D3

Offers a dining experience blending artisan noodles made from ancient grains with tasty Asian-inspired broths and sauces, all served in a stylish, art-infused setting. *12.15-2pm & 7-10pm Tue-Sat*

Local Favourites

Atelier Maître Albert €€
37 C2

This contemporary rotisserie near Notre Dame offers refined traditional cuisine in a historic 14th-century setting, complete with a medieval fireplace. *noon-2.30pm & 6.30-10pm*

Bar à Iode €
 D3

Laid-back with friendly staff, locals come for the platters of very well priced oysters, prawns and whelks, as well as hearty fish-focused mains like fish and chips. *noon-3.30pm & 7pm-midnight Tue-Sat*

TRAM €
39 C4

Open from breakfast to teatime, this coffee shop serves homemade fare, from chia bowls in the morning to fresh ceviche, salads and

Odette

9am-7pm Mon, Tue, Thu & Fri, to 1pm Wed, 11am-8pm Sat & Sun

Odette
 B2

An upstairs tearoom dishing out cream-filled choux (puff pastries) inside a charming 17th-century abode. *9am-8pm*

Chanceux
 C2

Replacing the popular Circus Bakery is the duo behind stylish and Michelin-approved Café Compagnon's second location where it serves top-notch coffee, cakes and sandwiches to sit in or go. *hours vary*

Café Maa
 B2

Nordic design, local art and Finnish flavours meet at the Finnish Institute. Try the rye tartines, cinnamon buns, pine chai latte. *11am-6pm Tue-Sat*

Student Vibes

Le Violon Dingue
 C3

'The crazy violin' is a studenty bar with sports showing on big screens upstairs and pub quizzes downstairs. *6pm-5am Tue-Sat*

cake. *9am-7pm Tue-Sat, 10am-5.30pm Sun*

Drinking

Pubs & Beer

Bombardier
 C4

An old English pub with the best view of the Panthéon, located right across from the blockbuster monument. Also serves food. *hours vary*

Margen's
 C5

A small, dark, neon-lit pub right on rue Mouffetard that serves cocktails and pints and jumps into action to the early hours. *5pm-5am Tue-Sun*

Le Chouff'Bar
 C5

A relaxed tavern serving Belgian beers, including extra-strong La Chouffe, and shots of all kinds. *4pm-2am*

Brewberry
 C5

A more modern bar, with over 20 craft beers from Paris and beyond on tap. *5pm-2am Tue-Sun*

Coffee & Tea

Nuage
44 C3

Lures digital nomads with its cosy, homey spaces in an old church (where Cyrano de Bergerac apparently studied).

Le Piano Vache
 C4

A 1970s rock den with live music on the weekends; it's a favourite on the student circuit. *5pm-2am Mon-Sat*

Pub St-Hilaire
50 B3

A buzzy bar, usually packed out with students who come for a game of pool and the hearty food. *5pm-2am Tue-Thu, 4pm-3am Fri, 1pm-3am Sat*

Shopping

Gourmet Treats

Brûlerie des Gobelins
51 C7

Established in 1957, this artisanal coffee roaster near rue Mouffetard has legions of devoted regulars who stock up on speciality blends. *9.30am-7.30pm Tue-Sat*

Fromagerie Androuet
52 C6

Launched in 1909, Androuet is a cornerstone on the Parisian cheese scene, with multiple locations including rue Mouffetard. Not just a *fromagerie* selling delectable varieties from across France, it also ages its own cheeses in maturing cellars. *hours vary*

La Maison d'Isabelle
53 C3

Winner of a butter-croissant competition in 2018, Isabelle's *viennoiseries* still attract crowds. The hot-from-the-oven organic baguettes and flakey croissants are hard to beat. *6am-8pm Tue-Sat, 6am-6pm Sun*

Au Bonbon du Palais
54 C3

Straight out of yesteryear, this sweet shop is reminiscent of a 1950s French classroom. Stocks specialised candies from French regions, including candied fruits and rose petals. *hours vary*

Offbeat Gifts

Messy Nessy's Cabinet
55 C3

A charming boutique run by Anglo-American Vanessa Grall, founder of the digital magazine *Messy Nessy Chic*. Heaps of quality and made-in-France Paris mementos to take home. *11am-6pm Mon-Sat*

Bourgine
 A3

This independent women's fashion label, inspired by overlooked historical figures, has a cult following. Self-described as the 'last neighbourhood *couturière*'. *11am-7pm Mon-Sat, from noon Sun*

Comic Books, Cassettes & Vinyl

Le Club K7
 C3

'The future rewinds here' goes the tagline at this unique boutique, dedicated to the lost world of the cassette tape. A guaranteed trip down memory lane. *11am-7pm*

Album BD
 B2

Comic-book fans appreciate the impressive selection of artwork and rare editions at this destination on rue Dante. *10.30am-7.30pm*

CrocoDisc
 B3

Vinyl collectors frequent this shop that's stocked with new and second-hand records covering a variety of genres, from funk to rock – everything but classical music. *11am-7pm Tue-Sat*

See p198 for eating, drinking and shopping listings

Explore
St-Germain & Les Invalides

Researched by
Nicola Leigh Stewart

In the Middle Ages, the Left Bank was considered the countryside, dominated by open fields, known in French as *prés* – hence the name St-Germain des Prés. But the development of the Abbey de St-Germain in the 6th century (where the Église St-Germain des Prés stands today) turned it into a spiritual and intellectual hub. The area really came into its own at the turn of the 20th century, when its cafe scene attracted creatives from across the globe for intellectual banter over carafes of cheap table wine. Today, St-Germain des Prés is home to some of the city's priciest real estate, and film stars, but reverberations of its colourful past still echo through its cobblestone streets.

Getting Around

Walking
Paris is a pretty compact city and easy to walk around, and St-Germain des Prés is one of the prettiest neighbourhoods for strolling.

Metro
The metro is quick, easy and cheap. The main St-Germain des Prés station (line 4) will put you in the heart of the 6e *arrondissement*. The Sèvres–Babylone station can be reached on the line 12 (running north–south in the city).

Bicycle
If you're comfortable cycling you can pick up Vélib' bikes across the city. Sign up online for a one- or three-day ticket.

Fontaine St-Sulpice, near Église St-Sulpice (p186)
OLIVEROUGE 3/SHUTTERSTOCK

★
THE BEST

FREE ART Église St-Sulpice (p186)

MUSEUM Musée d'Orsay (p183)

GARDEN Jardin du Luxembourg (p182)

SCULPTURE Musée Rodin (p187)

DEPARTMENT STORE Le Bon Marché (p193)

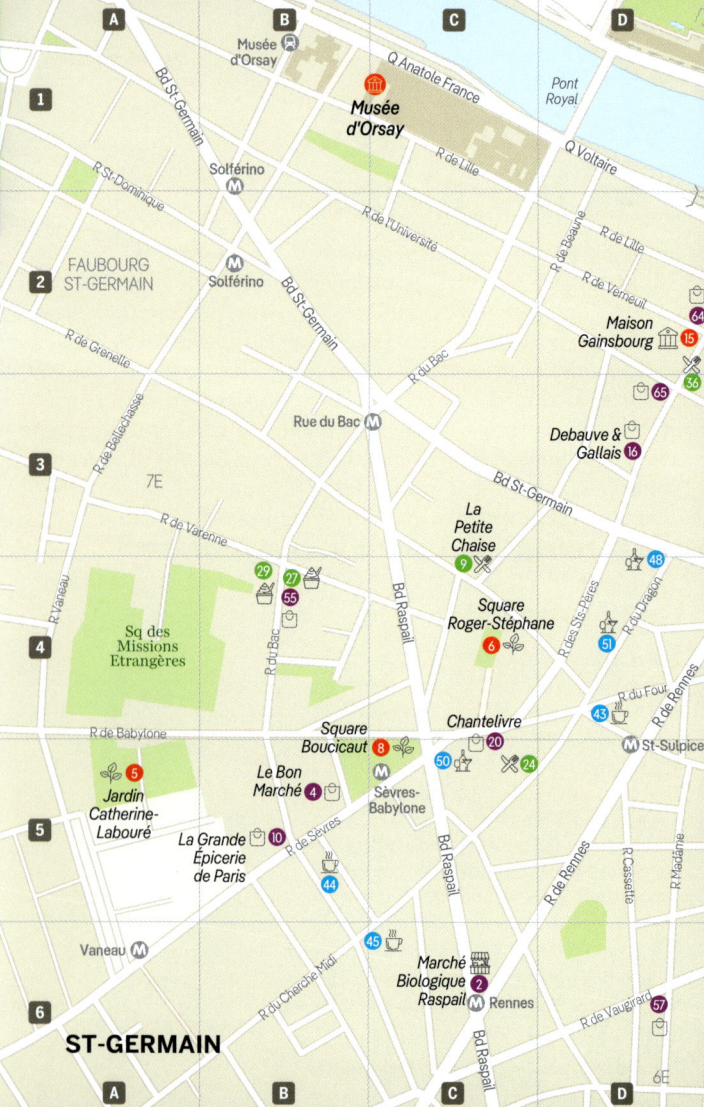

LES INVALIDES

ST-GERMAIN & LES INVALIDES

Musée Rodin

Hôtel des Invalides

Musée de l'Armée

Rosa Bonheur sur Seine

Pont de l'Alma

FAUBOURG ST-GERMAIN

Pl des Invalides

Q d'Orsay
R de l'Université
R St-Dominique
Pl du Palais Bourbon
R de Bourgogne
R de Grenelle
R de Varenne
R de Constantine
Av du Maréchal Galliéni
Bd des Invalides
Bd de la Tour Maubourg
R Fabert
R de Grenelle
R de l'Université
R St-Dominique
R Ernest Psichari
R Duvivier
R Cler
Av de la Motte-Picquet
Av Bosquet
R de Grenelle
R du Champ de Mars
Av Rapp
Q d'Orsay
Av de la Bourdonnais
R de Belgrade

ST-GERMAIN & LES INVALIDES

For more see
- Top Experiences p182
- Experiences p192
- Eating p198
- Drinking p199
- Shopping p200

★ TOP EXPERIENCE

Jardin du Luxembourg

A 22-hectare expanse along the southern edge of the Latin Quarter, the Jardin du Luxembourg is where formal French symmetry meets the softness of English landscaping. Children sail electric boats in the central pond or ride one of France's oldest merry-go-rounds, while locals play chess beneath a pergola.

MAP P178 **E6**

PLANNING TIP
Be mindful of designated picnic spots, as not all lawns are permitted for use – you might get whistled off by the keeper.

Thinking of Italy

Following the assassination of King Henri IV in 1610, Marie de' Medici became regent of France for her young son, Louis XIII. Feeling poorly housed at the Louvre and longing for the atmosphere of her native Italy, the queen decided to build an Italian-style palace of her own. In 1612 she acquired the Petit Luxembourg, a three-winged residence belonging to François, Duke of Piney-Luxembourg. A friend, she often visited him and his peaceful property with her young children, including future king Louis XIII, who loved to play and hunt in the duke's garden.

Get Your Bearings

The garden is full of quiet treasures: the 17th-century **Fontaine Médicis**, the **Orangerie** greenhouse, centuries-old trees, orchard, apiary and over a hundred statues scattered among tree-lined paths, each a quiet witness to the city's layered past. Honey from the garden's bees is sold at the end of September during the annual **Fête du Miel**.

Luxembourg Museum

This museum features contemporary exhibitions that frequently highlight the work of women artists. Past shows have explored the art of painter Tarsila de Aguiar do Amaral, the friendship between American writer Gertrude Stein and artist Picasso, and the women artists of the *années folles* (Roaring Twenties).

Scan this QR code for opening hours, which change seasonally.

⭐ **TOP EXPERIENCE**

Musée d'Orsay

The second-most-visited museum in France after the Louvre, the Musée d'Orsay is housed in a former railway station and contains one of the world's most important collections of impressionist and postimpressionist works. With sublime architecture and masterpieces, plan on spending at least half a day here.

MAP P178 **C1**

A Living History of Architecture

As you enter the Musée d'Orsay, take a pause to notice the layout of the ground floor, with sculptures in two straight rows, and small galleries annexed along the outer edges of the space. It was organised to mimic the layout of the original railway station within which it is housed. Given the sheer significance of the encasing building, it was decided from the outset that the Musée d'Orsay would elevate the history of architecture to the same revered rung as that of the history of art. Accordingly, galleries dedicated to the museum's impressive collection of architectural drawings by the likes of Gustave Eiffel and Viollet-le-Duc interject those allocated to fine art. At the end of the ground floor is a space dedicated to the history of Paris' urban development. Look below you and you'll notice an intricate scale model of the city as it stood in 1914 when the museum first opened.

The Impressionists

Most people visit the Musée d'Orsay for its collection of impressionist works and rightly so: the 5th floor of the museum is largely dedicated to the movement. By tracing the galleries in a clockwise direction you'll get a fairly comprehensive

PLANNING TIP
Book your ticket online in advance. The best time to visit is when it opens at 9.30am or on Thursday evenings when the museum is open until 9.45pm.

Scan this QR code for opening hours, exhibit information and tickets.

ALEXANDRA LANDE/SHUTTERSTOCK

overview of the development of the movement from impressionism to postimpressionism to neoimpressionism. Here is where the movement's masterpieces, such as Monet's *Londres, le Parlement;* Van Gogh's *Starry Night Over the Rhône;* and Edgar Degas' sculpture *La Petite Danseuse de Quatorze Ans* are exhibited alongside other fabled modern works like Cézanne's *Nature Morte* series.

Cinema as Art

Few people know that from its beginnings the Musée d'Orsay has devoted one of its sections to the history of cinema and cinematography, innovating an approach that considers film as art, and not simply as technique or entertainment. On the 5th floor, tucked away alongside the impressionist collection, is a gallery tracing

SEINE VIEWS
Don't miss the Parisian panorama through the giant glass clock face on the 5th floor – there's usually a queue of visitors waiting to take selfies here.

the medium's history and technical developments, with projections of short clips from pivotal films in the medium's history. To complement this venture, the Musée d'Orsay often holds screenings in its auditorium of some of the most important works of cinema from the early 20th century. Check the official website for a schedule.

A Contemporary Lens

Although the focus of the Musée d'Orsay is modern art from the period between 1848 and 1914, several times a year the museum invites the biggest names in today's contemporary art scene, such as Jean-Philippe Delhomme, Marlene Dumas and Peter Doig, to curate exhibitions featuring their own works interwoven with selections from the permanent collection. By placing contemporary art in direct dialogue with historical masterpieces, it urges us to consider the works with a fresh perspective while emphasising their enduring importance. On one Thursday evening per month, the museum also hosts 'Curious Thursdays', when young artists from other creative worlds (like dance and music) are invited to perform among the art. Check the website for schedule details.

Themed Tours

It's impossible to view the entire collection in one day – instead it's advisable to pick one or two themes as entry points to discover the collection. Alternatively, take one of the museum's themed guided tours. Held daily in English, French and Italian, the 1½-hour tours are centred around fun themes such as masterpieces, animals and parties. Check the museum's website for departure times.

QUICK BREAK
The museum's food options include the **Café Campana**, fantastically decorated by the renowned Brazilian designers, the sumptuous, frescoed **fine-dining restaurant**, and a casual **coffee shop** under the nave.

AUDIOGUIDE
Rent an audioguide to hear commentary from the museum's curators on over 300 works. For the temporary exhibitions, there's an audioguide to download on your phone.

★ TOP EXPERIENCE

Église St-Sulpice

Despite being just 1 sq metre smaller than the Notre Dame de Paris, the Église St-Sulpice has long lived in its shadow – until Dan Brown's *The Da Vinci Code* drew crowds to the monumental Roman Catholic church in search of the hidden treasures detailed in his epic novel.

MAP P178 **E5**

PLANNING TIP
It's free to enter the church, though best to time your visit outside of the Mass service, unless you wish to join in worship (and hear the splendid organ).

Six Different Architects

Construction of the current church began in 1642, but it passed through the hands of several different architects – which accounts for its unique mishmash of baroque and neoclassical references – until work was halted entirely by the French Revolution. In fact, the right tower on the church's western façade (designed by Italian architect Servandoni, who drew inspiration from London's St Paul's Cathedral) remains unfinished to this day.

Museum-Worthy Art

What's so special about Église St-Sulpice is the artwork contained within. Immediately to your right after entering, in the **Chapel of the Holy Angels**, are three well-preserved wax murals painted by French artist Eugène Delacroix between 1855 and 1861. Also look out for the peculiar pair of holy water fonts, located on either side of the nave and the giant clam shells, which were gifted to King Francis I by the Venetian Republic, and which sit atop stone bases hand-carved with sea motifs by Jean-Baptiste Pigalle. The marble statue of Mary, located at the far end of the church, was also sculpted by the prolific artist.

Classical Music

Throughout the year, classical-music recitals are held at the church, with tickets available from **L'Officiel des Spectacles** (*offi.fr*) or on-site before performances.

Scan this QR code for opening hours and visitor information.

⭐ TOP EXPERIENCE

Musée Rodin

In the heart of the 7e *arrondissement* is one of Paris' most serene museums, dedicated to the prolific oeuvre of French sculptor Auguste Rodin. The Musée Rodin is housed within the 19th-century Hôtel Biron, a former aristocratic mansion where Rodin had two showrooms.

Iconic Sculpture

Rodin is considered by many an art historian to be the founder of modern sculpture, known for his unparalleled talent for translating the complexities of human emotion into meticulously sculpted clay, bronze and plaster works. Among his most famous sculptures are *The Thinker, The Kiss* and *The Gates of Hell* – all of which are on show at the museum. There's also a room dedicated to sculptor Camille Claudel, who was at various points also Rodin's collaborator, muse and lover.

Idyllic Gardens

But what makes this museum so special is its tranquil sculpture garden, which is used to present some of Rodin's works. Although it's a beautiful space all year-round, and it's interesting to see how the sculptures catch the light in different seasons, the months of April and May are particularly lovely when the garden's Rodin roses are in full bloom. There's also a cafe with an outdoor terrace, which is a particularly lovely spot to stop for a coffee.

Also look out for two temporary exhibitions a year, one of which, **Atelier Rodin**, is designed with children aged six months to 10 years in mind to learn about sculpture in a fun, hands-on way.

MAP P180 **E4**

PLANNING TIP
Avoid Tuesdays, which are busy after the Monday closure. An entry ticket provides you with access to both the museum and the garden. Guided tours are available in French.

Scan this QR code for opening hours and to book tickets.

★ **TOP EXPERIENCE**

Hôtel des Invalides

The Hôtel des Invalides was built in the 1670s by Louis XIV to provide housing for 4000 *invalides* (disabled war veterans). Today, it houses several museums, including one devoted to France's military. At the southern end of the grassy Esplanade is the final resting place of Napoléon.

MAP P180 **D4**

PLANNING TIP
Entrance to Napoléon's tomb is included in the ticket to the Musée de L'Armée, as is entrance to the smaller Museum of the Order of the Liberation and Museum of Relief Maps.

Scan this QR code for opening hours, exhibition information and to book tickets.

Musée de L'Armée

On 14 July 1789, a mob forced its way into the building and, after fierce fighting, seized 32,000 rifles before heading on to storm the Bastille and start the French Revolution. This military history is on display at the Musée de l'Armée, France's national military museum. With over 500,000 artefacts, it boasts the third-largest collection of weapons and armour in the world. Don't be deterred from visiting if warfare and military paraphernalia are not your thing – the 8000-sq-metre complex is more of a gigantesque cabinet of curiosities with something to pique everyone's interest.

The museum is divided into various sections including French Classical Cannons, Ancient Armour and Arms (13th to 17th centuries), From Louis XIV to Napoléon III (1643–1870) and the two World Wars (1871–1990). It's impossible to cover it all in one day – you're better off concentrating on a single section or simply wandering aimlessly, pausing at whatever grabs your attention.

Among the curiosities are a taxidermy of Napoléon's last horse, Vizir (check out the Napoléonic branding on the horse's haunches), and Jean-Auguste-Dominique Ingres' painting *Emperor Napoléon on his Throne*. The museum hosts several temporary exhibitions, often centred around contemporary art, several times a year.

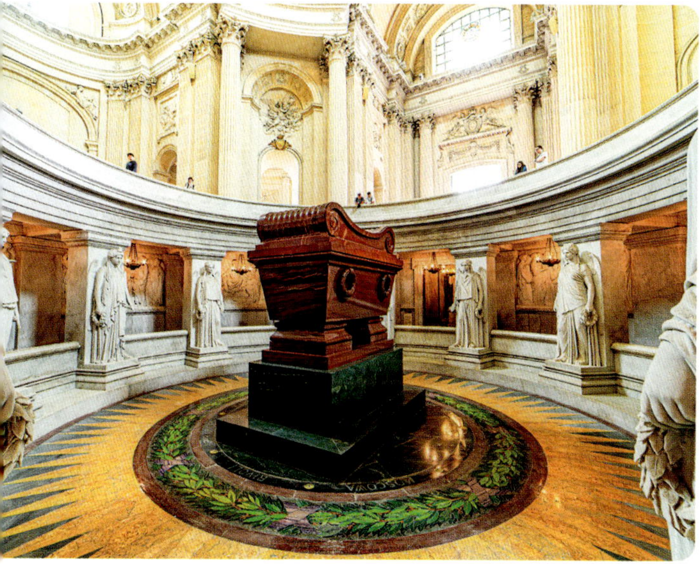

PAULOALBERTO82/SHUTTERSTOCK

Under the Gold Dome

Although Napoléon I died in exile on the island of St Helena in 1821, King Louis Philippe I ordered the repatriation of his remains to Paris in 1840, as per the emperor's wishes. His lavish tomb took more than 20 years to complete, during which Napoléon's remains were laid at the nearby **Chapelle de St-Jerôme**, due to the difficulties in importing the speciality stone used. The actual sarcophagus is made from Russian purple quartzite, the green granite base was sourced from Vosges, and the black marble bottom is from Sainte-Luce, Martinique. Surrounding the 6m-deep open crypt are 12 statues representing Victory; on the mosaic floor are tiled the names of the battles Napoléon fought in, with his insignia also laid into the marble floors.

QUICK BREAK
Café Max, founded in 1941 on the nearby av de la Motte-Picquet, was once the meeting place for Resistance fighters during WWII.

WALKING TOUR

Walk Quintessential St-Germain

This itinerary will take you to the beautiful and worthwhile landmarks in St-Germain des Prés. Experience hundreds of years of history, from stunning royal gardens to a secret courtyard where Enlightenment thinkers once caffeinated. As you wander and window-shop, soak up the vibe of this legendary district, particularly its lively cafe scene.

START	END	LENGTH
Jardin du Luxembourg	Monnaie de Paris	3km; 2 hours

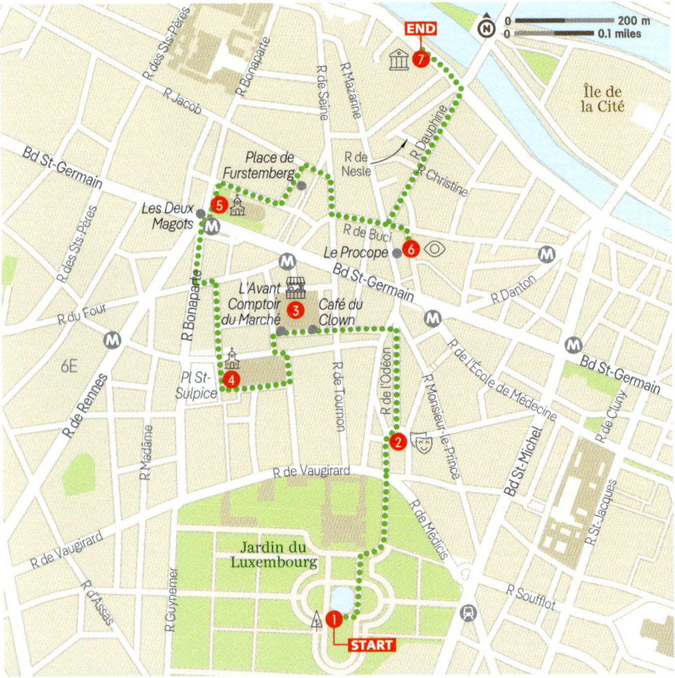

1. Garden Glory

Start off in the **Jardin du Luxembourg** (p182), the verdant wonderland that's the most popular park for Parisians. Grab a coffee from one of the kiosks and wander between the flower beds, linger by the pond filled with toy boats or watch a competitive game of pétanque. Exit to the north onto rue de Vaugirard and continue on pl Paul Claudel.

2. Monumental Theatre

The **Théâtre de l'Odéon** was opened in 1872 and many a famed French playwright debuted works here. In the summer months, the cobbled square in front of the neoclassical theatre is transformed into a giant cafe terrace. Continue on the rue de l'Odéon.

3. Market Munchies

Turn left onto the rue des Quatres Vents and continue to the **Marché St-Germain**. The covered market was built in 1511 but it was later destroyed by fire. The more modern version still has charm, despite the presence of big brands like Apple. Refuel at **Café du Clown** (p199) or graze on small plates at **L'Avant Comptoir du Marché**.

4. Delacroix Murals

The next stop is **Église St-Sulpice** (p186). The fountain in front of the church is as majestic as the Delacroix murals inside. Look for the gnomon, an astronomical marker, embedded in the floor – fictionalised by Dan Brown in *The Da Vinci Code* as 'the Rose Line'. Exit the church and make a quick detour to rue Férou to see the calligraphy wall mural of Arthur Rimbaud's poem 'Le Bateau Ivre' (The Drunken Boat).

5. The Oldest Church

Continue to bd St-Germain, the fabled Left Bank thoroughfare lined with restaurants and cafes that are destinations in themselves. Observe the people-watchers on the terrace at **Les Deux Magots** (p194), before ducking into the **Église St-Germain des Prés**, considered the oldest church in Paris. This was the site of a Benedictine abbey since 558, and the current edifice dates to the 11th century.

6. Cobbled Courtyard

Traverse the **cour du Commerce-St-André**, a cobbled lane that's almost impossibly charming, bordered by unique boutiques and restaurants, including **Le Procope**, where the likes of Voltaire, Benjamin Franklin and Thomas Jefferson dined. This is where Denis Diderot and Jean le Rond d'Alembert wrote the French *Encyclopédie* over endless cups of coffee.

7. Show Me the Money

Take gallery-lined rue Dauphine towards the Seine. Wander into the rue Christine and rue de Nesle to soak up the atmosphere of the district's tangle of historic back streets. Arrive at the Pont Neuf, the city's oldest bridge, where the **Monnaie de Paris** (p194) looms over the river.

EXPERIENCES

Step into the Artist's Atelier at Musée National Eugène Delacroix
MUSEUM

MAP: ① P178 E3

Tucked away in the charming place de Furstemberg is a small museum dedicated to Delacroix, **Musée National Eugène Delacroix** *(musee-delacroix.fr; adult/under-18 €9/free),* housed in the painter's former apartment, including the atelier in the garden. Delacroix chose the location to be close to Église St-Sulpice (p186) whilst he was working there on three large-scale murals, which you can still see today. It's also where Delacroix ended up spending the last few years of his life with his loyal housekeeper. None of his possessions remain, as they were all sold after his death. For Delacroix fans, seeing the smaller paintings here is a nice complement to viewing his more famous and much larger works in the Louvre (p72), and as you can imagine, a much quieter place to enjoy the artist's work. Note that although the museum is wheelchair accessible, Delacroix' atelier in the garden at the back isn't. If you'd like a guided tour in English, email the museum, which can organise a visit with an external guide.

Go Organic at the Marché Biologique Raspail
MARKET

MAP: ② P178 C6

Every Sunday between 7.30am and 2.30pm on the bd Raspail (between rue de Sèvres and rue de Rennes) is **Marché Biologique Raspail**, Paris' top organic food market. All the 50 or so stalls here must adhere to the national guidelines on organic produce. This, in turn, means that the prices are higher than at your usual neighbourhood market, but it's a great place for otherwise hard-to-find goods such as freshly baked gluten-free bread, vegan curries and superfood powders like spirulina and maca.

Read at France's Oldest Public Library
LIBRARY

MAP: ③ P178 F2

Located within the Institute of France (the national body conceived to protect French culture) is the oldest public library in the country: **Bibliothèque Mazarine**. Once the private reading room of Cardinal Mazarin, today it is both a public workspace and national archive, containing a stunning collection of rare and ancient manuscripts. The resplendent reading room is open to the public from 10am to 6pm, Monday through Friday, but you must register on-site for an access card (free for five days or €15 for an annual pass). All visitors are then required to wash their hands before entering the room in absolute silence. As you are not allowed to simply thumb through the treasured volumes, the library organises free (and wonderfully informative) daily guided tours in both French and English.

Explore the World's First Department Store

SHOPPING

MAP: ④ P178 **B5**

Le Bon Marché is a shopping temple whose elegant architecture matches the luxurious mix of fashion brands on display. Founded in 1838, it is where shopping was transformed into an *art de vivre*. In 1852 it was taken over by marketing maverick Aristide Boucicaut and his wife Marguerite who drastically improved the customer experience with their department store vision, introducing innovations such as a fixed-price system and a reading room for waiting husbands.

Even if you're not shopping, wander the store to experience the world of historic French luxury. The central escalators were designed by Andrée Putman with now-iconic square panels. Gustave Eiffel designed the wrought-iron ceilings – **La Librairie**, the store's bookshop, is said to hold more weight in iron than the Eiffel Tower.

And don't forget to stop in at the bathrooms (complete with an old-school powder room) – the Boucicauts were the first to innovate in-store separate-sex bathrooms. Now the store innovates with a regular events programme, including art exhibits and dance performances.

BEST SECRET GARDENS

Jardin Catherine-Labouré
MAP: ⑤ P178 **A5**

This little-known garden is located just a stone's throw from Le Bon Marché on the grounds of a former 17th-century convent.

Square Roger-Stéphane
MAP: ⑥ P178 **C4**

Another green oasis is square Roger-Stéphane, which you can find at the end of the pedestrian street rue Juliette Récamier, off rue de Sevrès.

Square Laurent-Prache
MAP: ⑦ P178 **E3**

It's easy to miss this little square even though it's hidden in plain sight right next to the Benedictine abbey of St-Germain des Prés.

Square Boucicaut
MAP: ⑧ P178 **C5**

This large square behind Sèvres–Babylone metro station is great for kids, or for enjoying an ice cream from the nearby Le Bac à Glaces.

Find Foodie Nirvana at La Grande Épicerie de Paris

GOURMET STORE

MAP: ⑩ P178 **B5**

If all the browsing at Le Bon Marché has made you peckish, pop next door (or across one of the connecting bridges) to **La Grande Épicerie de Paris**, Le Bon Marché's gourmet food store.

THE CITY'S OLDEST RESTAURANT
There are a handful of restaurants in Paris that lay claim to being the oldest. La Tour d'Argent (p172) is one of the most high-profile spots in Paris, thanks to a Michelin star and stellar views. But it was an inn when it opened in 1582. There's another contender on the Left Bank: **La Petite Chaise** (MAP: ⑨ P178 **C4**) was founded in 1680 by wine merchant Georges Rameau, who had the novel idea of serving food to accompany his wines for sale. And Le Procope (p191), founded in 1686, later the haunt of the intellectual elite during the Enlightenment, is the oldest cafe in Paris.

Indulge in Literary Libations in St-Germain
BARS

St-Germain is home to famous dining establishments beloved by the 20th century's greatest writers, artists and philosophers. **Les Deux Magots** (MAP: ⑪ P178 **E4**) is considered by many to be the birthplace of surrealism. Lost Generation writers James Joyce and Ernest Hemingway were also regular customers. Across the road, rival **Café de Flore** drew great existentialist philosophers like Simone de Beauvoir, Jean-Paul Sartre and Albert Camus. Today, it comes down to personal preference, but be warned that you might be queuing for a while. Ask for a terrace table if you want to people-watch over a coffee, or go for an evening apéritif. A few blocks away is **La Palette** (MAP: ⑫ P178 **F3**), a lesser-known bar that was frequented by artists such as Picasso and Cézanne. Although literary folklore would make it seem like artists subsisted entirely on coffee and dry sherry à la Ernest Hemingway, even the most starved of them had to eat at some point – which is why they'd head to **Brasserie Lipp**, conveniently located directly opposite Café de Flore.

Learn About the History of Money at Monnaie de Paris
MUSEUM

MAP:  ⑬ P178 **G2**
The **Monnaie de Paris** *(monnaiedeparis.fr; adult/concession €12/8),* or Paris Mint, was the first factory in Paris when it was

You can spend quite a while here just browsing the huge selection of high-quality French produce, luxury food brands, and breads and pastries made fresh on-site each morning. Its basement floor has one of the largest (and most expensive) wine selections in Paris (and top tip, there's also a toilet here – usually without a queue), while the upper levels are home to a restaurant and a selection of homewares. And if you've decided on an impromptu picnic, you can even find things like paper plates and napkins on the ground floor.

inaugurated in 1775. Although most of France's coins have been minted in a new factory in Bordeaux since 1972, celebration and collectors' coins are still made here, as were the Olympic medals. However, the building's main purpose now is to house a permanent museum showcasing coins and minting through the ages. There's quite a lot to see here, including the oldest coin in the world, gold coins and bullion recovered from shipwrecks, and on Fridays, dramatic demonstrations of someone pouring liquid molten metal into a cast. It's also a good one if you're travelling with kids: there's a stellar children's programme. Allow two hours to take in the exhibitions. Like a lot of museums in Paris, the evenings with late openings (which is Wednesday here) are a good time to visit. Also look out for an open-air cinema and concerts in the courtyard in summer.

Maison Gainsbourg

Make a Pharmaceutical Pilgrimage to Citypharma PHARMACY

MAP: 14 P178 E4

In the heart of St-Germain is the city's most famous pharmacy, **Citypharma**: a place of pilgrimage for both local and international beauty lovers looking to stock up on French beauty must-haves. The pharmacy has long held a reputation for offering the lowest prices in Paris and you'll still find some bargains, with hundreds, if not thousands, of products sprawled over two floors – it's a one-stop shop for all your beauty and pharmaceutical needs. Stock up on the usual cult favourites (Crème Embryolisse moisturiser, La Roche Posay, Caudalie, Nuxe) and don't hesitate to ask for help navigating the labyrinth of products – the staff are incredibly knowledgeable. Be warned that you'll need to brave the crowds, particularly at lunchtime and on weekends. Checkout lines tend to move quickly regardless of the packed aisles.

Step inside the Singer's Home at Maison Gainsbourg MUSEUM

MAP: 15 P178 D2

The heavily graffitied former abode of French singer Serge Gainsbourg, located at 5bis rue de Verneil, has long been a site of pilgrimage for the singer's

ROYAL HISTORY OF CHOCOLATE
St-Germain des Prés is one of the best neighbourhoods for buying chocolate, and we've partly got Marie Antoinette to thank for it. In 1779 when Sulpice Debauve was appointed Louis XVI and Marie Antoinette's pharmacist, the Versailles court had already adopted a chocolate habit. At the time chocolate was always drunk, not eaten, but when Marie Antoinette began to complain about her migraine medicine, Debauve had the idea to sweeten the remedy with cacao and almond milk. These round chocolate medallions, which were shaped like ancient coins, instantly won royal approval and Marie Antoinette's *pistoles,* as she called them, can still be found in the **Debauve & Gallais** (MAP: 16 P178 D3) shop today.

massive fan base. Now, **Maison Gainsbourg** (*maisongainsbourg.fr; adult/concession €12/6, house & museum from €16)* has been opened to the public by his daughter, the actress Charlotte Gainsbourg, who narrated the 30-minute audioguide to give visitors a poignant glimpse into his private life. After you've finished your tour of the house, head across the street to the museum, which showcases 450 personal objects from Gainsbourg's life and musical career. It's in French, so make sure to pick up the English-language booklet at the entrance. There's also a cafe and cocktail bar (named Le Gainsbarre), and it's free to pop by for a drink even if you're not visiting the house or museum. Bear in mind that as the house is small so only a few people are allowed in at a time, meaning that tickets sell out well in advance.

Partake in a Péniche Party on a Boat BOAT

Where the 6e and 7e *arrondissements* meet the Seine are several *péniches* – houseboats docked permanently along the riverbanks. Some are still private homes, while others have been converted into restaurants, bars and clubs – they're a great way to experience the city's famous waterway. **Rosa Bonheur sur Seine** (MAP: 17 P180 E1) is the most popular, known for its live music (with everything from salsa to jazz). Check out its Facebook page for the schedule. Tickets are required for certain events. Drinks and food can be purchased on board. If you're ready to dance all night, head next door to **Le Flow**, with its views of the glorious Pont Alexandre III. It regularly hosts live DJ sets on its rooftop and stays open until the early hours on the weekend. If you want a more ambient apéritif, then **La Balle au Bond** (MAP: 18 P178 F2)

La Balle au Bond

has a plant-lined rooftop terrace that's the perfect place to relax, drink in hand, while watching the sunset over the Seine. It's open daily for apéritifs and dinner, and on Saturdays and Sundays for brunch.

Browse a Bibliophile's Paradise   BOOKSHOPS

Given the famous literary names that once made St-Germain their font of inspiration, it's of little surprise that today the neighbourhood is the publishing heartland of French literature and home to some of the capital's most interesting bookshops. The English-language **Red Wheelbarrow** (MAP: 19 P178 **G6**), near the Jardin de Luxembourg, hosts regular author talks and signings. It also has a children's bookshop next door, **Red Balloon**.

Chantelivre (MAP: 20 P178 **C5**) has a children's section at the back, and an interactive book museum called La Maison des Histoires, for kids to play and attend story times. On rue Monsieur le Prince, **San Francisco Book Company** (MAP: 21 P178 **G5**) is a labyrinth of secondhand books. If you're looking for cool coffee-table books try the French brand **Assouline**, which has two Left Bank addresses, including one in Le Bon Marché (p193), or head to the Philippe Starck–designed **Taschen** (MAP: 22 P178 **F4**) boutique, which has hosted events and book signings for some of the biggest names in photography, fashion, art and more.

LISTINGS

See p178 for map of locations

Best Places for...

€ Budget €€ Midrange €€€ Top End

Eating

Bakeries

Maison Bergeron €
MAP P180 23 A3
Consistently voted as having one of the top 10 croissants by the Greater Paris Bakers' Union. *7am-8.15pm*

Poilâne €
MAP P178 24 C5
Perhaps France's most famous *boulangerie* (bakery), it's known for its sourdough *miches* (like a big round country loaf), *punitions* (butter cookies) and apple tarts. *7.15am-8pm Mon-Sat*

Boulangerie Liberté €
MAP P178 25 G4
Chic, new-wave *boulangerie* with buttery croissants made on-site. Locations around Paris. *7.30am-8pm Mon-Sat, 8.30am-5pm Sun*

Tapisserie €
MAP P180 26 C4
Delicious seasonal creations from the team behind seafood restaurant Clamato and one-Michelin-star Septime. *8.30am-7pm Wed-Fri, 9.30am-9pm Sat, 9.30am-5pm Sun*

Pastries & Sweets

Des Gâteaux et du Pain €€
MAP P178 27 B4
Sublime desserts, buttery croissants, freshly baked breads and even quiches for a quick lunch, Claire Damon has it all at her second fabulous address. *10am-7.30pm Mon & Wed-Sat, to 6pm Sun*

Mori Yoshida €€
MAP P180 28 D8
Some of the prettiest (and most delicious) desserts can be found at Mori Yoshida. Try Le Beige, his signature creation, or contemporary twists on French classics. *11am-7pm Wed-Sun*

Philippe Conticini €€
MAP P178 29 B4
The Gran Cru Vanille is the signature but it's hard to go wrong here. There are also giant (Instagrammable) croissants if that's your thing. *10am-7pm Tue-Sat, 10am-2pm Sun*

La Pâtisserie Cyril Lignac €
MAP P180 30 F8
French celebrity chef Cyril Lignac is now also well known for his delicious pâtisserie. *7am-7pm Mon, to 8pm Tue-Sun*

Picks in St-Germain des Prés

Café Pavane €
MAP P178 31 F5
Run by the daughter of chocolatier Jean-Paul Hévin, the menu features Russian-inspired dishes such as borscht followed by Hévin's wonderful chocolate desserts. *11am-7.30pm Wed-Sun*

Le Christine €€€
MAP P178 32 G3
Young chef Rodolphe Despagne serves up surprising, gastronomic creations (and plant-based options) in an unpretentious setting. Service is fantastic, as are the wines. *noon-2pm & 7-10pm*

Breizh Café Odéon €
MAP P178 (33) F4

This Paris-wide crêperie serves the best galettes and crêpes in Paris. A great spot for lunch or dinner, and dining in groups or with kids. *10am-11pm*

Huîtrerie Régis €€€
MAP P178 (34) F4

Not the cheapest oysters in Paris, but they are the best. Make sure to reserve, as the place is tiny and can quickly get booked out. *noon-2.30pm & 6.30-10.30pm Mon-Fri, 2-10pm Sat & Sun*

Bistros & French Classics

La Boissonnerie €€
MAP P178 (35) F3

A contemporary bistro serving seasonal dishes alongside a great wine list and in a friendly, lively setting. *12.30-2.30pm & 7-10.30pm*

Le Comptoir des Saints-Pères €€
MAP P178 (36) D2

A bustling classic St-Germain des Prés bistro that pulls in a very local crowd. Hemingway and Picasso also used to pop by. *7am-11pm*

Polidor €€
MAP P178 (37) G5

A historic address and affordable bistro, frequented by the likes of Rimbaud, James Joyce and Ernest Hemingway. The prix-fixe menus are good value. *noon-3pm & 7pm-midnight*

Le Comptoir du Relais €€
MAP P178 (38) F4

Classic French dishes served nonstop, which is hard to find in Paris, with a selection of natural wines. *noon-11pm*

Drinking

Best Apéro Spots

Freddy's
MAP P178 (39) F3

Fantastic wine list and sharing plates. Enjoy a drink and a nibble or make a whole dinner out of it. Arrive early to get a table. *12.30pm-midnight*

L'Avant Comptoir de la Terre
See (38) F4

Side-by-side with **L'Avant Comptoir de la Mer** (*la terre* focuses on meat, *la mer* on fish), these addresses serve small sharing dishes. Look out for huge mounds of butter on the counter. *noon-11pm*

Bar Etna
MAP P178 (40) F4

A buzzy and cosy *bar à vins* serving natural wines and small plates. *5pm-2am Tue-Sat*

La Crèmerie
MAP P178 (41) F5

Very cute wine bar (you can't miss the original façade) that fills with locals. Great cheese and charcuterie boards. *6.30-10.30pm*

Original Coffee Shops

Café du Clown
MAP P178 (42) F4

Great coffee, and a good spot for people-watching from the terrace outside the Marché St-Germain. Note that the toilet is inside the market. *8am-6pm*

Cafe Nuances
MAP P178 (43) D4

A hole-in-the-wall coffee shop for picking up freshly baked pastries and cups to go. Beans packed in reusable cloth bags make great gifts. *8am-7pm Mon-Fri, 9am-7pm Sat & Sun*

Maison Fleuret
See (16) D3

A cute coffee shop inside a historic former bookshop. There are plant-based dishes and pastries from Maison Fleuret's

own baking school. *9am-6.30pm Wed-Sun*

Wani
MAP P178 44 B5

Cute and stylish coffee shop serving breakfast, lunch, pastries and Japanese teas. *11am-5.30pm*

Speciality Coffee

Ten Belles
MAP P178 45 C6

The Left Bank outpost of beloved British-Franco bakery Ten Belles, famed for its delicious sourdough loaves. *8.30am-4.30pm Mon-Fri, 9am-5pm Sat & Sun*

Coutume
MAP P180 46 F6

One of the original speciality coffee shops, situated on the street where Yves Saint Laurent once lived. It also serves breakfast, brunch and cakes. *8.30am-5.30pm Mon-Fri, 9am-6pm Sat & Sun*

L'Arbre à Café
See 49 F4

Serious coffee lovers will appreciate the menu of organic speciality beans from this artisan coffee roaster and producer, which even has its own plantation. *10am-7.45pm Mon-Sat, 11am-7.45pm Sun*

Terres de Café
MAP P180 47 A4

Another pioneer in Paris' artisan coffee movement, Terres de Café has the largest range of speciality coffees in France and offers coffee workshops. *8am-7pm Mon-Fri, 9.30am-7pm Sat & Sun*

Cocktail Bars

Cravan
MAP P178 48 D4

The big sister to the original Cravan in the 16e. Expect cool design and excellent cocktails and as a bonus, you can even book. *5pm-1am Tue-Fri, noon-1am Sat*

Castor Club
MAP P178 49 G4

Look out for an unnamed wood-panelled door to find this hunting lodge–inspired bar, where drinks are served to a soundtrack of laid-back country music. *7pm-2am Tue & Wed, 7pm-4am Thu-Sat*

Bar Joséphine
MAP P178 50 C5

Once frequented by the likes of Picasso and Josephine Baker, this palace hotel bar serves up excellent cocktails and draws a local (sometimes celebrity) crowd. *5pm-1am*

Le Bar
MAP P178 51 D4

Chef Cyril Lignac is better known for his restaurants and patisseries but his intimate and sexy cocktail bar (not to be confused with restaurant Bar des Prés across the road) is a great spot for starting – or ending – the evening. *7pm-1am Wed-Sat*

Shopping

Beauty Products

Biologique Recherche
MAP P178 52 F5

This is the second Paris location from French beauty brand Biologique Recherche, whose cult products include the celebrity-approved exfoliating Lotion P50. *9.30am-7.45pm Mon-Sat, 10.30am-6.15pm Sun*

Caudalie
MAP P178 53 E5

You can easily pick up Caudalie products in the pharmacies, but fans might also want to book into the newly opened Left Bank spa. *10am-7pm*

L'Officine Universelle Buly 1803
MAP P178 54 E2

Originally founded by French perfumier Jean-Vincent Bully in 1803, the brand's beautifully packaged body lotions and soaps make great gifts. *11am-7pm*

Oh My Cream!
MAP P178 55 B4

This fashionable beauty shop can now be found across Paris thanks to its well-curated selection of high-end and hard-to-find organic, natural and cult beauty products. *10.30am-7.30pm Mon-Sat*

Homeware
Cire Trudon
MAP P178 56 F5

Once the official candlemaker for the royal courts; the rue de Seine shopfront was founded in 1643. *10.30am-7.30pm Tue-Sat, 11am-7.30pm Mon*

Marin Montagut
MAP P178 57 D6

Beautiful hand-painted porcelain and other decorative objects created by the French illustrator Marin Montagut. *11am-7pm Mon-Sat*

La Soufflerie
MAP P178 58 F5

Hand-blown artisanal glassware: 100% of proceeds benefit the glassmakers to help keep the dying art alive. *11am-7pm Mon-Sat*

Astier de Villatte
MAP P178 59 F5

Artisanal ceramics crafted in the store's own Paris workshop, as well as a small selection of stationery, perfumes, candles and homeware. *11am-7pm Mon-Sat*

Speciality Food
Compagnie Française des Poivres et des Épices
MAP P178 60 F3

Stop by for high-quality peppercorns, spices, French Guérande salt, *herbs de Provence*, vanilla and sugars. The gift boxes make great souvenirs. *11am-1pm & 2.15-7pm*

Lafitte
MAP P180 61 C4

Specialists in foie gras, *rillettes*, duck *confits* and pâtés since 1920. It also sells bottles of wine if you want to ask about a pairing. *2-7pm Tue, 10am-1pm & 2-7pm Wed-Sat*

La Belle-Iloise
MAP P180 62 B4

Founded in 1932, this *conserverie* sells multi-packs of canned fish from Quiberon, Brittany, in charmingly old-fashioned packaging. *10am-7.30pm Mon-Sat, 10am-1.30pm & 2.30-7.30pm Sun*

L'Agrumiste
MAP P180 63 F8

Harder-to-find organic citrus fruits as well as fresh and zingy citrus-based products – think marmalades, yuzu granola, lemon-infused gin and delicious citrusy cakes. *11am-7pm Tue-Sat*

Antiques & Vintage Design
L'Atelier 55
MAP P178 64 D2

Vintage shop specialising in mid-century and designer furniture (Gio Ponti, Charles Eames and so on) as well as easier to pack lamps, ceramics and posters. *10am-8pm Mon-Sat, to 6pm Sun*

Galerie Stéphane Olivier
MAP P178 65 D3

The showroom exhibits a mix of Scandinavian furniture from the 1950s to the '70s and works by contemporary designers. *10.30am-1pm & 2-7pm Mon-Sat*

Yveline Antiques
See 1 E3

Opened in 1954 on the charming place de Furstemberg, this neighbourhood institution is filled with antiques and curiosities, including workshop mannequins. Now run by Agathe Derieux, who took over from her grandmother in 2013. *11am-7pm Mon-Sat*

★ WORTH A TRIP

Les Catacombes

Paris' most spine-prickling sight are these skull- and bone-lined underground tunnels in old limestone quarries. Les Catacombes is one of the largest ossuaries in the world. Sure, it is gruesome, ghoulish and downright spooky, but it remains one of Paris' most visited attractions. All in all, it's an incredible experience.

PLANNING TIP
Note that the Catacombes are not wheelchair accessible. Bring sturdy shoes and a light jacket; don't carry large bags. Reserve online tickets in advance. The closest metro is Denfert-Rochereau.

Scan this QR code to book your ticket online for a guaranteed time slot.

History

In 1785 subterranean tunnels of an abandoned quarry were upcycled as storage rooms for the exhumed bones of corpses that could no longer fit in the city's overcrowded cemeteries. By 1810 the skull- and bone-lined catacombs – resting place of an estimated six million anonymous Parisians – had been officially born. Tourism began in 1809 when visitors descended underground to tour the site in a sober contemplation of life and death inspired by poetry written on the walls. These visits were conducted by candlelight – can you imagine the eerie experience?

A Timeless Journey

Begin at the spacious entrance on av du Colonel Henri Rol-Tanguy, 14e. Walk down 131 spiral steps to the ossuary, with a mind-boggling number of bones and skulls neatly packed along the walls. *Arrête, c'est ici l'empire de la mort* ('Stop, here is the empire of death') – this inscription at the entrance to the ossuary inspires fear and respect. But there's more than skulls and bones. The site is also of great interest from a geological, philosophical, architectural and archaeological perspective. You can even see ancient marine fossils in the layers of rock.

TATIANA POPOVA/SHUTTERSTOCK

Visits cover about 1.5km of tunnels, at a cool 14°C. The exit is up 112 steps via a minimalist all-white 'transition space' with a gift shop at 21bis av René Coty. People with claustrophobia may experience anxiety in the confined environment.

Did You Know?

Les Catacombes only comprise a small area of the vast network of tunnels beneath Paris. These former quarries have been used for various purposes over the years, from mushroom farming to a secret headquarters for the Resistance during WWII. Nowadays the areas beyond the official Catacombes are illegal to access. So-called *cataphiles* (thrill-seekers who sneak underground to explore) are often caught and fined when they stage rave parties in 'rooms' decorated with graffiti and sculptures.

QUICK BREAK
When you exit onto the leafy av René Coty turn right onto rue Dareau to find **Le Vaudésir**, a friendly bistro straight out of Old World Paris.

WALKING TOUR

Walk the Villagey 14e

Montparnasse was a historic hub for artists and writers, who frequented its legendary brasseries like La Coupole and La Rotonde. Directly south, the 14e has lots of hidden corners and off-the-beaten-track areas that are well worth exploring on foot for their laid-back and bohemian atmosphere.

START	END	LENGTH
Cimetière du Montparnasse	Parc Montsouris	4km; 2–3 hours

1 Legends of Montparnasse

Begin in the **Cimetière du Montparnasse**, the final resting place of luminaries like writer Guy de Maupassant, playwright Samuel Beckett, sculptor Constantin Brancusi, photographer Man Ray, singer Serge Gainsbourg and philosophers Jean-Paul Sartre and Simone de Beauvoir. Lesser known than Père Lachaise (p126), it makes for a pleasant stroll along shady avenues, with **Tour Montparnasse** in the background.

2 Lively Market Street

Continue to **rue Daguerre**, where Paris' traditional village atmosphere thrives. Pedestrianised between av du Général Leclerc and rue Boulard, this narrow street is lined with florists, *fromageries* (cheese shops), *boulangeries* (bakeries) and classic cafes where you can watch the local goings on. Shops set up market stalls on the pavement. At No 63, you'll find the entrance to Cité Artisanale, a lovely cul-de-sac lined with workshops.

3 The Prettiest Street

Head south to square Ferdinand Brunot and the adjacent square de l'Aspirant Dunant. Both are playgrounds for kids when the sun is out. Head west to **rue des Thermopyles**, arguably the most photogenic street south of the Seine. With its small houses equipped with colourful shutters, flowery gardens and serene ambience, this paved street that screams rural France is a gem to wander.

4 Ivy-Clad Houses

Take the rue du Moulin Vert, named for an old mill and green *guinguette* (open-air dance hall) that existed here before this area was incorporated into the city of Paris in 1860. Turn into the **impasse du Moulin Vert**, flanked with houses whose façades are covered with ivy and vines.

5 Pedestrian Promenade

Walk east, crossing busy av du Général Leclerc, to reach rue Hallé. At No 12, there's a half-moon-shaped square flanked with houses reminiscent of a French provincial town. Continue to **av René Coty**, a thoroughfare with a leafy pedestrianised promenade loved by locals.

6 Artist Haven

Take the steps on the right side of the street to reach tiny **rue des Artistes**, flanked with *petites maisons* once occupied by artists. Nearby the **Atelier Chana Orloff** is where the Ukrainian-born sculptor once lived and worked.

7 Charming Park

Continue to another picturesque street, the square de Montsouris. This residential lane adjacent to **Parc Montsouris** is lined with remarkable art deco villas built in the 1920s. Finish your walk in the sprawling lakeside park. Planted with horse-chestnut, yew, cedar, weeping beech and buttonwood trees, it's a delightful picnic spot and has endearing playground areas.

★ WORTH A TRIP

Château de Versailles

Sprawling over 900 hectares, the monumental, 400-year-old Château de Versailles is France's most famous palace. It's situated in the bourgeois suburb of Versailles, 22km southwest of central Paris. The estate is divided into three main sections: the palace; the gardens, canals and pools; and the Trianon Estate to the northwest.

History

Once a royal hunting lodge, Louis XIV transformed the property into a vast, baroque château. Some 30,000 workers and soldiers toiled on the palace, the bills for which all but emptied the kingdom's coffers. The Château de Versailles was the kingdom's political capital and the seat of the royal court from 1682 up until the fateful events of 1789 when revolutionaries massacred the palace guard. Louis XVI and Marie Antoinette were ultimately dragged back to Paris, where they were ingloriously guillotined.

PLANNING TIP
Versailles is best reached by the RER C line, which ends at Versailles Château Rive Gauche (some trains go elsewhere).

The Palace

Work on the palace began in 1661 under architect Louis Le Vau (Jules Hardouin-Mansart later took over in the mid-1670s); painter Charles Le Brun (whose interior decor was ostentatious); and landscape artist André Le Nôtre, whose workers flattened hills, drained marshes and relocated forests as they laid out the seemingly endless gardens, ponds and fountains. Few alterations have been made since its construction, apart from the furniture disappearing during the Revolution and many of the rooms being redecorated by Louis-Philippe (r 1830–48), who opened part of the château to the public in 1837. The château is in the final stages of a €400 million restoration.

Scan this QR code for tickets at a dedicated time slot – otherwise admission is not guaranteed.

KKULIKOV/SHUTTERSTOCK

Hall of Mirrors & State Apartments
The palace's opulence peaks in its shimmering **Galerie des Glaces** (Hall of Mirrors). This 75m-long ballroom shines with 17 sparkling mirrored features comprising 357 individual mirrors on one side and an equal number of windows overlooking the gardens and the setting sun on the other. Luxurious appointments adorn every feature of the palace's **Grands Appartements du Roi et de la Reine** (the King's and Queen's State Apartments). Rooms are dedicated to Hercules, Venus, Diana, Mars and Mercury.

Gardens & Estate
A walk through the sprawling and artful formal gardens, natural areas, huge Grand Canal and the Trianon palaces is a highlight for many visitors.

QUICK BREAK
Book Alain Ducasse's contemporary restaurant **Ore** in the château or lunch at **La Petite Venise** on the Grand Canal, or pack a picnic for the park.

Paris Toolkit

Family Travel	210
Accommodation	211
Food, Drink & Nightlife	212
LGBTIQ+ Travellers	214
Health & Safe Travel	215
Responsible Travel	216
Accessible Travel	218
Nuts & Bolts	219
Language	220

Cyclist, Latin Quarter (p157)
OLIVEROUGE 3/SHUTTERSTOCK

Family Travel

Paris is made for kids. Not only is there playground equipment in every park, but there's also a bonanza of fun things to see and do – from zoos to boat rides on the Seine.

Theme Parks

Disneyland Paris is a natural magnet for families. Located 32km east of the city, it's easily reached on the RER A. **Parc Astérix**, a summer-opening theme park 35km north of the city, features six 'worlds' of adrenaline-pumping attractions and shows. **Jardin d'Acclimatation** (p66), situated in the Bois de Boulogne, is the only amusement park within Paris proper.

MUSEUM MULTITUDE

You're spoilt for choice when it comes to Paris museums, many of which are free for kids. Dedicated children's workshops are engaging and entertaining.

Scan this QR code to find a full list:

Accommodation

Note that Paris hotel rooms can be smaller than you expect, so keep that in mind as you think about sharing the room. Some establishments offer rooms aimed specifically at families. Rental apartments will give you – possibly – more space and let you self-cater for younger tastes and habits. Consider lift (elevator) options if you'll be dealing with prams.

Park Paradise

Playgrounds, puppet shows, carousel: the legendary **Jardin du Luxembourg** (p182) has pandered to children for generations. Its vintage toy sailing boats are heart-stealers.

Treasure Hunt

Look for pixelated mosaics created by French street artist **Invader** (p116), racking up points on the app.

Public Transport

Children under four travel free on the metro, RER and buses. Kids under 10 travel at half-price. Buses have low-floor entrances; good for prams. The metro is chaotic at rush hour; some stations have many stairs.

PRYZMAT/SHUTTERSTOCK

Accommodation

Paris has a huge choice of accommodation, from hostels to palace hotels. Apartments are popular for those looking to self-cater and for more space.

Where to Stay if You Love...

 Artistic treasures and epicurean treats
Louvre & Les Halles (p69) Central Paris location with excellent transport links, major museums, fashion and food shopping galore. Given the real estate, it's not cheap.

Lofty views and lively multicultural quarters
Montmartre & Northern Paris (p89) Hilly streets, village charm. Some parts are very touristy. Good budget options. The red-light district around Pigalle won't appeal to everyone.

Hip boutiques and buzzing nightlife
Le Marais (p107) History-steeped streets, secret squares, copious drinking and dining choices make this district incredibly popular. Can be noisy near bars.

History, jazz and literary connections
Latin Quarter (p157) Energetic student area with scores of eating, drinking and entertainment options. Well situated to explore Paris on foot. Good mix of accommodation styles.

Stylish shopping and cafe life
St-Germain & Les Invalides (p177) Quintessentially Parisian quarter close to the Seine and the Jardin du Luxembourg. High-end prices match the chic retail offerings.

OUR PICK

We love to stay in...

outlying districts, such as the 16e in western Paris (p39), the 14e in southern Paris and the east (p123), offer great value. Paris is a compact city, meaning it's relatively easy to get from one district to the next. While tourist-loved neighbourhoods like St-Germain have the highest prices, less touristy areas offer cheaper rates and a chance to immerse yourself in the local lifestyle.

HOW MUCH FOR A NIGHT IN

Hostel dorm bed from **€32**

Boutique midrange hotel from **€160**

Studio apartment from **€130**

Food, Drink & Nightlife

⚠ Allergies & Intolerances

Common allergens are often listed on menus and dietary restrictions are taken seriously. Communicate your allergy to servers, and – if possible – email establishments in advance. French chefs generally do not modify dishes; alternatives are found.

HOW TO SAY
I'm allergic to... Je suis allergique aux...
nuts noix
shellfish crustacés
dairy produits laitiers
wheat blé

> **? HOW TO ASK...**
> **Is this gluten free?**
> Est-ce sans gluten?
> **Does this contain nuts?**
> Est-ce que ceci contient des noix?
> **Is there a vegan option?**
> Proposez-vous une option végétalienne?

--- **RESERVATIONS** ---

Reservations are essential to guarantee a table. Book a few days in advance for midrange spots, and one or two months ahead for popular/high-end restaurants. Some request a reconfirmation closer to the date, either by email or telephone: do pick up if a strange French number calls your mobile.

Fixed-Price Lunch Menu

Daily *formules* or *menus* (prix-fixe menus) typically include two- to four-course meals. The *plat du jour* (dish of the day) is invariably good value. Lunch *menus* are often a fantastic deal and allow you to enjoy *haute cuisine* at very affordable prices.

Pay the Bill

Trying to get *l'addition* (the bill) can be maddeningly slow. The French consider it rude to bring the bill immediately – you have to be persistent when it comes to getting your server's attention. Ask for *'l'addition, s'il vous plaît'* (the check, please) when you're ready.

Splitting the bill It's not uncommon for individuals in a group to pay separate amounts. Indicate to your server the amount you'd like to pay.

Tipping Service is included in the bill so a *pourboire* (tip) is not necessary, though leaving 5–10% for good service is appreciated.

PRICE RANGES

The following price ranges refer to the average cost of a main course.

€ less than €20
€€ €20–50
€€€ more than €50

OPENING HOURS

Cafes 7am to 11pm

Restaurants noon to 2.30pm and 7pm to 11pm; may close Sunday or Monday

Restaurants *en service continu* (nonstop service) noon to 11pm

Going Out

Cafe life For most Parisians living in tiny apartments, cafes and bars have traditionally served as the *salon* (living room) they don't have – a place to meet with friends over *un verre* (glass of wine), read for hours over a *café au lait* or swill cocktails during *apéro* (apéritif; predinner drink).

Club scene A variety of venues offer music and ambience for all types. The arrival of new dance-all-night destinations, like the Berlin-style electro **Mia Mao** (p100), housed in a cavernous industrial hall in La Villette, has utterly transformed the scene.

Tiered pricing Drinking in Paris means paying for the space you take up. So it costs more to sit at a table than to stand at the counter, more for coveted terrace seats, more in the 8e than the 18e.

Closing time Cafes and bars close around 2am, though some have licences until dawn. Club hours vary depending on venue and event, but start late.

HOW MUCH FOR A

Baguette
€1.20

Beer in a cafe
€6

Decent bottle of wine in a store
€10

Espresso in a cafe
€3

Crêpe
€5

Main in a bistro
€15–22

Two-course meal
€24–50 or more

LGBTIQ+ Travellers

'Gay Paree' lives up to its name. Paris is so open that there's less of a defined 'scene' here than in other cities.

 ### Festivals & Events

By far the biggest event on the LGBTIQ+ calendar is **Gay Pride** in late June, when the annual Marche des Fiertés through Paris via Le Marais provides a colourful spectacle, and plenty of parties take place over a two-week period.

Look for these events at other times of the year.

May **Le Bal de l'Amour** is a festive event celebrating marriage equality organised by the City of Paris that's open to all and free of charge.

May **Paris Ass Book Fair** brings together artists, booksellers, publishers and zinesters at the Palais de Tokyo.

October to November **Jerk Off** is a huge series of events devoted to queer and alternative culture.

November **Chéries-Chéri** is an annual, international LGBTIQ+ film festival supported by the French Ministry of Culture.

OUR PICKS

Must-Visit Gaybourhood

Le Marais, especially the areas around the intersection of rue Ste-Croix de la Bretonnerie and rue des Archives, and eastwards to rue Vieille du Temple, has long been Paris' main centre of LGBTIQ+ nightlife and is still its epicentre.

 ### POLITICAL PRIDE

In 2001 Paris was the first European capital to elect an openly gay mayor. The city itself is very open – same-sex couples commonly display affection in public.

GAY LOCALS

For an insider's perspective on gay life in Paris, take a tour with the **Gay Locals**. English-speaking residents lead tours and can provide itinerary planning.

NEW AFRICA/SHUTTERSTOCK

Resources

- **Gay Cities** (paris.gaycities.com) This travel guide offers reviews of all kinds of venues, from bars and clubs to bathhouses.
- **Gay and lesbian cultural venues** (parisjetaime.com/eng/article/gay-and-lesbian-cultural-venues-a652) The Paris Tourist Office lists 'the gayest spots in the French capital'.
- **Spartacus International Gay Guide** (spartacus.travel) Travel site with recommendations for gay-friendly accommodation in particular.

Health & Safe Travel

Paris is a safe and well-lit capital city, but always use common sense and pay attention to your surroundings.

Insurance
Citizens of the EU, Switzerland, Iceland, Norway and Liechtenstein receive free or reduced-cost, state-provided health-care cover with the European Health Insurance Card (EHIC), should medical treatment become necessary while in France. Each family member will need a separate card. Citizens of non-EU countries should check if there is a reciprocal arrangement for free medical care between their country and France.

STRIKES & PROTESTS
Sporadic strikes can disrupt travel. Paris is the focus of public protests, some drawing huge crowds from across France. Although there's a long tradition of peacefully protesting, these events can become unsafe. Routes are usually announced in advance.

Tap Water
Tap water is safe to drink. Order a free *carafe d'eau* (pitcher of water) at restaurants.

Pharmacies & Hospitals
For minor health concerns and to fill prescriptions, see a local *pharmacie*. For more serious problems, go to *urgences* (emergencies) wards at Paris' *hôpitaux* (hospitals).

Pharmacies are marked by a large illuminated green cross outside. At least one in each neighbourhood is open for extended hours; find a complete listing on the Paris tourist office website.

PICKPOCKETS
Stay alert for pickpockets, especially on the metro/RER and crowded, touristy areas. Don't keep your phone in your back pocket or out on a terrace table.

QUICK INFO

Security
Always lock bicycles, and keep a hand on your valuables on the metro.

Privacy
Always ask permission before taking pictures.

Alcohol
Locals drink wine at picnics despite the law against consuming alcohol in public.

Responsible Travel

Follow these tips to leave a lighter footprint, support local and have a positive impact on communities.

Sustainable Dining

Dine farm-to-fork at **Le Perchoir Porte de Versailles** at Europe's largest urban rooftop farm, Nature Urbaine.

Buy fresh produce at Paris' *biologique* (organic) markets, such as **Marché Biologique Raspail** (Sunday; p192), **Marché Biologique des Batignolles** (Saturday) and **Marché Biologique Brancusi** (Saturday).

Vegetarian and vegan restaurants are blossoming in Paris. **Franck Adandé**, aka @vegantouristparis, offers guided vegan tours, a newsletter and a dedicated Vegan Tourist Map.

Meet the Locals

Explore Paris *(exploreparis.com/en)* offers tourism activities and guided tours that break away from the Paris classics, with an emphasis on meeting locals and artisans in the Greater Paris region.

OUR PICK ★
No-Waste Bargains
Snap up bargain-priced unsold items at merchants such as bakeries via the app **Too Good to Go** *(toogoodtogo.fr)*, which helps prevent food waste.

Diverse Paris

Discover Black Paris on a guided tour with **Entrée to Black Paris** *(entreetoblackparis.com)*, take a walking or kick-scooter tour of Paris' multicultural northeastern neighbourhoods with **Ça Se Visite** *(ca-se-visite.fr)* and learn about Islamic culture on tours with the **Institut des Cultures d'Islam** *(institut-cultures-islam.org)*.

Resources

- **parisjetaime.com** Search 'sustainable tourism' for a list of initiatives.
- **bdmma.paris/en/les-prix/le-label-fabrique-a-paris** Products sporting the Made in Paris label.
- **welovegreen.fr** Zero-waste, renewable-energy-powered festival.

SKY HIGH

Look out over Paris from 150m up in the air aboard the helium-filled **Ballon Generali de Paris** *(ballondeparis.com).* Tethered in the Parc André Citroën, this sightseeing balloon monitors Paris' air quality as a 'flying laboratory'.

Smart Shopping

Paris has a plethora of vintage and secondhand boutiques. Le Marais caters to every budget, from the **Room** to **BIS Boutique Solidaire** (p115). Hit up the **Marché aux Puces de St-Ouen** (p94), the world's largest antiques market.

Browse over 1000 exquisite handcrafted items all made in French designers' studios, at **Empreintes** *(empreintes-paris.com).*

Climate Change & Travel

It's impossible to ignore the impact we have when travelling, and the importance of making changes where we can. Lonely Planet urges all travellers to engage with their travel carbon footprint. Many airlines and booking sites offer travellers the option of offsetting the impact of greenhouse gas emissions by contributing to climate-friendly initiatives around the world. We continue to offset the carbon footprint of all Lonely Planet staff travel, while recognising this is a mitigation more than a solution.

There are many carbon calculators online that allow travellers to estimate the carbon emissions generated by their journey; try **resurgence.org** using the QR code, right.

DRINKING FOUNTAINS

Refill your reusable water bottle at gorgeous green Wallace fountains all over Paris. Some contemporary fountains even offer sparkling water. In addition, 1000 establishments offer free refills as part of the **Ici, je choisis l'eau de Paris** (I choose Paris water) network.

Scan this QR code to find a fountain near you.

Accessible Travel

Public Transport
First opened in 1900, the vintage metro system is not fully accessible. Older stations have stairs and lack elevators. The driverless line 14, which now connects to Orly airport, is the only metro line that is fully accessible. Paris buses, however, are all accessible, with low floors and wide doors.

Accommodation
Hotels and rental apartments are a mixed bag for accessibility. Typically chain hotels in modern buildings meet international standards. But properties in older buildings, especially rental apartments, may lack lifts and other accessibility amenities.

TOURISME & HANDICAP LABEL
Monuments like **La Monnaie de Paris** (p194) and museums such as the **Louvre** (p72) have been recognised with the Tourisme & Handicap label for the quality of their amenities for those with disabilities.

Accessible Culture
Many cultural attractions, including the **Arc de Triomphe** (p58), offer free admission for people with disabilities and their companions, along with special discovery tours (booked in advance).

OUR PICK
The **Musée de la Marine** (p51), following a six-year closure for renovations, reopened at the end of 2023 with dazzling interiors that are accessible for everyone. Activities and exhibits are adapted to people with every type of disability. For example, those who wear hearing aids can borrow a hearing loop from reception. Wheelchairs are available, and there are regular guided tours in sign language. The museum even pioneered special amenities for children with autism.

TAXIS
Taxis G7 (g7.fr) has hundreds of low-base cars and over 100 cars equipped with ramps, and drivers trained in helping passengers with disabilities. Guide dogs are accepted in its entire fleet.

Resources
my.parisjetaime.com/handicap
The Paris tourist office has compiled a wealth of useful information.

Nuts & Bolts

Opening Hours

The following list covers approximate standard opening hours. Many businesses close in August for summer holidays.

Banks 9am-1pm and 2-5pm Monday to Friday; some open on Saturday morning

Bars and cafes 7am-11pm or 2am

Museums 10am-6pm; closed Monday or Tuesday

Restaurants Noon-2pm and 7-10.30pm; may close Sunday or Monday

Shops 10am-7pm Monday to Saturday; hours are longer in tourist zones

Ouvert(e) Open
Fermé(e) Closed

Smoking

Smoking is illegal in all indoor public spaces, including restaurants, cafes and bars. As of July 2025, smoking is also banned in outdoor places where children are present, including parks, beaches, bus stops, schools and stadiums. However, it's legal on restaurant terraces.

QUICK INFO

Time zone Central European Time (GMT/UTC +1)

Country calling code 33

Emergency number 112

Population 2.1 million

ELECTRICITY

230V/50Hz

Public Holidays

New Year's Day (Jour de l'An) 1 January

Easter Sunday & Monday (Pâques & Lundi de Pâques) Late March/April

May Day (Fête du Travail) 1 May

Victory in Europe Day (Victoire 1945) 8 May

Ascension Thursday (L'Ascension) May (celebrated on the 40th day after Easter)

Whit Monday (Lundi de Pentecôte) Mid-May to mid-June (seventh Monday after Easter)

Bastille Day/National Day (Fête Nationale) 14 July

Assumption Day (L'Assomption) 15 August

All Saints' Day (La Toussaint) 1 November

Armistice Day/Remembrance Day (Le Onze Novembre) 11 November

Christmas (Noël) 25 December

Language

French basics

Hello
Bonjour *bon·zhoor*

Goodbye
Au revoir *o·rer·vwa*

Yes
Oui *wee*

No
Non *non*

Please
S'il vous plaît *seel voo play*

Thank you
Merci *mair·see*

Excuse me
Excusez-moi *ek·skew·zay·mwa*

Sorry
Pardon *par·don*

Fast Phrases

Do you speak English?
Parlez-vous anglais? *par·lay·voo ong·glay*

I don't understand.
Je ne comprends pas. *zher ner kom·pron pa*

What's your name?
Comment vous appelez-vous? *ko·mon voo·za·play voo*

My name is ...
Je m'appelle ... *zher ma·pel ...*

Where's ...?
Où est ...? *oo ay ...*

Can you show me (on the map)?
Pouvez-vous m'indiquer (sur la carte)? *poo·vay·voo mun·dee·kay (sewr la kart)*

Help!
Au secours! *o skoor*

Cheers!
Santé! *son·tay*

What would you recommend?
Qu'est-ce que vous conseillez? *kes·ker voo kon·say·yay*

Numbers

 un *un*

 deux *der*

 trois *trwa*

 quatre *ka·trer*

 cinq *sungk*

Good to Know

Must-know grammar French has a formal and informal word for 'you' (*vous* and *tu*, respectively). It distinguishes between masculine and feminine forms of words; eg *beau/belle* (beautiful).

Warning Many French words look like English words but have a different meaning altogether; eg *menu* is a set lunch, not a menu (which is *carte* in French).

Time
What time is it?
Quelle heure est-il? *kel er ay til*
It's (8) o'clock Il est (huit) heures *il ay (weet) er*
It's half past (10) Il est (dix) heures et demie *il ay (deez) er ay day·mee*
morning **matin** *ma·tun*
afternoon **après-midi** *a·pray·mee·dee*
evening **soir** *swar*
yesterday **hier** *yair*
today **aujourd'hui** *o·zhoor·dwee*
tomorrow **demain** *der·mun*

FRENCH SLANG
What's up?
Quoi de neuf?
Drop it/nevermind!
Laisse-tomber!
I can't be bothered/ am feeling lazy
J'ai la flemme
Enjoy your meal!
Bon app!
No way!
C'est pas vrai!
Let's go/do it!
C'est parti!
Perfect! It's good!
Nickel!
Oh god! La vache! (literally 'the cow')
Good luck/break a leg Merde
There you go/there you have it Et voilà

Signs
Entrée Entrance
Fermé Closed
Ouvert Open
Sortie Exit
Toilettes/WC Toilets

WHO SPEAKS FRENCH?
French is an official language of 29 countries, including France, Belgium, Canada, Democratic Republic of the Congo and Vanuatu.
Eighty million people speak French as their first language and fifty million speak it as their second.

 six *sees*   **sept** *set*   **huit** *weet*   **neuf** *nerf*   **dix** *dees*

Index

Sights p000   Map pages p000

See also separate subindexes for:
- Eating p225
- Drinking p226
- Shopping p227

A

accessible travel 218
accommodation 27, 210, 211
airports 28
African heritage 101
Aquarium Tropical 133
Arc de Triomphe 58, 61
archaeology 35
architecture 6, 32, 48-9, **48**
Arènes de Lutèce 165, 166
arriving 28
art 11, 33-4, 51-2, 118-19, 170-1
Association pour la Sauvegarde et la Mise en Valeur du Paris Historique 111
Au Marché de la Butte 97
Avenue des Champs-Élysées 62

B

Basilique du Sacré-Cœur 93
Bastille 123-37, 124-5
  drinking 136-7
  experiences 130-5
  food 136
  shopping 131, 132, 137
  transport 123
Batignolles 102
Bibliothèque Mazarine 192-3
bicycle travel 30
boat tours 46-7, 102
boat travel 30
Bois de Boulogne 66-7
Bois de Vincennes 138-9
bookshops 168-9, 197
Bourse de Commerce 82-3
bus travel 28, 29
business hours 219

C

Canal St-Martin 102
Catacombes, les 202-3
Cathédrale Notre Dame de Paris 144-9
Caveau de la Huchette 169
Centre Pompidou 81
Césure 171
Champs-Élysées 60-1
Champs-Élysées area 55-65, **56-7**
  drinking 65
  experiences 62-4
  food 65
  highlights 58-9
  itineraries 60-1, **60**
  shopping 65
  top experiences 58-9
  transport 55
  walking tours 60-1, **60**
Château de Versailles 206-7
children, travel with 19, 210
chocolate 196
Cimetière du Montparnasse 205
Cimetière du Père Lachaise 126-7
cinemas 170
Cinémathèque Française 134-5
Cité de l'Architecture et du Patrimoine 49
climate 26, 217
Clos Montmartre 97
clubs, see nightlife
coach travel 28
Collège des Bernardins 165, 167
Conciergerie 151
Corbusier, Le 49
costs 25, 31, 211, 213
Coulée Verte René-Dumont 130-1
Cour Damoye 129
cour du Commerce-St-André 191
currency 25
cycling 30

D

Dalí Museum 98
disabilities, travellers with 218
drinking 16, 212-13, see also individual neighbourhoods, Drinking subindex
Duc des Lombards 83

E

Eastern Paris 123-37, 124-5
  drinking 136-7
  experiences 130-5
  food 136
  highlights 126-7
  itineraries 128-9, **128**
  shopping 137
  top experiences 126-7
  transport 123
  walking tours 128-9, **128**
Église de la Madeleine 61
Église St-Antoine des Quinze Vingts 131
Église St-Étienne du Mont 165, 166
Église St-Germain de Charonne 135
Église St-Germain des Prés 191
Église St-Médard 168
Église St-Séverin 166
Église St-Sulpice 186, 191
Eiffel Tower 42-7
  transport 39
electricity 219
Enceinte de Philippe Auguste 32, 111
events, see festivals & events

F

family travel 19, 210
fashion 63-4, 115
Faubourg St-Antoine 128-9
festivals & events 26-7
  Fête de la Musique 132

Fondation Cartier pour l'Art Contemporain 83
Fondation Henri Cartier-Bresson 118-19
food 8, 212-13, *see also individual neighbourhoods*, Eating subindex
free attractions 19
French language 220-1

G

Galerie Amélie du Chalard 171
Galerie Emmanuel Perrotin 119
Galerie Kreo 171
Galerie Vivienne 79
gardens, *see* parks & gardens
gay travellers 118, 214
Grande Mosquée de Paris 165, 169
Grand Palais 63
Grands Boulevards 55
Ground Control 135

H

Halle St-Pierre 97, 98
health 215
highlights 6-19, *see also individual neighbourhoods*
history 32, 34, 111, 118, 130, 196
holidays 219
Hôtel de la Marine 63
Hôtel de Lamoignon 111
Hôtel de Sens 111
Hôtel de Sully 111
Hôtel de Ville 114
Hôtel des Invalides 188-9
Hôtel Lambert 153

I

Institut du Monde Arabe 170-1
insurance 215
Islands, the 141-55, **142-3**
  drinking 155
  experiences 154
  food 154, 155
  itineraries 152-3, **152**
  shopping 154, 155
  top experiences 144-51
  transport 141
  walking tours 152-3, **152**
itineraries 20-3, *see also individual neighbourhoods*

J

Jardin Catherine-Labouré 193
Jardin des Plantes 161-3
Jardin des Tuileries 80
Jardin du Luxembourg 182, 191
Jardin du Palais Royal 80
Jeu de Paume 81
jazz 170
Jean Fidler building 49
Jewish Paris 112-13
Joseph Migneret Garden 113

L

La Cigale 98-9
La Galerie Dior 63-4
La Maison Rose 97
Lafayette Anticipations 119
language 220-1
Latin Quarter 157-75, **158-9**
  drinking 174-5
  experiences 166-71
  food 172-4
  highlights 160-3
  itineraries 164-5, **164**
  shopping 168-9, 175
  top experiences 160-3
  transport 157
  walking tours 164-5, **164**
Le Carreau du Temple 118
Le Cordon Bleu 62-3
Le Marais 107-21, **108-9**
  drinking 121
  experiences 114-19
  food 117, 120
  itineraries 110-11, 112-13, **110, 112**
  nightlife 118
  shopping 115, 117, 119, 121
  transport 107
  walking tours 110-11, 112-13, **110, 112**
Le Trianon 99
Les Disquaires 131-2
Les Halles 69-87, **70-1**
  drinking 85-7
  experiences 80-3
  food 84-5
  highlights 72-7
  itineraries 78-9, **78**
  shopping 87
  top experiences 72-7
  transport 69
  walking tours 78-9, **78**

Les Invalides **180-1**
  highlights 188-9
  top experiences 188-9
LGBTIQ+ travellers 118, 214
literature 169, 194
live music 83, 98-9, 101, 131-2, 169
Louvre, the, *see* Musée du Louvre

M

Madame Arthur 98
Maison de Balzac 50
Maison de Nicolas Flamel 111
Maison de Victor Hugo 115
Maison Européenne de la Photographie 118
Maison Gainsbourg 195
Maison La Roche 49
Marché aux Fleurs 154
Marché aux Puces de St-Ouen 94-5
Marché Biologique Raspail 192
Marché des Enfants Rouges 117
Marché Président Wilson 50-1
markets 18, 116
medical services 215
Mémorial de la Shoah 113
metro travel 29
money 25
Monnaie de Paris 191, 194-5
Montmartre 89-105, **90-1**
  drinking 105
  experiences 98-103
  food 104-5
  highlights 93
  itineraries 96-7, **96**
  shopping 105
  top experiences 93
  transport 89
  walking tours 96-7, **96**
Montparnasse 204-5, **204**
Moulin Rouge 98
Mur des Je t'aime 97
Musée Carnavalet 114-15
Musée Cognacq-Jay 115
Musée d'Art et d'Histoire du Judaïsme 113
Musée de Cluny 165, 166-7
Musée de la BNF 81
Musée de la Chasse et de la Nature 115
Musée de la Vie Romantique 99

Musée de l'Histoire de l'Immigration 133
Musée de l'Orangerie 81
Musée de Montmartre 99
Musée des Arts et Métiers 116
Musée des Arts Forains 133-4
Musée d'Orsay 183-5
Musée du Louvre 69, 72-7
Musée Marmottan Monet 50
Musée National de la Marine 51
Musée National des Arts Asiatiques Guimet 52
Musée National Eugène Delacroix 192
Musée National Picasso-Paris 115
Musée Rodin 187
museums 11, 35
music, *see also* live music
   Banlieues Bleues 27
   Fête de la Musique 26

N
new attractions 14
nightlife 16, 100, 212-13, *see also individual neighbourhoods*
Northern Paris 89-105, **92**
   drinking 105
   experiences 98-103
   food 104-5
   highlights 94-5
   nightlife 100-1, 103
   shopping 94-5, 101, 105
   top experiences 94-5
   transport 89
Notre Dame 144-9

O
offbeat attractions 35
Olympic Games 80
opening hours 219

P
Palais de Chaillot 51
Palais de la Porte Dorée 133
Palais de Tokyo 51-2
Palais Garnier 59, 61
Panthéon 160, 165
Parc de Bercy 133
Parc de la Villette 103
Parc des Buttes-Chaumont 100

Parc Montsouris 205
Parc Zoologique de Paris 139
parks & gardens 10, 193
perfume 117
Petit Palais 61, 62
Petite Ceinture 99
pickpockets 25, 215
place Dauphine 153
Place de la Bastille 130
place de la Concorde 61
place de la Contrescarpe 168
Place de la République 114
Place des Vosges 114
place du Tertre 97
planning
   booking 24
   clothes 24
   etiquette 24
   Paris basics 24-5
   tips 24
Point Ephémère 103
Polka Galerie 119
Pont Alexandre III 64
Pont Neuf 153
Pont St-Louis 153
population 219
protests 215
public holidays 219
public transport 30-1

Q
quai de Bourbon 153

R
responsible travel 216-17
river cruises 46-7, 102
rue des Ursins 153
rue Mouffetard 167-8
rue St-Blaise 135

S
safe travel 25, 215
Sainte-Chapelle 150
Seine River 17, 46-7, 102, 134, 154, 196-7
shopping 18, *see also individual neighbourhoods*, Shopping subindex
smoking 219
Square Boucicaut 193
square du Vert-Galant 153
Square Laurent-Prache 193
Square Roger-Stéphane 193

St-Germain des Prés 177-201, **178-9**
   drinking 194, 196-7, 199-200
   experiences 192-7
   food 198-9
   highlights 182-7
   itineraries 190-1, **190**
   shopping 193-4, 195, 197, 200-1
   top experiences 182-7
   transport 177
   walking tours 190-1, **190**
St-Julien-le-Pauvre 166
street art 33-4, 116
strikes 215
Sunset/Sunside 83
surprises 32-5
sustainability 216
swimming 33, 134

T
taxis 28, 30
Théâtre de l'Odéon 170, 191
Théâtre des Abbesses 98
theft 25, 215
time 25
tipping 25
Tour de France 26
train travel 28, 29
transport 28, 29-31
travel seasons 26
traveling with kids 19, 210

U
underground sights 35

V
vegetarian & vegan travellers 85, 120, 216
Versailles 206-7
viewpoints 12
Village St-Paul 111

W
walking 29
walking tours
   16e architecture 48-9, **48**
   Champs-Élysées to Palais Garnier 60-1, **60**
   eastern Paris artisan history 128-9, **128**
   Islands, the 152-3, **152**
   Latin Quarter 164-5, **164**
   Le Marais history 110-11, **110**

Le Marais Jewish traditions 112-13, **112**
Les Halles covered passages 78-9, **78**
Monmartre 96-7, **96**
Montparnasse 204-5, **204**
St-Germain 190-1, **190**
western Paris architecture 48-9, **48**
weather 26
Western Paris 39-53, **40-1**
  drinking 53
  experiences 50-2
  food 53
  highlights 42-7
  itineraries 48-9, **48**
  top experiences 42-7
  transport 39
  walking tours 48-9, **48**
World's Fairs 51

 Eating

A
19 SAINT ROCH 84
Aki Boulangerie 82
Aléa 104
Amarante 136
Arnaud Nicolas 53
Atelier du Geste à l'Émotion 154
Au Petit Bar 84
Au Pied de Cochon 82
Au Rocher de Cancale 82
Aux Bons Crus 136
Aux Petits Cakes 154

B
Bistrot Instinct 120
Bouillon Chartier 65
Bouillon Pigalle 104
Boulangerie Liberté 198
Boulangerie Manobaké 136
Boulangerie MieMie 136
Boutique Yam'Tcha 84
Brasserie Baroche 65
BrEAThe 85
Breizh Café Odéon 199
Brutus 120
Buvette Gastrothèque 104

C
Café Antonia at Le Bristol 65
Café Campana 185
Café de l'Industrie 136
Café Leone 145
Café Mollien 73
Café Pavane 198
Café Saint Régis 154
Caillebotte 104
Capitaine 120
Carré Pain de Mie 120
Chez Aline 136
Chez Eating 120
Chez Miki 85
Comice 53
Comme un Bouillon 84
Comptoir Général 105

D
Daroco 84
Des Gâteaux et du Pain 198

E
Early June 104-5
Eats Thyme 84
Eric & Lydie 85

G
Glaces Glazed 163

H
Huîtrerie Régis 199

J
Jantchi 84

K
Kitchen 120
Kitchen Izakaya 85
Kodawari Ramen Tsukiji 85

L
La Boissonnerie 199
La Brasserie de l'Îsle Saint-Louis 154
La Collective Parisienne 120
La Dame de Paris 145
La Galerie at Hôtel Plaza Athénée 65
La Part des Anges 104
La Pâtisserie Cyril Lignac 198
La Petite Chaise 194
La Rotonde 103
La Rotonde de la Muette 53
La Tour Montlhéry – Chez Denise 84
Land&Monkeys 120
L'As du Fallafel 113
Le Bon, La Butte 104
Le Bouillon du Coq 95
Le Canon d'Achille 104
Le Christine 198
Le Comptoir des Saints-Pères 199
Le Comptoir du Relais 199
Le Coq d'Or 95
Le George at Four Seasons Hotel George V 65
Le Grand Colbert 79
Le Jules Verne 43
Le Mâche-dru 154
Le Petit Bouillon Pharamond 85
Le Petit Rétro 53
Le Progrès 104
Le Sergent Recruteur 155
Le Servan 127
Le Vaudésir 203
Les Dessous de la Robe 85
Les Deux Abeilles 53
Les Deux Colombes 155
Les Enfants Perdus 105
Les Marches 53
Les Rêveuses 135
L'Escargot Montorgueil 82

M
Madame Brasserie 43
Maggie 104
Magnolia 104
Maison Bergeron 198
Marché des Enfants Rouges 117
Maslow 85
Matin des Oliviers 84
Michi 85
Moon Croissant 120
Mori Yoshida 198

N
Notre Café Marais 120

P
Pantobaguette 101
Pâtisserie Viennoise 165
Pavyllon 65
Pépite 136
Petite Île Boulangerie 120

Philippe Conticini 198
Poget & De Witte 155
Poilâne 198
Polidor 199
Postiche Bistrot 85

Restaurant Paul 155

Sacha Finkelsztajn's 113
Stohrer 82
Substance 53

Tapisserie 198
Tata Burger 118

Udon Jubey 85

VG Pâtisserie 136

Yann Couvreur 120

 Drinking

Artesano 121
Au Soleil de la Butte 105

Bar 8 86
Bar 228 86
Bar des Ferrailleurs 136
Bar Etna 199
Bar Hemingway 85-6
Bar Joséphine 200
Bombardier 174
Brewberry 174

Café de Flore 194
Café du Clown 199
Café Joyeux Opéra 87
Café La Perle 119
Café Maa 174
Cafe Nuances 199
Café Nuances 65

Café Richelieu 73
Caffè Stern 79
Candelaria 121
Castor Club 200
Causeries 121
Chanceux 174
CopperBay at Hotel Lancaster 65
Coutume 200
Cox 118
Cravan 53, 200
Culottées Panoramas 86

Delicatessen Place 121
Dernier Bar avant la Fin du Monde 86
Duplex Bar 118

Elles Bar 118
Experimental Cocktail Club 86

Freddy's 199
freedj 118

Golden Promise Whisky Bar 86

Ha Noi 1988 Flowers & Archives 121

Klover Coffee Showroom 137

La Balle au Bond 196-7
La Crèmerie 199
La Mutinerie 118
La Palette 119
La Tropicale Glacier 137
L'Arbre à Café 200
L'Avant Comptoir de la Terre 199
Le Bar 200
Le Bar du Caveau 155
Le Barav 121
Le Baron Rouge 137
Le Belair 53
Le Café des Deux Moulins 105
Le Chouff'Bar 174
Le Cœur Fou 86
Le Pavillon des Canaux 105
Le Piano Vache 175

Le Procope 191
Le Progrès 119
Le Saint-Gervais 119
Le Sedaine Bar 137
Le Tagada 105
Le Très Particulier 105
Le Violon Dingue 174
Les Aimant·e·s 118
Les Ambassadeurs at Hôtel de Crillon 65
Les Cuves de Fauve 136
Les Deux Magots 194
Les Souffleurs 118
Little Red Door 121

Maison Fleuret 199
Margen's 174
Martin 121
Mia Mao 100
Midi-Minuit 53
Minicafé 155
Mokochaya 137

Napa 155
Noir 155
Nuage 174

Odette 174

Paname Brewing Company 105
Pub St-Hilaire 175

ROOF 86
Rosa Bonheur sur Seine 196

Septime La Cave 137
Sister Midnight 105
Sotto 121
Spootnik Bar 121
St James Paris 53
Stéréo 101

Ten Belles 200
Terra Bar à Vins 121
Terres de Café 200

Wani 200

Shopping

 A

À La Mère de Famille 82
Abbey Bookshop 168
Album BD 175
Alix D Reynis 117
Assouline 197
Astier de Villatte 201
Athanase 87
Au Bonbon du Palais 175
Au Nain Bleu 87

 B

Biologique Recherche 200
BIS Boutique Solidaire 115
Bobby 115
Book Off 82
Bourgine 175
Brigitte Tanaka 87
Brûlerie des Gobelins 175
BRUT 115

 C

Calligrane 119
Candora 117
Caudalie 200
Caviar Kaspia 65
Chantelivre 197
Chapellerie De Punta en Blanco 137
Cire Trudon 201
Citypharma 195
Clair de Rêve 155
Compagnie Française des Poivres et des Épices 201
CrocoDisc 175
Cul de Cochon 82

 D

Debauve & Gallais 196
Design & Nature 87

 E

Empreintes 117

F

Flash Vintage 105
Fleux 121
Fragonard 117

Frederic Malle 117
Free 'P Star 115
Fromagerie Androuet 175

 G

Galerie Stéphane Olivier 201
Galeries Lafayette 61, 64
Graineterie du Marché 137

 J

Jamini 102
Junku 87

 K

Kure Bazaar 87

 L

La Belle-Iloise 201
La Fermette 82
La Grande Épicerie de Paris 193-4
La Laiterie de Paris 105
La Maison de la Truffe 65
La Maison d'Isabelle 175
La Samaritaine 87
La Soufflerie 201
Lafitte 201
L'Agrumiste 201
L'Atelier 55 201
L'Auguste Cave 137
Lavrut 79
Le BHV Marais 121
Le Bon Marché 193
Le Club K7 175
Le Parti du Thé 137
L'Éclaireur Sévigné 121
Legay Choc 118
Les Drapeaux de France – Noxa 87
Librairie du Temple 113
Librairie Ulysse 155
Liquides Bar à Parfums 117
L'Officine Universelle Buly 1803 200

M

Macon & Lesquoy 105
Maison Wa 82
Marché aux Fleurs Reine Elizabeth II 154
Marché aux Puces de St-Ouen 94-5
Marché Biologique Raspail 192

Marché d'Aligre 132
Marché Président Wilson 50-1
Marché St-Germain 191
Marin Montagut 201
Marius Fabre 117
Mélodies Graphique 119
Merci #2 87
Messy Nessy's Cabinet 175

 N

Nishikidori – Le Comptoir des Poivres 82

 O

Oh My Cream! 201
Olympia Le-Tan 79

 P

Papier Tigre 119
Plastic Soul Records 137
Praline 117
Printemps 61, 64

 R

Red Wheelbarrow 197
Rickshaw 87
Room 115
RSVP 117

 S

Sabre 117
San Francisco Book Company 197
Shakespeare & Company 168-9
Système Solaire 115

 T

Taschen 197
Tucked Friperie 137

 U

Un Jour, une Vieillerie 137
Ursa Major Chocolats 137

 V

Viaduc des Arts 131

 Y

Yoyaku 101
Yveline Antiques 201

NOTES

NOTES

Send Us Your Feedback

We love to hear from travellers – your comments help make our books better. We read every word, and we guarantee that your feedback goes straight to the authors. Visit lonelyplanet.com/contact to submit your updates and suggestions.

Note: We may edit, reproduce and incorporate your comments in Lonely Planet products such as guidebooks, websites and digital products, so let us know if you are happy to have your name acknowledged. For a copy of our privacy policy visit lonelyplanet.com/legal.

Acknowledgements

Cover photograph: Eiffel Tower, seen from Marché Président Wilson area. Amir Hamja for Lonely Planet

Back photograph: Banks of the Seine. OKcamera/Shutterstock

THIS BOOK

The 9th edition of Lonely Planet's *Pocket Paris* guidebook was researched and written by Mary Winston Nicklin, Alexis Averbuck, Jean-Bernard Carillet, Fabienne Fong Yan, Rooksana Hossenally, Nicola Leigh Stewart, Rowan Twine and Peter Yeung. This guidebook was produced by the following:

Destination Editor
Annemarie McCarthy

Coordinating Editor
Anita Isalska

Cartographer
Dave Connolly

Production Editor
Joel Cotterell

Image Editor
Nicolas D'Hoedt

Assisting Editors
Janet Austin, Jenna Myers, Charlotte Orr

Cover Researcher
Giada de Agostinis

Thanks to
Isabella Noble, Darren O'Connell

Although the authors and Lonely Planet have taken all reasonable care in preparing this book, we make no warranty about the accuracy or completeness of its content and, to the maximum extent permitted, disclaim all liability arising from its use.

All rights reserved. No part of this publication may be copied, stored in a retrieval system, or transmitted in any form by any means, electronic, mechanical, recording or otherwise, except brief extracts for the purpose of review, and no part of this publication may be sold or hired, without the written permission of the publisher. Lonely Planet and the Lonely Planet logo are trademarks of Lonely Planet and are registered in the US Patent and Trademark Office and in other countries. Lonely Planet does not allow its name or logo to be appropriated by commercial establishments, such as retailers, restaurants or hotels. Please let us know of any misuses: lonelyplanet.com/legal/intellectual-property.

Paper in this book is certified against the Forest Stewardship Council™ standards. FSC™ promotes environmentally responsible, socially beneficial and economically viable management of the world's forests.

Published by Lonely Planet Global Limited
CRN 554153
9th edition – Mar 2026
ISBN 978 1 83869 912 3
© Lonely Planet 2026
10 9 8 7 6 5 4 3 2 1
Printed in China